# AN ANTHOLOGY OF
# GERMAN POETRY

*An Anthology of*

# GERMAN POETRY

1730–1830

Jethro Bithell, M.A.

*Formerly Reader in German*
*University of London*

METHUEN & CO LTD
*36 Essex Street, Strand, London WC2*

*First published 1957*

CATALOGUE NUMBERS
5908/U (Best) 8137/U (School)

PRINTED AND BOUND IN GREAT BRITAIN BY
BUTLER AND TANNER LTD, FROME AND LONDON

# PREFACE

IF this Anthology is to have the effect it is intended to have, it must be read as a companion volume to my *Anthology of German Poetry 1830–1880.* In this, post-romantic poetry was fully represented, but not romantic poetry proper; the present Anthology ends where its successor begins, and romanticism is preceded by classicism, and so on backwards. The only poet who is included in both anthologies is Heine; and he is represented here by one book; but this was, at the lowest estimate, one of the most important books of lyrics of the eighteen-twenties. To get a complete picture of the history of the lyric in the first half of the century Grillparzer, Annette von Droste-Hülshoff and Lenau are needed, but they have their proper place in the 1830–80 Anthology.

The difficulty for the anthologist was the vast scope of the material to be dealt with in a space necessarily limited. This period of the German lyric is of course, according to the accepted academic view, that which for importance and interest transcends all others. Here I can hear some of the sixth-form boys and girls, whom for thirty years it was the greatest delight of my life to examine orally, saying: 'importance, yes (for examinations), but interest, no . . .!' In these poets of over a hundred years ago there is not, it is true, the modernity of mood that we find today in (say) Rilke or Hofmannsthal; but Goethe, for instance, was in every respect in advance of his period; indeed, his series of poems *Gott und Welt* has been quoted recently by our most advanced scientists as the nearest that can be reached to an interpretation of the universe that will accord with the knowledge we have. Then there is the modern preoccupation with psychology; and here it is generally agreed that Hölderlin—for instance again (Platen and others might be instanced) —is as fascinatingly modern as the most complicated innovators of the moulding of verse form of recent years.

Because I think it is essential that the student should learn to probe into the mind and soul of the poet I have taken care to tell as much of his life story as is needed. Very important too in the period the anthology covers are the lines of development of philosophical concepts. Every German poet has his *Weltanschauung* or *Weltbild*; and groups or circles of poets are linked by their adherence to the system of some philosopher or other, with the result that their poetry cannot be adequately understood unless students have some idea of the principles involved. If it were urged that philosophy is too heavy going for candidates at school-leaving age— and it is for them principally that the anthology is intended, though it is also planned to help them for their finals—I would say that I always remember a boy who, years ago, came into my oral examination room for Higher School Certificate (as it was then) and began emphatically with: '*Ich möchte über Philosophie sprechen. Ich interessiere mich dafür.*' And he did it, for half an hour, and did it well. He had pieced his knowledge together mainly from his set books.

But of course the final criterion is not the thought.

but the feeling and the way it is put to shape in form and phrasing. The basic fact is that poetry is poetry in all its periods; and if 1730 to 1830 is indeed the greatest period, then this must be the greatest poetry the Germans have. And certainly my first concern in my discussion has been to bring home: What *is* poetry? This, I think, is what should be discussed and probed in all class work in schools and universities. In any case this great period is what students do need for their examinations, and I have had it in my mind all the time to provide them with the information they require.

J. BITHELL

*Paignton*
*12 November 1956*

# CONTENTS

# INTRODUCTION

In the seventeenth century the chief centre of German literature had been in Silesia. Here MARTIN OPITZ (1597–1639) had written his *Buch von der deutschen Poeterei* (1624), which set the pattern of poetry for a hundred years or more. Opitz's chief rule—a startling innovation at the time—was that in German verse lift and dip correspond to long and short in classical verse; that is, he established the fact that German verse is accentual, not quantitative. Before him there had been no regular scansion in the modern sense; the more academic verse had often depended on the number of syllables counted to the line; natural versification had survived only in the *Knüttelverse*, the traditional line of an unfixed number of syllables with a norm of two chief stresses and two subsidiary stresses coming wherever the sense placed them, and in the *Volkslied*, which, ignored by poets conscious of their calling, went on singing its way through the centuries till Herder and the romanticists put it in the forefront of interest as the lyric form indigenous to German song. Since Opitz shared the admiration of his period for the Renaissance forms of Italian and French verse, and since his immediate model was Dutch poetry, then in the heyday of its classical glory, it was inevitable that his chief lyric line should be the alexandrine, which is made up of twelve syllables swinging with rigid regularity to and from a caesura dead in the middle of the line. The French alexandrine with its discreet stresses glides along rapidly; it has approximately the tempo of a German decasyllabic iambic line; the Dutch and German alexandrine, with its resonant retardatory stresses, is heavily weighted and often sluggishly slow;

nevertheless, it lasted as the most reputed metrical line till well over the middle of the century ; Goethe still uses it in his student days at Leipzig.

The lyric poets who, together with Opitz, wrote in Silesia, and the contemporary Silesian dramatists, wrote in a richly ornate and heavily rhetorical style, which is classed as Baroque [1] ; much of it—in the Silesian drama particularly—is turgid bombast (*Schwulst*). Baroque literature, gloomed by the devastation of the Thirty Years War, is pessimistic : nature contrasts with God, and is therefore evil ; there is disharmony of world and spirit ; the world is dust and ashes. By the end of the seventeenth century this Baroque despair gives way to two spiritual movements : Pietism, which continues to be a force during the eighteenth century, and the teleological [2] philosophy of GOTTFRIED WILHELM LEIBNIZ (1646–1716), the deepest thinker of his day. According to Leibniz the world is made up of indivisible monads, which are irradiated by God's spirit, and which, by interacting on one another, create what he calls pre-established harmony (*die prästabilierte Harmonie*) ; that is, harmony between matter—the world of sense—and spirit—which is God. Since God is good, and since the world of automatically acting monads is God, this must be the best of all possible worlds (*mundus optimus*).

Leibniz wrote his works in Latin and French ;

---

[1] Baroque as a phase of literature has been revived after the two great wars of our own period ; it may be defined as a representation of the clash of opposites, flesh and spirit or body and soul in particular, which is the rule of all being. Thus there are marked elements of Baroque in the poetry of the Viennese poet Josef Weinheber (1892–1945), with his dramatization of the contrast of *Tier oder Geist* or *Fleisch und Geist*.

[2] Teleology = the philosophy of final causes (*causae finales*) as defined by Christian Wolff (*Zweck- oder Zweckmässigkeitslehre ; Lehre von der zweckmässigen Einrichtung der Welt*). The contrary concept of creation ('mechanism controlled from outside' or mechanically self-acting ; see p. xx) would be Wolff's *causae efficientes*.

CHRISTIAN THOMASIUS (1655–1728), a professor at Leipzig and afterwards at Halle, created a sensation by lecturing (1687) in German ; and he edited (1688–9) the first literary journal in German, *Scherzhafte und einfältige Gedanken über allerhand lustige und nützliche Bücher und Fragen* ; as the title indicates, the review attempted a light touch ; and it marks the beginning of German journalism. Thomasius' period of office at Halle gave that university a lead in literary matters ; and here another professor, CHRISTIAN WOLFF (1679–1754), a pupil of Leibniz, popularized the monadic doctrine. He describes his system as *utilis et certa* ; he means that, reason by its nature being certain, all that accords with reason must be certain and therefore useful. Man's happiness is achieved by the application of reason ; to be happy is to be reasonable ; and therefore human happiness is the highest good. This theory that reason is the foundation of certainty in knowledge is known as rationalism. German rationalism (*Aufklärung*) during the first part of the eighteenth century derives also from English philosophy ; particularly from Locke and Shaftesbury, and, in the second half of the century, from the Voltairean intellectualism of the encyclopaedists, more particularly Diderot ; it signifies emancipation from dogmas imposed by the church and hidebound tradition. Frederick the Great was a rationalist out and out—Voltaire was for some time (1750–1753) in residence at his castle of Sans Souci ; but, though he wrote in French (his pamphlet *De la littérature allemande*, 1780, is one of the curiosities of literature), the wave of national feeling which his victories aroused was a potent factor in the eclipse of rationalism. This was brought about mainly by the vindication of the claims of imagination in the critical works of the Swiss writers Bodmer and Breitinger, and by the cult of feeling which sweeps the country after the first successes of Klopstock. Pietism had, with its religious sense of sin and sadness, faced rationalism throughout the period of its triumph ; in Klopstock an inrooted pietism blends harmoniously with an optimism and robust joy in life which springs from the conviction that, since Christ has redeemed us, we are free to get the best out of the world.

As the eighteenth century proceeds Baroque is displaced by Rococo (*das Rokoko*). The style of Rococo is florid but conventional, all flourishes and furbelows, but lightly and gracefully worn as against the downweighting and grotesque over-ornamentation of Baroque. In much of the lyric verse of Rococo there is an elegance and a light touch which is, so to speak, standardized, though the individuality of good poets breaks through the hackneyed moulds. Rococo, after the extravagance and the obscenities of Baroque, is the literature of ' good taste ', of urbanity, of a refined social order.

Between Baroque and Rococo comes JOHANN CHRISTIAN GÜNTHER (1695–1723). There is still, in his early verse and in the poems which he wrote copiously for ceremonious occasions (*Gedichte*, 1724), something of Silesian *Schwulst*. He was himself a Silesian, the son of a doctor who detested poetry and despised his son for indulging in it ; he forced him to study medicine. Günther was dissipated from his schooldays onwards ; and from his schooldays dates his love for Leonore, whom he immortalized in the finest love-songs since the days of the Minnesingers. For the first time for centuries the love lyrics of a poet spring from his own passionate experience ; here indeed we have *Erlebnisdichtung*. Günther has ample variety ; his lyrics range from drinking songs to religious hymns and poems in which repentance for his wastrel's life rings tragically true. There is the *carpe diem* motif in *Studentenlied*, the most famous of his student songs— it is still, with *Gaudeamus igitur*, of which it is an

adaptation, in the *Kommersbuch*. Günther declared—
and the freshness of his lyrics bears him out—that he
owed more to the *Volkslied* than to the rules of Opitz.
His verse indeed leaps beyond the anacreontic poets
who directly follow him to herald the poets of the
Hainbund ; these, following Herder's directions, go
back to the Minnesong and the older patterns of native
verse. Cast off by his father, Günther died in his
twenty-eighth year. ' *Er wusste sich nicht zu zähmen*,'
wrote Goethe at the end of his warm appreciation in
*Dichtung und Wahrheit*, Part 2, Book 7, ' *und so
zerrann ihm sein Leben wie sein Dichten* '.

Günther died seven years before our period begins ;
but as the first real modern poet he belongs to it.  He
is the last Silesian poet before Eichendorff at the
beginning of the next century ; the representative
poetry of the thirties has its home in Hamburg, a city
culturally more closely linked with the literature and
rationalistic philosophy of our own Silver Age.  Not
in Hamburg only, as we shall see, Pope's *Essay on Man*
provides a model for philosophical poetry, while his
*Windsor Forest* and *Pastorals*, and still more Thomson's
*Seasons*, set the fashion of descriptive nature poetry.

It would be hard to find a more glaring contrast than
that between the wastrel Günther and the next
important poet of the century, BARTHOLD HEINRICH
BROCKES (1680–1747).  Solid and severe as a public
official and as a Town Councillor of Hamburg, he was
still more solid and severe as a poet.  After studying
at Halle under Thomasius, he made the *grand tour* of
Holland, France, and Italy, and made his *début* in
literature with a translation of Marini's *La Strage degli
Innocenti* under the title of *Bethlehemitischer Kindermord*
(1715) ; this to some extent harks back to the blood
and fury of the Silesian school.  He then wrote an
oratorio which was set to music by Handel and produced
at Hamburg, where at that time German opera was

beginning its course. His translations from English
come late in his career : that of Pope's *Essay on Man*
in 1740, that of Thomson's *Seasons* in 1745. The first
edition of Thomson's *Seasons* had appeared in 1726 ;
the first volume of Brockes' *Irdisches Vergnügen in Gott*
appeared in 1721, so that Brockes was before Thomson
in the field of descriptive nature poetry. But Brockes
did not complete his voluminous work—there are nine
volumes—till 1748, so that the influence of Thomson
is possible in the main body of the work. In Brockes'
work, however, nature description, minute as it is, is
subordinate to the main purpose, which is to demon-
strate the truth of Pope's dictum : ' Whatever is, is
right.' Thus in *Die himmlische Schrift* in the 1727
volume, an astronomical rhapsody, God's love and
greatness are shown to be written on the face of the
skies ; the workings of the universe are laid bare ; the
plan and purpose of all that is and happens is demon-
strated ; all that is, is good, for the good of God, and
therefore for the good of God's creature man. Evil
itself is good, for it is part of the plan and purpose ;
since all that God made is good—runs the general
reading of the book—and since God made the raging
tiger, even the raging tiger is good. The poet con-
templates the overwhelming immensity of the heavens,
and by contrast a little red worm running with invisible
legs over his hand ; he examines it through a magni-
fying-glass, and lo ! it is as perfect in its anatomy and
every purpose of its parts as the vasty universe is
perfect in its harmony of controlled masses ; he
remembers that even a grain of pepper is in itself a
universe in miniature ; and therefore God is infinitely
great and glorious in the minutest particle as in the
vastest entity. And this gives surety to man, that
wretched clod of earth, that God's love upholds him.
The poet plunges his gaze into the endless heights of
heaven and the bottomless abyss of space ; and despair

folds over him as do the dense masses of the sea over a sinking ship; he dwindles to a speck of dust; but, having lost himself in humility, he finds himself again in God. This is the theme of these endlessly unrolled contemplations: to find God and to praise God in the panorama of nature. Not nature is lovely, but God in nature.

Nevertheless, in the history of poetry Brockes stands out not so much for his insistent teaching of the doctrine of utility as because he is the first German poet of nature. To the poets before him nature had been a sealed book; Brockes describes nature with untiring patience and with an endless wealth of detail drawn from accurate observation and poetically coloured; his technique has often been compared with that of the Dutch genre painters, whom he loved. What detracts from the merit of the poem is that the description of nature is didactic, not idyllic (as it is to be in Kleist's *Frühling* and Gessner's *Idyllen*), while the rationalistic or teleological idea—that God, being Himself Reason, has created everything for the purpose of Reason, which is servability to man—is wearily repeated from instance to instance, and is made more weary by the grinding out of the eternal alexandrines, though the rhythm is relieved by lines of varying length.

The philosophic note of Brockes is continued by his friend KARL FRIEDRICH DROLLINGER (1688–1742), who wrote didactic poetry at Basel (*Gedichte*, 1743), and still more by ALBRECHT VON HALLER (1708–77), who was born at Berne, graduated at Leyden, made a stay of two years in England, and, the most famous scholar of his day, was in 1736 called to Göttingen as professor of botany, anatomy, physiology and surgery. He wrote his letters and his diary in French, his scientific works in Latin. As a Swiss he found difficulties in writing German verse, and this he hints at in the title of his *Versuch schweizerischer Gedichte*, ' An

Attempt at Swiss Poems' (1732), and indeed his vocabulary has Swiss dialect elements. In 1753 Haller returned to Berne, where he died in 1777. The second edition of the *Versuch* (1734) included the most famous of his poems, *Die Alpen*. It is the first [1] description of Alpine scenery before Rousseau's *La nouvelle Héloïse* (1761) ; but Haller has no lyric enthusiasm for the landscapes he describes ; his native mountains are depicted as stern and wild. He owed the conception of the poem to a botanical expedition in the Alps in 1728 ; in his diary he had written : ' *Heureux peuple que l'ignorance préserve des maux qui suivent la politesse des villes* ' ; and in the poem he contrasts the simple life of Swiss peasants with the depraved life of town dwellers : *Seht ein verachtet Volk zur Müh' und Arbeit lachen,* | *Die mässige Natur allein kann glücklich machen.* This is of course the idea which, a score of years later, Haller's fellow-countryman Rousseau was to make the base of his sensational doctrine that man is happiest in the state of primitive nature, and is corrupted by the loose morality of town life ; and it is interesting that Haller, who was the reverse of revolutionary, indignantly rejected, when they were the topic of the day, the doctrines and person of Rousseau.

Haller continues the descriptive nature poetry of Brockes ; but whereas Brockes takes the universe apart and deals with it piecemeal, Haller has a sweep and grandeur of vision commensurate with his command of all the scientific knowledge of his time. *Die Alpen* loses, not so much by any defect of description as by the trailing length of the alexandrines, the heavy hammering of the metal. Haller by his pitiless cataloguing of details provided Lessing with an object lesson —important, too, for the consideration of the poetry of Matthisson and Salis-Seewis and the romanticists

---

[1] The first Alpine *lyrics* are those of Lenau, but they describe the Austrian and Styrian Alps.

—for his possibly not quite fair condemnation of descriptive poetry as a literary genre. In his *Laokoon* (1766) Lessing shows that Haller's minute description of the blue gentian, though in its way it is a masterpiece, fails to give us the instantaneous picture that we get, for instance, from a Dutch flower-piece ; he has split the whole into parts ; but in poetry the parts remain as parts, and the exact picture of the part as it passes fades out, so that we do not see the flower itself—unless we have seen it before, and in that case it is memory which creates or restores the picture, not the poem. Romantic poets, and still more the poets of our own day, agree with Lessing when he says, in effect : ' Do not describe, suggest ' ; which means, again, that the reader, with the help of memory and imagination, creates together with the poet.

As a writer of deeply thought out didactic and philosophical poetry Haller pairs rather with Schiller than with Brockes. What he has in common with Brockes is his teleological conception of the *mundus optimus*. But he is not so cock-sure as Brockes ; he sums up *Über den Ursprung des Übels* (one of the poems of the 1734 edition) by a series of *vielleicht* . . . The idea of this poem follows up Leibniz's *Essais de Théodicée sur la bonté de Dieu, la liberté de l'homme et l'origine du mal* (1710), which had been translated into German in 1720, and had been dealt with by Brockes in his poem *Der Ursprung des menschlichen Unvergnügens bei dem Ausgange des 1720sten Jahres.* Haller's poem—it has the colours and contours of modern verse—begins with a description of a prospect viewed from a pine-clad mountain crowned with shadows on the sky-line, the yellow lustre of cornfields gleaming between wooded hills, and the river Aar brightly winding through the far-stretched valley—peace and plenty spread to view, with mossy huts where labour is blessed with enjoyment. There follows a picture of

Creation, and the proof that evil is possible because man's will is free; for God saw that if the world were to be left to work like a clock it would be mechanism controlled from outside, and there would be no virtue, for man would have no power to sin. [A comparison with Goethe's poem *Proömion* (p. 74)—*Was wär' ein Gott, der nur von aussen stiesse* is inevitable]. God willed that we should love Him, not impelled by the blind force of imposed urges, but from the inspiration of knowledge; and therefore God gave man a will free to love Him. We should not praise God if we were forced to praise Him. Thus He created the angels; and they, being perfect, felt no urge to evil. But on man—' *zweideutig Mittelding von Engeln und vom Vieh* ' —God impressed His own image, but also the love of self, and, deep within, a watchful feeling that is ever prone to evil. Thus the love of beauty drove us to forbidden lusts. ' Perhaps . . .' man's soul is to be purified by long torment; ' perhaps . . .' his will shall turn from evil to good. The weight of thought in Haller's didactic poetry might give the impression that he was remote from common feeling; but in two poems there is an upwelling of deep human affection: in *Doris* (1730), his one love poem, addressed to the lady who was to be his wife, and the elegy *Trauerrede beim Absterben meiner geliebten Marianne*, in which he enshrines the grief he felt when she died just as he was settling in Göttingen.

Much less solid and serious than Brockes was his contemporary and fellow-townsman FRIEDRICH VON HAGEDORN (1708–54). During his three years as secretary of the Danish Embassy in London he made himself familiar with English literature. He returned to his native city of Hamburg in 1731, and in 1733 he was appointed secretary to *der englische Hof*, an old-established trading company. This comfortable post afforded him leisure for his literary pursuits. *Johann*

*der muntere Seifensieder*—in the title of which there is a
famous mistranslation of Lafontaine's *savetier*—is the
best known of his fables (*Fabeln*, 1738), which have the
metrical form of his model Lafontaine ; his lyrics
(*Versuch einiger Gedichte oder erlesene Proben poetischer
Nebenstunden*, 1729 ; *Sammlung neuer Oden und
Lieder*, 1742 ; *Moralische Gedichte*, 1750) are moulded
to the pattern of the French *poésies fugitives* of Chaulieu
and La Fare and the light verse of Prior and Gay ;
but his great master was Horace, whose odes he trans-
posed with great dexterity and occasionally with a
charm of imagery and a mastery of melody new then
and still delightful today. Much of Hagedorn's verse
falls into the anacreontic manner of the forties, and he
is classed as the first of the anacreontic poets of the
century. In his later years he wrote unrhymed
anacreontic verse in Gleim's manner.

All the literature of the thirties bears the stamp of
JOHANN CHRISTOPH GOTTSCHED (1700–66), the literary
dictator of the period. A native of East Prussia and
educated at the University of Königsberg, he saved
himself (1724) from the press-gang of the King of
Prussia—he was over six feet tall, and such men were
required for the Guards—by flight to Leipzig, where
he became professor of logic and metaphysics. In his
*Versuch einer kritischen Dichtkunst vor* [1] *die Deutschen*
(1730) he applied, with cold logic, the rationalism of
Christian Wolff to all the branches of literature. Since
everything serves a purpose, the argument ran, so too
does poetry ; and this purpose is to fit all that is
written to the service and the moral betterment of
mankind. The poet's aim must be, not to move, but
to improve. The theme or ' fable ' must be devised
by the understanding ; what is not at the first glance
clear must be rejected as dust and mist over the idea ;

[1] In the eighteenth century *vor* (O.H.G. *vora*) and *für* (O.H.G.
*furi*) were confused.

and once the theme is devised it may be evolved either in the sense of comedy or of tragedy. Gottsched's utter negation of the senses and of sensuality, of feeling and passion, indeed of all that is not the planned product of the reasoning faculty, was bound to lead to cut-and-dried rules which have the form of recipes. He describes Baroque poetry as a vertical region with wild peaks straining to the skies, with plunging abysses, mist-shrouded valleys and forests gloomed with mystery, whereas the Rococo poetry of which he is the expositor is a level landscape with all its features geometrically ordered, and with nothing hid or strange : the river drives the mill, which grinds the corn, which the baker bakes into bread that man consumes in a pleasant arbour. The revolt which led to the dictator's down-fall had begun guardedly with *Die Discourse der Mahlern*, a journal, on the model of Addison's *Spectator*, published in Zürich (1721–23) by JOHANN JAKOB BODMER (1698–1783) ; the break-away gathered momentum in 1740, the year of Frederick the Great's accession to the throne of Prussia, with the appearance of Bodmer's *Kritische Abhandlung von dem Wunderbaren in der Poesie*, and of JOHANN JAKOB BREITINGER'S (1701–76) *Kritische Dichtkunst*. From now onwards Bodmer and Breitinger, two staunch friends and allies, carry on their campaign for a new literature which shall not be tied down by pedantic rules ; to us today they may themselves seem pedants, but in their day they were iconoclasts. Bodmer's reading of Addison had led him to Milton ; and the result was his prose translation of *Paradise Lost* (1732). Round this mass of Baroque bombast, as it appeared to Gottsched, the battle of the Swiss and the Leipzig men (*Streit der Leipziger und Schweizer*) surged and raged.

Both schools agreed as to the main tenet that art imitates nature (for Aristotle had said so) ; but the Swiss urged that nature had existed before art, that

the best writing had not been built up mechanically
by the observance of rules, but that, on the other hand,
rules had been deduced from writings; nature is in
the poet, and nature in the poet writes; in other
words, the poet is inspired, not directed. Bodmer's
interpretation of the miraculous (*das Wunderbare*)
swept the field, and Germany awaited its own Milton,
whom the revelation of the new doctrine should bring.
In Bodmer himself there was nothing of Milton, nor
of the wonderful; but he had what may be called
critical imagination, and certainly insight; and he saw
deeper into the essentials of poetry than any German
critic had done before him. His doctrine of imagination and of emotional inspiration is that of the literary
movements to come—of Klopstock and the Hainbund,
of *Sturm und Drang*, and of romanticism. From now
on poetry wells up from the deep spring of inspiration,
and is not channelled and confined.

Breitinger in his *Kritische Dichtkunst* stresses the
importance of descriptive poetry—' *poetische Gemälde* ';
and he too explores the difference between logical
reasoning, which is the handmaid of science, and
imagination, which is the *fons et origo* of poetry. This
treatise of Breitinger's is amusingly summed up in
Book 7, Part 2, of Goethe's *Dichtung und Wahrheit*:
poetry imitates nature; but nature is crude, and therefore the poet must imitate what is significant or
important (*bedeutend*) in nature; but what *is* important? Obviously that which is new. Now what
is new is always more *wonderful* than anything else.
But what is wonderful may be without significance
for the fate of man; a poet, therefore, must select
from what is new that which is of a nature to improve
his fellow-men; and from this it follows that the
highest form of poetry is the fable; for the fable links
with a miraculous happening (animals speaking, &c.)
the betterment of humanity by the moral inculcated.

In the light of this verdict it is not surprising that a *Blütezeit* for the fable follows—though ‘ fable ’ was really intended to include any invented story, the plot of a drama, &c. Lafontaine and Hagedorn were already there as past masters of the genre, and GOTT-HOLD EPHRAIM LESSING (1729–81), the greatest critic of the century, not only wrote fables of his own, but wrote an illuminative essay, *Abhandlung über die Fabel* (1759). In this essay Lessing disproves Breitinger’s thesis that if animals speak in fables this is something wonderful : it is assumed, and therefore it is a common-place idea, that they do so. What Lessing criticized in the fables of his day was the deviation from concision and the plain statement of truth to the poetically embellished manner of Lafontaine and Hagedorn and the rest ; what charms us in these fables, it is true, is often not the moral, but the poetry ; the fable of the period is in the nature of a *jeu d’esprit*, like the con-temporary anacreontic verse. The fables which accom-pany Lessing’s essay are in concise prose ; but, in spite of logic, his earlier verse fables (*Fabeln und Erzählungen*, 1753) are much more pleasing.

Blest with no thrill of lyric feeling, Lessing’s rhyming can only be rated low. As a critic he is in the first rank : his *Hamburgische Dramaturgie* (1767–69) paves a way to the appreciation of Shakespeare, and his *Laokoon* (1766) is the very groundwork of modern aesthetics ; here Lessing argues against the thesis *Ut pictura poesis*, which Bodmer and Breitinger and Brockes had made their doctrine. Identity of poetry and painting is impossible, Lessing proves ; for while painting is contiguous poetry is consecutive. Painting represents bodies, poetry actions. Painting can repre-sent actions only by allusion (*andeutungsweise*), poetry can only represent bodies allusively by actions. And this, Lessing demonstrates, is Homer’s technique.

Lessing’s starting-point for *Laokoon* had been his

reading of JOHANN JOACHIM WINCKELMANN'S (1717–
1768) *Geschichte der Kunst des Altertums* (1764), a work
which, following this great scholar's *Gedanken über die
Nachahmung der griechischen Werke in der Malerei und
Bildhauerkunst* (1754), laid the foundation for a new
interpretation of the Greek classics and at the end of
the century gave shape and colouring to the new
classicism of Goethe and Schiller (p. lxxvi) with its sacred
text taken from Winckelmann : *Edle Einfalt und stille
Grösse.*

The classical writer of fables was to be CHRISTIAN
FÜRCHTEGOTT GELLERT (1715–69), like Gottsched a
professor at Leipzig ; he was the darling of his day,
and everybody's poet. There is a musicality and
charm in his fables (*Fabeln und Erzählungen*, 1746,
1748), which comes near to what is best in Lafontaine ;
the moral lesson is lightly conveyed, and the verse,
with its lines of unequal length (*vers libres*), is varied
and touched with sly humour.

Gellert contributed to the *Bremer Beiträge* (1745–59),
a journal which was edited in Leipzig but owed its
title to the fact that it was published in Bremen.
Those who wrote for the journal—among them
Johann Adolf Schlegel, the father of the romanticist
brothers Schlegel ; his brother, the critic Johann Elias
Schlegel (1719–49) ; and the critic and satirist Gottlieb
Wilhelm Rabener (1714–71)—, though their aim was
still correctness of form and moral betterment, had
fallen away from Gottsched to take sides with the
Swiss.

The fable, particularly as handled by Lessing, was
a vehicle of satire ; but the satire of the period was
most direct and pungent in the epigram (*das Sinnge-
dicht*). In the year that saw the publication of his
*Fabeln* (1759) Lessing had edited the *Sinngedichte* of
the seventeenth-century satirist FRIEDRICH VON
LOGAU (1605–55). Lessing's own epigrams are often

hackneyed or even trivial ; but sometimes they have a telling effect ; e.g.

> *Wer wird nicht einen Klopstock loben ?*
> *Doch wird ihn jeder lesen ? — Nein.*
> *Wir wollen weniger erhoben*
> *Und fleissiger gelesen sein.*

Since the epigram, if it is to strike home, must be concise and adroitly turned and pointed, it is not surprising that the most brilliant epigrammatist of the time was a professor of mathematics (at Göttingen)—ABRAHAM GOTTHELF KÄSTNER (1719–1800). The epigram of Rococo is not a lyric genre ; its only music is the swish of the rapier. This is still true of Bürger's epigrams (p. xlv ff.) ; these, however, may have a tragic personal note. The epigram rises to poetry when the rhymed form, paired or crosswise, gives way to distiches (hexameter + pentameter) which cradle the idea in a melodious flow and tone down the raw invective, though they may not blunt the rapier's point. Klopstock's distiches are still rough-hewn, or even lumbering. The epigram reaches its height in Goethe's and Schiller's *Xenien* ; but some of the poets who come after them also excel in this typically German genre, notably Platen and Rückert, though the latter is usually persuasively didactic rather than fiercely combative.

The university of Halle, at the turn of the century the cradle of pietism, had been the centre whence rationalism radiated ; here, after a period at Leipzig, Thomasius had taught ; here Christian Wolff diluted the philosophy of Leibniz ; and here ALEXANDER GOTTLIEB BAUMGARTEN (1714–62), a pupil of Wolff, following the lead of Bodmer and Breitinger, laid the foundations of the new science of aesthetics (*Æsthetica*, 1750). And now, in the forties, poets who had been *alumni* of Halle—' the Halle poets ', ' die preussische Dichterschule '—broke away from the applied rationalism of Gottsched, and, for the most part with easeful grace and wit, produced a body of lyric verse which, though not quite new in type—for Hagedorn had been a master of much the same styles—practised an elegant irrationalism. Two of them, JAKOB IMMANUEL PYRA (1713–44) and SAMUEL GOTTHOLD LANGE (1711–81), anticipated the *Odes* of Klopstock by attempting rhymeless metres modelled on those of Greek and Roman poetry : *Thirsis und Damons freundschaftliche Lieder*, their joint work, was published by Bodmer in 1745. But what the Halle poets—JOHANN WILHELM LUDWIG GLEIM (1719–1803), JOHANN PETER UZ (1720–96), and JOHANN NIKOLAUS GÖTZ (1721–81)— are best remembered for is their anacreontic verse. The light Greek lyrics attributed to Anacreon had been first edited by a member of the Pléiade, Henri Estienne, in 1554, and Remi Belleau had translated them in French verse ; but the first adequate German translation was *Die Oden Anakreons in reimlosen Versen* (1746) ; it bears the name of Götz, but Uz had collaborated.

Gleim was the most famous of the *Anakreontiker* ; his emoluments as Cathedral Secretary (*Domsekretär*) at Halberstadt—he held the post for fifty-five years —enabled him generously to befriend impecunious poets ; guests were continuously installed in his hospitable home, and through the second half of the century he was known as Vater Gleim. His reputation as a poet rested mainly on his *Fabeln* (1756), poor by comparison with those of Hagedorn, Gellert and Lessing, and above all on his patriotic *Preussische Kriegslieder von einem Grenadier* (1756–57). These ballads sing the victories of Frederick the Great ; today they have the glitter of tinsel, partly because of their blend of folksong patter—the Chevy Chase stanza [1] is used, but the rhythm is monotonously level and regular—and

---

[1] The Chevy Chase stanza was introduced by Klopstock, but unrhymed.

classical mythological trimming. Gleim tried his hand
at narrative poems (*Romanzen*), but these are rather
travesties or *Bänkelsängerlieder* ; their ironic handling
was continued with greater vigour and coarseness by
Bürger (p. xlix).

The anacreontic poetry (*die Anakreontik*) really
begins with Gleim's *Versuch in scherzhaften Liedern*
(1744). Included are adaptations of poems by the
Minnesingers, who were to be published by Bodmer
(*Proben der Minnesänger*, 1748 ; *Sammlung von Minnesingern aus dem schwäbischen Zeitpunkte*, 1759) ; such
free translations, often marvellously attuned to the
lyric note of the time, appear in the other anacreontic
poetry, and in that of the Hainbund and of Bürger.
Gleim's later anacreontic verse (*Lieder nach dem
Anakreon*, 1766 ; *Gedichte nach den Minnesingern*,
1773 ; &c.), trochaic or iambic, is usually in four-
lined stanzas, the first and third lines unrhymed with
feminine endings, the second and fourth with masculine
rhymes. The *Lyrische Gedichte* (1749) of Uz, a legal
official (*Justizbeamter*) in Ansbach, followed Gleim's
*Versuch*. Götz's lyrics—except for *Versuch eines
Wormsers in Gedichten*, published without his name in
1750—did not appear till after his death (*Vermischte
Gedichte*, 1785) ; as a parson he had needed anonymity.

In this considerable body of anacreontic verse, which
is continued, though less exclusively, by the poets of
the Hainbund, the *carpe diem* motif recurs continuously.
It finds its loveliest expression in Hölty's *Rosen auf
den Weg gestreut* ; it echoes to this day, as it has done
through the ages, in the students' song *Gaudeamus
igitur*. But the main tenor is a frank hedonism, which
logically derives from the comparative optimism of the
Age of Enlightenment : in the best of all possible
worlds the best of all is the pleasure of the senses ;
' *Wein, Weib, Gesang* ', as Luther had phrased it.
The love element, however, is impersonal, an airy

fiction. Whereas Günther's love for Leonore had been intensely personal, the anacreontic poet sings, not of a girl, but of girls ; to him a girl is a toy, or at best an idea. Was it indeed to be expected that a high official of the church, or a legal luminary, or a gowned parson could love so lightly and drink so potently ? Hagedorn indeed, a wealthy patrician with no moral obligations, may have had his girls and his banquets ; Gleim was a bachelor and a water-bibber ; Hölty, an ungainly ill-dressed recluse, had to collect information from his experienced friends as to the configuration and function of bosoms. Like the love of the knights for the wives of other knights, which is the monotonous theme of the troubadours as of the Minnesingers, these peri-wigged functionaries follow a fashion ; it is all just a phase of lyric verse. What makes the attraction of anacreontic verse is the conceit, the elegant turn of phrase, the wit, and in the best of it the melody (as : Kleist's softly suggestive *Und auf Rosen ruhn*). So much a fashion of the day are these *amatoria et potatoria* that even Lessing (*Kleinigkeiten*, 1751) had his fling at it ; his verses of this sort, as might be expected, have point and pungency, but their cold cleverness sets in relief the little masterpieces of the anacreontics proper.

EWALD CHRISTIAN VON KLEIST (1715–59), an officer in the Prussian army, died of wounds received in the battle of Kunersdorf ; like Theodor Körner at the beginning of the next century he lives on in the memory of his nation as one who might have achieved so much more had he not been a soldier with a nobler fate than that of a poet. A close friend of Gleim as of Lessing, he was more than an *Anakreontiker*, though he began with anacreontic verse. He is remembered more as the first German poet after Brockes to write a descriptive nature poem in the manner of Thomson's *Seasons* ; he too planned a poem on the full cycle of the year, but only *Der Frühling* (1749) was completed. The metrical form is an innovation : it is in hexameters beginning with an unstressed syllable (*Vorschlagssilbe, Auftakt,* anacrusis). To us it must be surprising that with the intense study of English poetry at this time Kleist did not choose blank verse—the metre of Thomson's *Seasons* ; decasyllabic verse had indeed been attempted sporadically, but how difficult it was to make it run smoothly we can see from Lessing's *Nathan der Weise* (1774), which jolts along like a cart over cobbles. The unrhymed iambic line of the *Anakreontiker,* on the other hand, had come out smooth and melodious ; but they were not decasyllabic—lines with a short breath were required by the volatile social spirit of such verse. Certainly Kleist's hexametric line is more pleasing to the ear than Brockes' and Haller's Dutch-patterned alexandrines ; the greater readability of *Der Frühling,* however, is rather due to the fact that the poem is an idyll, whereas Brockes' and Haller's nature poetry had been weighted down with teleological philosophy.

Very close to Gleim was JOHANN GEORG JAKOBI (1740–1814). His lyrics—delicately limned and tinted like the most precious porcelain—have sometimes a loveliness of form that was unmatched till Goethe came ; and indeed one of them, *Der Sommertag,* was so like one of his own that Goethe innocently annexed it. His *Sagt, wo sind die Rosen hin ?* is still a popular song.

It is a far fling from the *vers de société* of the anacreontic poets to the priestlike solemnity and apostolic fervour of FRIEDRICH GOTTLIEB KLOPSTOCK (1724– 1803). Born at the ancient city of Quedlinburg, at the northern foot of the Harz Mountains, he was educated—like the *Bremer Beiträger* (p. xxv) Adolf and Elias Schlegel and, nearer our own time, Nietzsche— at the famous Saxon school of Schulpforta. Here he assiduously practised the writing of Greek and Latin

verse ; and his reading of Bodmer's translation of
*Paradise Lost*, added to his study of Homer, fired his
ambition to be a great epic poet. As a student at
Jena (1745) he wrote, in prose, the first three cantos of
his epic *Der Messias*. After six months at Jena he
transferred to Leipzig, where he came into contact with
the *Bremer Beiträger*, who were mightily impressed by
what he had written of the *Messias* ; and, acting on
the advice of his Leipzig friends, he rewrote his three
cantos in verse—not, however, in Miltonic blank verse,
but in hexameters. The *Messias* was the first long
poem to be written in this metre ; for the three cantos
appeared in the *Bremer Beiträge* for 1748, and Kleist's
*Frühling* appeared the year afterwards. The first five
cantos appeared in volume form in 1751, and the
remaining volumes in 1756, 1769, and 1773.

What above all is significant in *Der Messias* is the
theme and the way it is handled. Klopstock was a
deeply religious man, and by his upbringing and the
depth of his convictions he belonged to pietism ; but
against this he was temperamentally incapable of
asceticism, and he had the simple faith that the
Redemption had freed man from the burden of the sin
of Adam, and that by the Redemption we are con-
secrated to great joy and to delight in being and doing.
The tone of the epic, therefore, is triumphant ; there
is throughout the resonant note of God's victory over
fallen angels and devils on earth. Christ's victory is
our victory, and therefore we may be joyful ; the
purpose of life is not to wail and moan, but to develop
one's personality, to be conscious of this personality
and to express it with all the force that is given us.
But Klopstock's joy in life is not that of the anacreontic
poets ; their pleasures, indeed, were for the most part
a pretence ; their feelings were fictitious, while Klopstock's feelings are exuberant, almost dizzy, or, to
use his own word, seraphic. To him the passionate

upwelling of feeling is the best of life ; and thus he is
the chief exponent of that *Gefühlskultus* which, after the
meticulous rationalism of the thirties and the dainty
trifling of the forties, is the mark of the fifties.    What
makes the national enthusiasm for Klopstock significant
in the history of literature is the conviction it brought
with it that a true poet is dowered with a divine
nature ;  inspired himself, his task is to inspire and to
elevate his fellow men.    This ideal of moral betterment
remains over from the teleological school ;  but the
means to it is no longer reason, it is feeling.

The *Messias* was the literary sensation of the day ;
it was something new, it had the sound of trumpets.
Today the epic lies honoured but unread on our
shelves ;  few, even of scholars, get past the first seven
lines.    It has not the qualities of an epic ;  indeed it
is not an epic at all, for the action is slight ;  nothing
can happen, because there are no characters in the
epic or dramatic sense ;  there are merely angels or
devils who roll out reels of high-sounding hexameters ;
what thrills is not the conflict of character, but the
voice of the Lord or of Jesus out of the circumambient
mist.    The poem is just a lyric stretched out to weary-
ing dimensions.

It would be hazardous to say that the renascence of
wonder realized by Klopstock would not have been
possible if the Swiss critics had not broken the ground
for it ;  for Klopstock was a poet born, and a poet
incapable of being cramped by rules and reason ;
nevertheless in the writings of Bodmer and Breitinger
he found justification for his intuitive conception of
the sublimity of poetry.    His personal contact with
them, however, led to disillusion—on both sides.
Klopstock had been in correspondence with Bodmer,
and had, in particular, confided to him his love for
his cousin (the Fanny or Cidli of the *Odes*) ;  and
Bodmer had told his friends of an Ode he had seen

which the Messias himself might have written, had He been a lover. In the upshot Bodmer sent an invitation to visit Zürich, and Klopstock accepted. A letter from the poet should have put the old scholar on his guard : *Wie weit wohnen Mädchen Ihrer Bekanntschaft von Ihnen, von denen Sie glauben, dass ich einen Umgang mit ihnen haben könnte ?*, Klopstock asked. He adds that he would not like the girls to be told of his love for Fanny, as they might hold back. The guest arrived, in 1750 ; and Bodmer was shocked to find that, in addition to flirting, he drank wine and smoked tobacco, and he came to the conclusion that the *Messiasdichter* was, after all, no saint. Today, instead of being shocked, we should speak of his muscular Christianity ; and at all events his zest in outdoor sports dates from his proficiency in riding, skating, and swimming from his boyhood's days. What the Swiss did not realize was that Klopstock was a new sort of man ; he was more than a poet, he was a character ; and though today we may find it a heavy task to read his poetry, though we may agree with Lessing that his work is so full of feeling that we feel nothing, we must honour him as the great liberator he was.

The social tension at Zürich was relieved when a letter arrived in which Klopstock was informed that King Frederick V of Denmark had granted him a pension of 400 Thaler a year to enable him to complete the *Messias*, inviting him to live in Copenhagen. In February, 1751, Klopstock left Switzerland ; and on his passage through Quedlinburg to Hamburg he met Meta Moller, whom he married in 1754. She, too, is the Cidli of his poetry. She died in 1758. In 1770 Klopstock retired to Hamburg, where he still received his pension ; and here his epic was in the fullness of time (1773) brought to an end. With Lessing, too, resident in Hamburg as the *Dramaturg* of the new

3

repertory theatre the Free City was again for a time the literary centre of Germany. The poet's one grief in the last years of his life was the course of the French revolution, which he had hailed with enthusiasm; like Schiller he had been elected a citizen of the republic; but he was to curse what he had praised. In 1791 he married his wife's niece, Johanna von Winthem; and she cared for him till his death in 1803. There was a great funeral in the churchyard at Ottensen near Altona, where the poet lies with his two wives.

Today there is general agreement that Klopstock's outstanding achievement lies in his *Oden*. They, too, are difficult to read—not a few are frankly unreadable; but they mark a turning-point in the history of the German lyric, both as regards form, vocabulary, and themes. After the playful dalliance of the anacreontic poetry they return to the high seriousness of Brockes and Haller; but they are not philosophical, they are religious. Klopstock at his best cannot be classed as a thinker; historically considered his thinking, and still more his show of scholarship, was naïve. There is naïveté, too, in the conception of the native superiority of all that is German which, for the first time in German poetry, runs riot in these odes; but they go back to the roots of German history, they build up a German national consciousness, and a reverence, never again to die out, for *das Altgermanische*. Equally important is that, from first to last, they bring to the forefront the personality of the poet; he is not merely the mouthpiece, he is himself the theme. Klopstock is thus the first self-crowned *vates* of German poetry. He built up, too, a new poetical vocabulary and diction; he invented words, he gave new turns to syntax; he was, as a true poet must be, a creator of style.

Of the greatest possible importance historically is Klopstock's re-creation of lyrical form. He follows in

the wake of Pyra's and Lange's experiments, but he
has a more instinctive sense of rhythm and melody ;
and what he does essentially achieve is a rediscovery
of the natural rhythms of the German language.   His
starting-point is a declaration of war on rhyme.   The
classical languages, he says, in an ode to Johann Heinrich Voss, had ' *Wohlklang und Silbenmass* ' ;  and he
continues :

> *Die spätern Sprachen haben des Klanges noch wohl ;*
> *Doch auch des Silbenmasses ?  Statt dessen ist*
> *In sie ein böser Geist, mit plumpem*
> *Wörtergepolter, der Reim gefahren.*

> *Red' ist der Wohlklang, Rede das Silbenmass,*
> *Allein des Reimes schmetternder Trommelschlag,*
> *Was der ?  Was sagt uns sein Gewirbel,*
> *Lärmend und lärmend mit Gleichgetöne ?*

The metrical line itself, he means, constitutes the
melody and the rhythm ;  if the lines are varied, the
rhythm is varied ;  and so he casts aside the monotonous
iteration of iambus with iambus and trochee with
trochee and (in intention) makes the line more wavy
or fluid by blending them with choriambs and dactyls.
In theory he introduced—or rather established, for the
Anacreontics had already practised them—the classical
strophes of Greek and Latin poetry (Alcaic, Sapphic,
Asclepiadic) ;  but, phonetically considered, these complicated combinations of classical feet are illusory
—what we get, if we read with natural accentuation,
is a line with chief-stressing of the syllables which
convey the vital meaning together with depression of
subsidiary syllables.   Kleist's hexameter with anacrusis, too, was often illusory : *Führ' mich in Gängen
voll Nacht zum glänzenden Throne der Tugend* has no
*Vorschlagssilbe* at all, for *Führ'* is more highly stressed
than *mich* ;  and so, too, in Klopstock's lines a chief
stress often falls, according to the metrical scheme, on

what is grammatically and phonetically an unstressed syllable : thus he frequently depresses the grammatically stressed syllable of a separable verb : *Und still anbetend, da wo die Zukunft ist* (scansion : $\times\frac{\prime}{-} \mid \times\frac{\prime}{-}\times \mid \frac{\prime}{-}\times\times \mid \times\frac{\prime}{-} \mid \times\frac{\prime}{-}$); *Mit einweihendem Blick, als er geboren ward,* where the first two syllables are an iambus, whereas the scansion requires a trochee. This assumption of a main stress on a naturally unstressed syllable is technically a deviation from Opitz's rule that metrical and natural stress coincide ; but actually there is no need whatever, in reading Klopstock's Odes, to think of the ancient metrical scheme to which his poem has been fitted ; and the lines read naturally—as ' free rhythms ' (*freie Rhythmen*)—are almost always unclogged and musical. In other Odes Klopstock discarded classical scansion and wrote confessedly free rhythms (' *Klopstocksches Silbenmass* '), with lines shortened or lengthened by the surge or ebb of feeling, with bold enjambments, and with accentuation and breath-pauses fixed by the sense only. Such free verse—and we must stress that the classically scanned strophes, too, tend to be this free verse—are in the native Germanic pattern of lifts attached to the syllables that bear the sense—some higher, some lower—with intervals of slurred syllables. But, master of form as he is (and no one who follows him has such a resonant roll of rhythms), Klopstock is yet a pioneer ; and it remained for Matthisson, Hölderlin, and Platen to perfect and mellow his assertive and masculine technique.

There is considerable diversity of theme in the Odes ; but they can be chronologically classed and graded. Of the earliest (they date from 1747 and first appeared in collected form—*Sammlung der Oden*—in 1771) the most striking are not so much the love poems to Fanny or Cidli as those devoted to friendship (*An des Dichters Freunde*, 1747, later revised as *Wingolf*, with classical mythology replaced by Scandinavian); *An Ebert*, 1748. Here we have a craze of the fifties (*Freundschaftskultus*), which binds together the poets of the Hainbund and shows again in the correspondence of der junge Goethe. *Der Zürchersee* (1750) uses the landscape loosely as a background for a panegyric on friendship and joy. The very soul of Klopstock is in the odes which quiver to feelings stirred by meditations on God and creation and the Saviour (*Der Erlöser*, 1751). *Die Frühlingsfeier* (1757), in magnificently handled free rhythms, culminates in a vision of the Almighty coming in the roll of thunder. This is visionary verse, rapt, ecstatic; the meaning shifts, and may float away. ' *Klopstock zieht allem, was er behandelt, den Körper aus, um es zu Geist zu machen* ', says Schiller; and indeed in these seraphic poems all is spirit. More accessible to beginners are the odes in which the poet breathes out his robust zest in the common things of life; he takes their commonness away, but in such a poem as *Der Eislauf* (1764) there is delight in open-air exercise and something of that robustiousness which had horrified Bodmer. More directly appealing with their magic of mood and imagery are *Der Jüngling* (1764) and the two short poems in which the poet's lasting grief for his dead wife is veiled: *Die frühen Gräber* (1764) and *Die Sommernacht* (1766); these three lyrics at least are indisputably masterpieces.

The patriotic poems have no parentage, but they have a great progeny. They include eulogies of the German language (*Unsere Sprache an uns*, 1775, together with the rhymed ' epigram ' *Unsere Sprache*); these express the idea, developed later in a crisis of history by Fichte in his *Reden an die deutsche Nation*, that as the language is so is the nation, and that the German nation is thus the noblest of all. Curious is the ode *Die beiden Musen*: there is a race between

the British Muse and the German Muse ; Klopstock
spares us the finish, but we remember Herder's verdict
that one ode of Klopstock outweighs all the lyric
literature of Britain. The most dubious of the odes
are those in which classical mythology is discarded as
alien, and supplanted by that of the *Eddas* ; in his
discovery of primitive Germany Klopstock confused
Scandinavian scalds and Celtic bards ; the Celts, being
Nordic, were also German. The *Eddas* had become
known from P. H. Mallet's translation in his *Introduction à l'histoire de Dannemarc* (Copenhagen, 1755–56) ;
in England we find this new interest in medieval
Scandinavian lore reflected in Gray's bardic poems
*The Fatal Sisters* and *The Vegtam's Kivitha*. The
Celtic craze derives from Macpherson's *Ossian*, first
translated in 1764, and later on by the Austrian ' bard '
MICHAEL DENIS (1727–1800), who, together with his
fellow bard KARL FRIEDRICH KRETSCHMANN (1738–
1809) (*Gesang Rhingulfs des Barden, als Varus geschlagen
war*, 1768), popularized the bardic bellowing by his
*Lieder Sineds des Barden* (1772).

This interest in ancient poetry, Germanic or other-
wise, was to lead to a revolution in literature. No one
was more convinced of the authenticity of Ossian,
who in Germany had a greater vogue than he had in
England, than JOHANN GOTTFRIED HERDER (1744–
1803), by profession a clergyman who rose to high rank
in the church, and, after Lessing, the most inspiring
and fruitful German critic of the century. But how
different a critic from Lessing ! In Lessing, proof
patiently marshalled and illumined by the clear light
of reason ; in Herder criticism fortified by wide reading, but generated by a wild rush of feeling ; dynamic
and lyrical criticism, supplementary to Klopstock
rather than to Lessing. After Klopstock's poetry of
feeling, Herder's intuitive criticism precipitated by
pent-up feeling. Herder, the son of an elementary

schoolmaster in East Prussia, had been educated at the university of Königsberg ; he had been a pupil of Immanuel Kant (1724–1804), whose philosophy was soon to deepen German conceptions of literature ; and he owed much to a strange countryman of his, a way-ward genius, JOHANN GEORG HAMANN (1730–88), ' der Magus im Norden '. Hamann had been a rolling stone and something of a wastrel until, during a stay in London, down and out and desperate, he had turned to the Bible and there found illumination. His frag-mentary musings, often incoherent, often charged with the spark of inspiration, he grouped, on his return home, in aphoristic form, in *Sokratische Denkwürdig-keiten* (1759), *Kreuzzüge des Philologen* (1762), and *Aesthetica in nuce* (1772). Some of his *Genieblitze* ; none, perhaps, more than his saying ' *Poesie ist die Muttersprache des menschlichen Ge-schlechtes* '; this is the germ of Herder's essay *Über den Ursprung der Sprache* in his *Fragmente über die neuere deutsche Literatur* (1767–8). To Hamann Herder owed his first acquaintance with English literature ; he learned English by spelling his way through *Hamlet* under the guidance of his teacher ; and his English reading gives the main substance of much of his early work, particularly in *Von deutscher Art und Kunst* (1773). This work is made up of two essays by Herder, one on *Ossian und die Lieder alter Völker*, and the other on Shakespeare, followed by an essay by a young friend of his, then a student at Strassburg—Goethe— entitled *Von deutscher Baukunst*, in essence a rhapsody on ' Gothic ' architecture as exemplified by Strassburg Cathedral. Two English works of the time, which had incalculable influence on the break-through of new ideas in the German literature of the late sixties and early seventies, were Young's *Conjectures on Original Composition* (1759) and Percy's collection of old British ballads, *Reliques of English Poetry* (1765). The old

ballads were a revelation, particularly to Herder ; they
showed what wealth of genuine poetry there was in the
old popular poetry of Britain ; and it was Herder's
mission to proclaim that the *Volkslieder* of all nations
—hitherto scorned as barbaric—were primitive but for
that very reason delightful poetry—for ' poetry *is* the
primitive language of mankind '. Herder got together
a comprehensive collection of such folk-songs of all
the nations and published them in 1778–9 as *Volkslieder* ; the later title is *Stimmen der Völker in Liedern*.
Herder's conception of the *Volkslied* is catholic ; he
includes the Minnesong, which is for the most part
aristocratic and artificial rather than popular, as are
also the medieval scaldic lays he takes into his net ;
his lyrics from Shakespeare's plays, in his own apt
translation, are much more in the nature of songs of
the people, but not the misty meanderings of Ossian,
which Goethe nevertheless (in *Werthers Leiden*) transformed by the magic of his own mood.

Herder's original poetry is second-rate ; it is metric-
ally good, but hackneyed ; his themes are often morally
edifying, but they have no thrill of vision, no unex-
pectedness of imagery. The mass of it is good clergyman's verse, with here and there, where Klopstock's
mood is on him, an alluring note of modernity, the
illusion of a great mind plunging into mystic deeps.
In the best of his verse he is a *Nachempfinder* : one
who re-creates with the most delicate perception of
the qualities of his model. This is obvious, for instance,
if one compares his *Der Eistanz*—a good poem—with
Klopstock's *Der Eislauf* ; metre and rhythm are quite
different ; but the motifs and the images are taken
over quite literally—one might say shamelessly if
Herder were not such a respectable person. It is just
this knack of re-creating differently, and yet alike,
what has been intensely felt that makes a perfect verse
translator ; and that Herder certainly was. And

nowhere more so than in *Der Cid* (1808), his re-creation
of the national epic of Spain, which he rendered, not
from Spanish, but from a French prose version.

Klopstock's rhapsodic cult of friendship, his hatred
of tyrants, his mythical worship of the ancient poetry
and customs of his race, were shared to the full by a
band of disciples, for the most part present or past
students of the university of Göttingen, who are known
in literary history as *der Hainbund* and *der Göttinger
Hain*. (Actually the term Hainbund was first used
by J. H. Voss in 1804 as a parallel to Greek Olympus.)
The ancient Germans had celebrated their rites and
held their tribal deliberations in groves of oak, the
Hainbund believed ; and hence the name they adopted.
Not literally in an oak-grove, but in a festive chamber
with a vacant chair wreathed with flowers to represent
the throne of Klopstock as master bard, they solemnly
declared war on all that was not German to the core,
and in particular on CHRISTOPH MARTIN WIELAND
(1733–1813), who, in their view, was an immoral man
and a panderer to French taste ; for which reason at
this convivial gathering in 1773 they burned his
portrait and his poem *Idris* (1768). The poets of the
Hainbund shared Herder's belief that poetry should
reach the heart of the people ; and there is a per-
ceptible approach to the folk-song in their lyrics, some
of which (e.g. Hölty's *Rosen auf den Weg gestreut*) have
been genuine *Volkslieder* since the time they were
written. These poets still play with anacreontic genres,
but there is a richer fund of experience ; or, where
there is still a lack of it (as in Hölty's erotic verse), it
is compensated for by a haunting expression of yearning which, after all, is itself experience in the best
sense of the word. Even their adaptations of old
Minnelieder ring true ; and in their frequent handling
of the *carpe diem* motif and their elegiac verse the tone
is deeper and more intense. The sombre colouring and

the plaintive melancholy of their verse at its best is palpably influenced by Young's *Night Thoughts* (1742), which had been translated (in prose) by JOHANN ARNOLD EBERT (1723–95), one of the *Bremer Beiträger*, in 1751 ; and they owe much of their popular appeal to their study of Percy's *Reliques*. In their handling of the classical strophes introduced by Klopstock there is less force but a more melodic cadencing of the rhythm. How completely German these strophes are, and how appropriate for elegiac themes, comes out clearly if Hölty's parallel handlings of *carpe diem*, *Lebenspflichten* and *Der rechte Gebrauch des Lebens* are compared ; the former (*Rosen auf den Weg gestreut*), in alternately rhymed quatrains, has, perhaps, too light a lilt for its serious import, while the latter (*Wer hemmt den Flug der Stunden ? Sie rauschen hin*) in the alcaic strophe has, with its slower motion, more of the gradual shadowing of life by death. Hölty and his fellow-poets develop the adaptations, rhymed or unrhymed, of the Minnesang which Gleim and others had initiated.

The organ of the Hainbund, the *Göttinger Musenalmanach*, had already (1769) been founded by HEINRICH CHRISTIAN BOIE (1744–1806 ; pronounce [bɔjə]), a poet now of no account but the leading spirit in the inception of the league ; the journal was afterwards edited by Voss (1775), then (1776–78) by Göckingk, and was then carried on (1778–94) by Bürger. The Göttinger Musenalmanach played a great part in the contemporary history of the lyric ; for the best poets of the day, including Klopstock, wrote for it, and Goethe contributed to the issue for 1774, in which, too, Bürger's *Lenore* made its sensational appearance. Moreover, other *Musenalmanache*—particularly that of Schiller—followed, and in them appeared much of the representative verse of the period.

The revolutionary hotheads of the Bund were two

Reichsgrafen, the brothers CHRISTIAN (1748–1821) and
FRIEDRICH LEOPOLD (1750–1814) ZU STOLBERG.
They belonged later to the *Sturm und Drang* movement,
and were friends of der junge Goethe, whom they
accompanied on his Swiss journey in 1775. Fritz
Stolberg, as a student at Göttingen, was a fiery
republican ; and as such he hurled dithyrambic songs
of hate at the heads of tyrants. Nevertheless, there
is the martial ardour of his class in other poems which
were long popular : *Lied eines schwäbischen Ritters an
seinen Sohn* and *Lied eines deutschen Knaben.* Like
Klopstock, he was cured of his fervour for freedom by
the course of the French revolution ; and towards the
end of his life, to the horror of his friends, he allowed
himself to be converted to Catholicism.

If it had not been for Boje's help JOHANN HEINRICH
VOSS (1751–1826) would not have been able to study
at Göttingen ; he was the grandson of a serf in Mecklenburg. At the university Voss kept up a lively correspondence with Boje's sister Ernestine ; he fell in
love with her before he met her ; in the course of
time he married her, and their simple but happy
domestic life is reflected in his idylls. Voss was a
typical hard-featured and hard-natured Mecklenburg
man ; and his peasant stock and upbringing comes to
the surface even in his most scholarly work. The
grinding poverty of his youth filled him with life-long
hatred of the nobility ; this rings out unpleasantly,
for instance, in his vituperative ' idyll ' *Die Leibeigen-
schaft.* Voss indeed is said to have fixed—he certainly
helped to fix—the opprobrium which since his days
attaches to the term Junker. He owed his appointment as headmaster of the Gymnasium at Eutin in
Holstein to Fritz Stolberg ; but when the latter turned
Catholic he attacked him tooth and nail as a reac-
tionary. Voss ended his days at Heidelberg, where he
was loosely associated with the university. Today

Voss is best remembered for his longer village idylls in hexameters : *Der siebzigste Geburtstag* (1781) and *Luise* (1795), the latter Goethe's direct model for *Hermann und Dorothea*. In his shorter *Idyllen* there is a rough realism which is in stark contrast with the Arcadian idylls of Gessner (see p. li). His lyrics too are often in the nature of genre pictures of North German rural life ; typical is *Die Kartoffelernte*— Goethe praised it—, in which the nutritive properties of the homely potato and the hectic harvesting of its tubers are celebrated. Voss was a pioneer, too, in dialect (*Plattdeutsch*) poetry ; he was soon to be followed here by Maler Müller and Hebel (pp. lii–liii). And this rough-hewn poet wrote translations of Homer (*Homers Odüssee*, 1781 ; *Ilias*, 1793) ; the hexameters are as rough-hewn as he was himself, and today the smoother versions of Rudolf Alexander Schröder or Thassilo von Scheffer are preferred ; but Voss's *Homer*, reprinted continuously in cheap editions, was and remained the one German epic after Klopstock's *Messias* which was read by the people ; indeed it might be said that till recent times the only national German epics—for the *Messias*, as we have seen, was not an epic at all—were the *Nibelungenlied* and Voss's *Homer*, though one might perhaps add Herder's *Der Cid*.

At the opposite pole to Voss was the gentle poet LUDWIG HÖLTY (1748–76), the son of a village parson ; he died of consumption at the age of twenty-eight. The delicately cadenced rhythm of his classical strophes is matched only by Matthisson and surpassed by none but Hölderlin. The patience with which he bore deprivation and disease shows in his verse ; only in such a poem as *Der Tod* is there a faint note of rebellion against his fate.

The best work of JOHANN MARTIN MILLER (1750–1814) was in his adaptations of the Minnesong. Several of his lyrics (*Was frag' ich viel nach Geld und Gut* and *Das ganze Dorf versammelt sich*) still survive as folk-songs. LEOPOLD FRIEDRICH GÜNTHER VON GÖCK-INGK (1748–1828) had a vein of pointed wit and satire, which shows in his verse *Episteln* ; in his lyrics (*Lieder zweier Liebenden*, 1777, and *Gedichte*, 1780–2) there is more of anacreontic playfulness than of the genuine feeling of the Hainbund poets. The last lyric in Herder's *Volkslieder* is the *Abendlied* of MATTHIAS CLAUDIUS (1740–1815) ; by its very nature, Herder judged, this poem, though freshly written, was a folk-song ; and time has confirmed the verdict. Matthias Claudius is to this day one of the most popular of German poets ; and it would be hard to think that some of his lyrics could ever fade out of the public mind. To a note of hearty familiarity he joins a simple Christianity which has endeared him all the more to wide circles of readers ; and, light-hearted as his general moods may seem, there is in some of his lyrics a sense of deeper things which touches the inmost chords of feeling ; nowhere else in the German language is the awesomeness of death brought home to us so solemnly as in the four simple lines of *Der Tod*. He was somewhat loosely associated with the Hain-bund—he had not studied at Göttingen. One of the first popular journalists in the history of German literature, he was known as der Wandsbecker Bote, this being the name of the journal he edited (1771–5) at Wandsbeck, near Hamburg.

More closely associated with the *Hainbündler,* though not actually one of them (his style was aggressive and dramatic rather than elegiac) was GOTTFRIED AUGUST BÜRGER (1747–94) ; like Boie, Hölty, and Miller he was a son of the manse. He first studied theology at Halle, and then law at Göttingen. At Halle he was associated, to his moral detriment, with the disso-lute Professor Klotz, whom we know from Lessing's

relentless attack in the *Literaturbriefe* as a superficial
and fraudulent species of scholar.   But Klotz was well
aware of Bürger's gifts, and he won him over from his
ostensible field of studies to literature.   At Göttingen
Bürger founded a Shakespeare club—the members
were so drunk and uproarious at the first meeting that
they found themselves in gaol the morning after.   At
Göttingen, too, he studied Italian and Spanish and
began to translate Homer ;   and here he dived deep
into the one book which was to shape him as the first
and best of modern ballad writers—Percy's *Reliques*.
In 1771 he contributed a poem to the *Göttinger
Musenalmanach*, and he was represented in the following issues.   In 1772 Boie procured him an appointment
as judge (*Amtmann*) at Altengleichen, near Göttingen.
He was no business man, and he got into financial
difficulties from which he suffered for the rest of his
life ;   nevertheless he held out in this uncongenial post,
neglecting his dossiers for his literary avocation, for
twelve years.

In 1773 there were two literary events of momentous
importance :  the publication of Goethe's drama *Götz
von Berlichingen* and of Bürger's ballad *Lenore*.   With
*Lenore* the *Göttinger Musenalmanach* presented something absolutely new, and from now on Bürger had to
be reckoned with as one of the poets of the day.   In
1774 he married Dorette Leonhart.   We know from
his own confession that he was already in love with
his wife's younger sister Molly.   The result was a
*mariage à trois*, a marital complication which in those
early days of *Sturm und Drang* was much to the fore ;
it is the solution of the dramatic problem in Goethe's
drama *Stella*.   Dorette died in 1784, and in 1785
Bürger married Molly, who had already borne him a
son ;  but after six months of happiness she too died.
A knowledge of this unsavoury story is needed for any
adequate comprehension of the most vivid of Bürger's

lyric verse ; immoral as the inspiration was, the poems which reveal the poet's passion for Molly have the throb and thrill of tragic experience, while those which have Dorette and her child for theme make clear the anguish of his conflict and desperation. Before his marriage to Molly Bürger had been forced to give up his post as judge ; and he then took up residence at Göttingen to try his luck in what should have been a more congenial profession, that of university lecturer (*Privatdozent*). He lectured on aesthetics and metrics ; and he was one of the first university teachers to lecture on Kant. In 1789 he was given the title of professor, but still without salary. His most brilliant pupil was August Wilhelm Schlegel, who, in particular, learned from Bürger that mastery of sonnet form which was to give him distinction among the romanticists. Together, as intimate friends, they studied English, Italian, and Spanish ; together they translated Shakespeare's *Midsummer Night's Dream* ; and to these joint activities we may trace at least one source of that intensive study and translation of the masterpieces of world literature which is one of the outstanding achievements of romanticism. Bürger's function at the university was thus to stimulate literary studies ; academically judged he was a man of wide reading in many languages, but with no strict discipline of research or indeed of exact scholarship. He was, however, one of the first *Germanisten* ; he had whatever knowledge was then possible of old German literature. Bürger hailed the French revolution with exultation ; and, unlike Klopstock, he remained a political and social revolutionary. Like Voss he had come into collision with the petty nobility of his district, and like Voss he despised and detested their class. His political lyrics (*Empörungslyrik*) are among his best work. His hatred of tyrants rings out in such a poem as *Die Tode*, in which he cries out that the man who dies for

his king has the courage of a dog. Two events contributed to the disaster which finally overwhelmed
Bürger : Schiller's scathing critique of his poetry, and
his marriage to Elise Hahn, a Swabian girl who had
written to him declaring her admiration and offering
to be his third wife ; she was a light o' love who
carried on with students in his own home while he
was lecturing. He divorced her ; but he had always
been cold-shouldered by his colleagues at the university
—only two literary professors, the epigrammatist
Kästner and the satirist Lichtenberg, had treated him
with human decency ; and he was now completely
discredited and isolated, so that his death in 1794 was
a relief from hopeless misery. His effects were sold
by auction to pay his debts.

Bürger's rank as a lyric poet has been variously
estimated. It is agreed that his ballads are the best
in their kind, as they are the first in time ; and it is
agreed that he was the first to write perfect sonnets
(1788-9). But there has been a tendency to allow
him only the second rank as a lyric poet ; his lyrics,
it is urged, have the dramatic move, surge, and
resonance of his ballads, but they have also the violent
tone and the metrical tricks which fit the action that
ballads need but are out of place in lyric verse, which
must be judged by the indefinable magic of mood and
melody which we find, say, in Hölty's poems. That
is, Bürger's verse is contrived and cunningly elaborated,
not inspired ; in Schiller's terminology it is *sentimentalisch*, not *naïve*. There is some truth in this ;
but on the other hand we may argue that if lyric verse
is to be measured by the expression of the poet's
personality, by whatever means are available to the
particular poet, then there is very little in German
poetry that comes near to Bürger's love lyrics ;
Günther is perhaps, but in a more limited range and
on a lower note, his equal ; Goethe surpasses him,

though in Goethe's love lyrics there is not Bürger's direct and overpowering outburst of physical passion. In the love lyrics to and for Molly we have the most intensely personal and passionate love lyrics in the German language. Nothing is hidden ; there is shame, defiance, exultation, and despair. In judging Bürger's poetry we must remember his intentions. He was determined to be, first and foremost, a *Volksdichter*, a poet for the people. The popularity of a poetical work, he argues, is the seal of its perfection. The poet must write for the people, not for critics and scholars. Bürger was by his very nature (like Robert Burns, with whom he has striking points of contact) a poet with a direct appeal to a wide audience ; but he based his technique firstly on his intimate knowledge of Percy's *Reliques* and secondly on Herder's essay *Über Ossian und die Lieder alter Völker*. The latter he supplemented by his own disquisition *Aus Daniel Wunderlichs Buche : Herzenserguss über Volkspoesie*. His ballad *Lenore*, written at the age of twenty-five, was intended to realize Herder's programme of poetry for the people ; and literally it did so. There had been ballads in the Middle Ages ; that of *Tannhäuser*, for instance ; but this indigenous ballad had deteriorated, and survived only in the form of *Bänkelsänger-lieder* and *Gassenhauer* (street ballads and broadsheets), which were recited and sold at fairs and other gatherings by itinerant ballad-mongers. But the anacreontics had come across Góngora's humanist travesties of old Spanish ballads ; and Gleim in particular thought the Spaniards were the inventors of this form of burlesque ballad, which he imitated in his *Romanzen* (1756). Hölty and others had written such *Romanzen* (*Ballade* and *Romanze* were used indiscriminately for the same thing) ; and Bürger's semi-obscene *Prinzessin Europa* is literally shaped as a narrative recited by a ballad-monger to a crowd of gaping yokels ; his *Frau Schnips*,

4

modelled on the ballad of the *Wife of Bath* in Percy's *Reliques* and a scurrilous lampoon on Bible history, is of the same nature, while *Die Weiber von Weinsberg* treats lightly a theme which served Rückert and Chamisso for noble classical ballads. The importance of *Lenore* lies in the fact that it displaces this comical ballad or ' romance ' and provides the model, in form derived from the medieval ballad. *Lenore* marks the height of Bürger's achievement as a ballad writer; there is a masterly use of metrical devices—dialogue, onomatopoeia, anaphora, asyndeton. Important, too, is the first appearance here of an element which was to be a main ingredient of romanticism—the use of the supernatural (*Geisterromantik*); this we find too in another ballad of Bürger's, *Des Pfarrers Tochter von Taubenheim*, the theme of which—the murder of her new-born child by an unmarried mother—points forward to *Sturm und Drang*.

The main point of Schiller's devastating critique is that Bürger lacked a sense of the ideal; i.e. that his work is crude. Bürger, says Schiller, boasts of being a *Volkssänger*; but a *Volkssänger* should raise the people to his own level and not descend, as Bürger does, to theirs. To Bürger's contention that the popularity of a poem is its seal of perfection Schiller replies that the hall-mark of a poem is its inner worth; and the poet must perfect himself, if he would write perfect poetry. There is pith and purpose in Schiller's argumentation, but his conception of poetry as set forth in his critique is fundamentally false; the explanation is that in 1791 he had reached that conception of idealistic poetry which he was shortly to expound in his treatise *Über naive und sentimentalische Dichtung*; and in the light of this philosophical interpretation of poetry as a means of moral uplift he was bound to reject not only Bürger's poetry but the lyrics of his own youth, which had been influenced,

in part, by Bürger's verse. Schiller's condemnation
of Bürger's poetry might imply condemnation of Villon,
possibly of Burns, and certainly of not a few poets of
recent years. The critic is entitled to ask whether
ideality and moral uplift or readability and the thrill of
interest is more the true criterion of what is good verse.

In *Über naive und sentimentalische Dichtung* Schiller
deals with the pastorals of SALOMON GESSNER (1730–
1788); they are as moral and ideal as could be, he
admits; but their aim is to show man in a state of
perfection, not in the future, to which the path of
progress leads us, but in the Golden Age of a remote
past; in other words the Arcadian pastoral of Gessner
is retrograde. The Arcadian idyll had been introduced
by Opitz (*Schäferei von der Nymphe Hercinie*, 1630),
but Gessner derives primarily from the pietistic
idealization of nature in Brockes' *Irdisches Vergnügen
in Gott*, and his starting-point is that of his fellow-
countryman Haller. He had been captivated by
Brockes' work when he was a schoolboy, and he continued to study it during his stay in Berlin, where he
was learning his father's trade as a bookseller; on his
return to his native Zürich he made fame and fortune
as a bookseller, a painter, and as an engraver. His
*Idyllen* (1756 and 1772) made Gessner world-famous
and earned him the name of ' the German Theocritus '.
The scene of the idylls is ancient Greece; the pervading
idea is that which Haller had stressed—happiness is
found, far from the pomp and corruption of cities, in
rural peace; pleasure-lovers do not see the hollow back
of Dame World, whom they court, while labour hardens
the limbs of the patient peasant. The popularity in
France of the *Idyllen* was helped by the idealization
of nature in the works of Rousseau, Diderot, and
Bernardin de Saint Pierre; with its remoteness from
the rumbling problems of the day it was fit reading
for the perfumed boudoirs of Paris in the days of

Louis XV. Really, of course, there is in Gessner's Golden Age not nature at all, but nature de-natured. There is realism—a coarse realism—in the idylls or (sometimes) genre pictures of Theocritus ; but Gessner, as he wrote to Gleim, was pained by the mention of cheese and even of nuts in his old Greek models ; and so he cut out all that might smack of life as it is. ' Sugared over ' (*verzuckert*) is Herder's word for these soft and soothing dreamful visions. Gessner's pastoral picture is indeed in stark contrast with the robust though often unpleasant realism of Voss's Mecklenburg idylls. Today we read Gessner's idylls because they constitute a genre in literature ; for in spite of their prose form they are poems—poems in a softly gliding and cadenced prose that by its very rhythm calls up such pictures of lovely youths and maidens embowered in halcyon landscapes as we see figured in Gessner's engravings in the precious eighteenth-century editions of his works. There is historical importance in the fact that here we have the first instance of that rhythmic prose which in later periods does service for verse. There is rhythmic prose in *Werther* ; and there is something in Gessner's idylls, with their soft motion of long waves lapping a quiet shore, of the ' stretched verses ' (*Streckverse*) with which Jean Paul experimented in his novels.

Also in prose, but in prose redolent of the real soil of his native Palatinate, are the idylls of FRIEDRICH MÜLLER (1747–1825), known as MALER MÜLLER. To begin with he imitated Gessner, but in *Die Schafschur* (1775) he pokes fun at Arcadian idylls ; a shepherd discussing this literary phase with a schoolmaster declares roundly that ' shepherds cannot live on flowers and the dew on roses '. Equally close to the realities of rural life is *Das Nusskernen* (1811). Lyrics are interspersed ; one of them, *Soldatenabschied*, has to this day the vogue of a *Volkslied*.

Between the classicists and the romanticists dialect verse, later to be so important, begins to make headway. The first dialect classic in the lyric proper is JOHANN PETER HEBEL (1760–1826), who lived as a Church dignitary (*Kirchenrat*) in Karlsruhe; his *Alemannische Gedichte* (1803), with their homely humour, follow in the wake of Voss's idylls in dialect (p. xliv), but are closer to the people.

The cult of feeling, the irrationalism, the hatred of tyrants, the revolt against conventional morality and the assertion of the rights of personality which surge up in the works of Klopstock and of the Hainbund poets and Bürger reach a climax in the movement which is known as Storm and Stress (*Sturm und Drang*). It lasted about twenty years, beginning in 1767 with Herder's *Fragmente* and ending with Schiller's *Don Karlos* in 1787. The highest points of the movement are Goethe's *Götz von Berlichingen* (1773) and Schiller's *Die Räuber* (1781). The name *Sturm und Drang*—it is taken from the title of a drama (1776) by Maximilian Klinger—sufficiently indicates the nature of the movement ; what was proclaimed was a revolution in form and matter ; all rules are discarded and derided, and there is no restraint in the choice of theme. From the sibylline aphorisms of Hamann the doctrine was deduced that the man of genius, by reason of his genius, is a full and favoured personality free to create from intuition and in visionary ecstasy or from whatever stirs and shapes itself within his imagination. Herder's interpretation of primitive poetry (*Urpoesie*) and of *Volkspoesie* as poetry natural and untrammelled was accepted as gospel, and Klopstock's free rhythms provided a means of expressing passion and revolt against God and man in ejaculatory dithyrambic verse. Klopstock had, one might almost say, deified himself as poet-prophet ; and the *Stürmer und Dränger* in their turn proclaim the poet-creator as divinely privileged to overthrow whatever stands in the way of the expression of their inspired self; the rights of privileged personality are vindicated together with the rights of the senses (*Triebleben*); instinct, even brute instinct, is more right than reason. These poets and dramatists are *Originalgenies*, *Kraftgenies*; and *Sturm und Drang* is the *Genieperiode*. The eruptive and germinative force of Hamann and Herder is helped by Rousseau's doctrine of the return to nature; but nature as the *Stürmer und Dränger* understand it is not the denatured ideal nature of Gessner but nature luxuriantly wild; and nature in man is a chaos of primitive passion and of violence which bursts all bounds. Nature creates without plan, and from the sheer urge of fertility; and therefore nature is God. The result is a new realism—a realism which is too exasperated to be real—and a vigour of expression which is concentrated in a new type of drama and appears in the lyric (after Bürger) only in Schubart and Lenz and in the early verse of Goethe and Schiller. The new type of drama strikes fiercely away from the mathematically planned dramatic form of Lessing—which, rebel against the French unities as he was,[1] was still close to the French classical type of drama—and shapes itself to that of Shakespeare, which is declared to be the ideal drama because it is free from constricting rules and concerned only with the creation of characters.

CHRISTIAN FRIEDRICH DANIEL SCHUBART (1739–91) was a poet of revolt, and, as editor of the *Deutsche Chronik*, a pioneer in political journalism (p. xlv). Schubart's Klopstockian dithyrambs fail by sheer force of bombast; his lyrics in the *Volkslied* manner (*So herzig wie mein Liesel* | *Ist halt nichts auf der Welt*, &c.) have a simple but effective appeal to popular taste. He is more memorable for such poems as *Das Kaplied*, which has for theme the sale by Karl Eugen

[1] Lessing observes unity of place but not unity of time.

(p. lxxxvi) of his subjects to the Dutch, to fight their war in South Africa, and *Die Fürstengruft,* which Schubart wrote with the buckle of his belt on the wet wall of his prison.  JAKOB MICHAEL REINHOLD LENZ (1751–1792), a native of Livonia and therefore by nationality a Russian, wrote lyrics which so resembled those of Goethe that they were sometimes attributed to the latter.  Lenz aped Goethe to such an extent that he was called *Goethes Affe* ; he even tried to make love to Friederike Brion.  He made himself impossible at Weimar, went mad, and died in Moscow.

JOHANN WOLFGANG VON GOETHE (1749–1832) was born in the Free City of Frankfurt am Main.  (For *von,* see p. lxvi.)  Practically all the poets who have been dealt with here so far were the sons of poor people or they were of middle class origin, and it is customary to class Goethe, by way of exception, as a patrician by birth.  But he, too, is a plebeian by descent on the paternal side, for his great-grandfather was a farrier in Thuringia, while his grandfather settled in Frankfurt as a master tailor and married the well-to-do widow of an innkeeper.  His mother, however, was of good patrician stock ; she was the daughter of the chief magistrate (*Schultheiss*) of Frankfurt, Johann Wolfgang Textor.  Goethe's father, Johann Caspar Goethe, had the title of Imperial Councillor (Kaiserlicher Rat) ; he had a sufficient income to live comfortably without exercising his profession as a lawyer, devoting himself to learned hobbies and to collecting paintings and engravings.  The poet's mother, the ' Frau Rat ', was twenty-one years younger than the severely correct and pedantically stiff and formal Herr Rat ; she was gay and sociable and always bubbling over with high spirits, and as the writer of letters enlivened with frank wit and packed with interest she, too, has her place in literature.  It is customary to explain the contrasting elements in

Goethe's character and genius as the heritage of his father's high seriousness and business capacity and of his mother's lively imagination, love of story-telling, and volatile humour ; this was indicated by Goethe in the verse he set at the head of his autobiography : *Vom Vater hab' ich die Statur,* | *Des Lebens ernstes Führen,* | *Vom Mütterchen die Frohnatur* | *Und Lust zu fabulieren.*

The Herr Rat in person undertook or directed the education of Goethe and his sister Cornelia in their house in the Grosse Hirschgraben ; though as time went on it was necessary to engage private tutors. During the occupation of Frankfurt by the French (1759) in the war with Frederick the Great a French officer was quartered in the house, and the boy acquired a good speaking knowledge of French, partly by assiduous visits to the French theatre which had been set up, and for the performances of which his grandfather Textor had given him a season ticket. He was already a voracious reader ; his favourite book was the Bible, which throughout his life was ever present in his memory ; he revelled in the old German chap-books and Tasso's *Jerusalem Delivered* ; and surreptitiously he and his sister read and recited Klopstock's *Messias,* which the Herr Rat firmly excluded from his library as an unrhymed monstrosity. Goethe was already writing poetry ; his *Die Höllenfahrt Jesu Christi,* written, in smooth iambics, when he was sixteen, has a place in his *Complete Works.*

In the autumn of 1765, at the age of sixteen, Goethe was sent to Leipzig to study law. But his heart and soul were set on literature. Of the professors who might have been expected to be of use to him Gottsched was discredited, and Gellert's lectures had scant relation to literature as Goethe conceived it. Of more permanent influence on his intellectual development were the lessons in landscape sketching which he had from

the painter Adam Friedrich Oeser, a friend and disciple
of Winckelmann, whose pioneer writings on the art
of classical antiquity, by their revelation of the genius
of Greek plastic art as ' *edle Einfalt und stille Grösse* ',
had great influence on critical theory (p. xxv) and that
rejection of *Sturm und Drang* in favour of a new classicism which we shall find in the riper work of Goethe
and Schiller.   It was only because Winckelmann was
murdered at Trieste when he turned back in a fit of
nostalgia on his way from Rome to Germany, where
he was to visit Oeser, that student and critic did not
meet in person ;  Goethe, however, was to go through
the stage of Herder's directly opposite influence before
he could pass over—except in his practice of landscape
drawing—to classical restraint and clearness of form.
For the present his style in the verse he wrote was
that of the rococo fashionable at Leipzig.   In the
eighteen lyrics written in 1767, copied out by his friend
Behrisch but lost till they were discovered and published in 1895 under the title of *Annette*, there is
anacreontic pretence and a precocious familiarity with
erotic conceptions.   Annette was one of the two names
—the other is Käthchen—which Goethe gave, in his
verse and his very lively correspondence, to Anna
Katharina Schönkopf, the daugher of a wine merchant
and restaurant keeper at whose house in Leipzig he
dined daily in company with *bons vivants* of the town.
In Goethe's second small collection of his Leipzig
verse, *Neue Lieder* (1769), there is palpable reality
in the expression of sexual urge, though it is still
conventional in imagery and phrasing rather than
emotionally tense ;  and in several of the lyrics there is
that indefinable musicality (*klanggewordenes Gefühl*, as
Gundolf puts it) which, after Leipzig, is to distinguish
Goethe's verse from that of all other German poets.
In two lyrics there is the moon-magic of which Goethe
is to be a master.   In *Die schöne Nacht*, there is Goethe

at his best in his picture of birches bowing to spread
their incense to the moon :

> *Nun verlass' ich diese Hütte,*
> *Meiner Liebsten Aufenthalt,*
> *Wandle mit verhülltem Schritte*
> *Durch den öden, finstern Wald ;*
> *Luna bricht durch Busch und Eichen,*
> *Zephyr meldet ihren Lauf,*
> *Und die Birken streun mit Neigen*
> *Ihr den süssen Weihrauch auf.*

Every detail is perfect : the contrast of the mellow
moon and the dark forest ; the soft footfall of the lorn
lover ; and the melodic and visual climax of the last
two lines ; only the rococo terms of zephyr and Luna
have an antiquated but not unpleasing tinge.

As a result, not so much of emotional stress as of
student indiscretions, including addiction to Merseburg
beer and attempts to harden his body as prescribed by
Rousseau for *Naturmenschen*, Goethe fell seriously ill ;
he burst a blood vessel, and had to spend two years
recuperating at home, tenderly nursed by mother and
sister, brooding over the history and the nature of
religion, and delving into studies of alchemy and black
magic which later found their reflex in the study scenes
of *Faust*. When quite cured he went to Strassburg to
continue his law course. In Strassburg, a French
border town, he lost the French veneer he had acquired
in Leipzig, that ' Klein-Paris ', and learned to be a
German in feeling. His new-born enthusiasm for
things German emerges from an essay on the ' Gothic '
cathedral, *Von deutscher Baukunst*, which Herder later
included in *Von deutscher Art und Kunst*. From the
platform of the cathedral spire he could see the far-
stretched Alsatian landscape ; this filled him with a
new love of nature, which his wanderings and excur-
sions in the neighbourhood deepened and intensified.
But the greatest formative influence at Strassburg

was that of Herder, who was staying in the city to cure an affection of his eyes ; Goethe accosted him on the staircase of the inn Zum Geist, and meetings followed in which Herder opened the young poet's eyes to the difference between *Kunstpoesie* and *Naturpoesie* ; art and civilization (*Übernatur*), he was told, had defaced and debased nature ; and so the aim and purpose of a new poetry must be to return to nature, to primitive peoples, and to primitive folk who still sang poems that had come down through the centuries. And so Goethe set to work, as he wandered about the countryside, to collect folk-songs, which he handed over to Herder.

But Goethe's own lyric verse in the Strassburg days owed its inspiration to his love for Friederike Brion, one of the daughters of the Protestant pastor of Sesenheim, some twenty miles out from Strassburg, the distance of a six hours' sharp ride such as is described in *Es schlug mein Herz, geschwind zu Pferde*. The Leipzig poems had been exercises in a conventional style ; from now onwards all of Goethe's works are a dynamic expression of himself only ; fragments, as he himself put it, of a great confession. The intensity of the feeling creates the close-packed bold imagery of the language, the leap and fall of the rhythm ; nothing is derived ; the mood, and the melody which is faultlessly wedded to the mood, are startlingly new. No one poem resembles another, for each re-creates a deeply felt new experience ; that is, this first great burst of verse, as indeed all the verse of Goethe's best years and a good part of the verse of his old age, is directly inspired by a particular occasion or experience (' *Gelegenheitsdichtung* '). *Mit einem gemalten Band* has still traces of the playful anacreontic manner ; Scherer calls it ' *die Krone der deutschen Anakreontik* '. *Mailied* links love and springtime—love golden as the morning clouds on the distant Black Forest hills, and springtide

decked like a bride in a vaporous dress of blossoms,
with dances over the laughing lawns and from the
lover's heart a burst of new songs. *Willkommen und
Abschied* throbs with the vigour of youth, and every
detail of the vivid personification of nature (that
'anthropomorphism' which from now on is an essential element in Goethe's nature description) stands out
against the eerie background of dusk and darkness
through which the eager lover rides to his tryst. The
Sesenheim idyll could not last ; to Goethe Friederike
was indeed unspoilt nature ; but ambition was stirring
within him, and he was conscious that this simple
village maid could be no mate for him in the fullness of
the future he foresaw. That he felt the break as cruel
desertion of one whom he had taught to love him we
may infer from the tenor of works he was soon to write :
he is himself Weislingen who (in *Götz von Berlichingen*)
for the sake of his career is faithless to Maria ; he is
Clavigo who in the drama of that name deserts Marie.
Friederike never married. The immediate expression
of the poet's self-reproach can be heard in *Heidenröslein*,
the best known of the *Friederikenlieder*. Herder
printed a variant in his *Volkslieder* ; he regarded it as
an authentic folk-song ; and a folk-song it is, except
that it has not the patina of age ; but we have every
reason to believe that Goethe used the motif of *das
Rosenbrechen*, which in folk-songs is so common a
symbol of the deceiving of simple maidens by faithless
lovers, to give expression to his own poignant feelings
then and for long after ; in work after work, as in
passages of his correspondence, the pain stings.

In 1771 Goethe left Strassburg as licentiate of law
and returned to Frankfurt to practise, with the help of
his father, as an advocate. In the same year he
dashed off his play *Gottfried von Berlichingen*.
'*Shakespeare hat Euch ganz verdorben*', Herder wrote,
when he had read the manuscript, with its chaotic

welter of scenes ; Goethe rewrote the play, pulled the scenes together somewhat, and it was published in 1773 as *Götz von Berlichingen mit der eisernen Hand*. It created a sensation all over Germany ; it was the first *Sturm und Drang* tragedy.

From 1771 to 1775 we have poems which are the finest lyric expression of *Sturm und Drang*. The most remarkable, for form and theme, are those which, in ever-varied symbols, set forth Goethe's dogma of Titanism. All creation—the doctrine runs—wells forth from the passionate heart of Heaven-defying Titans, who are not bound down by obedience to whatever law and custom may ordain ; in fragment after fragment of dramas which were planned, but did not need to be finished, because one pulsing dithyramb or Pindaric hymn tore out the heart of them, Goethe sang the will to life, the will to creation, not so much of the titular hero of the poem as of himself as *grosser Kerl*, as *Originalgenie*, as (to use Nietzsche's term—but it occurs in *Faust*) *Übermensch*. The only one of these dramas which was completed, but not till the last year of the poet's life, was the *Urfaust* (1773–5) ; and *Faust* in its completed form in itself holds all that might have been pieced together from the other plans, if they had taken shape. Goethe, it is true, was not all Titan in his self-portraiture ; he is Prometheus, Caesar, the Wandering Jew, Mahomet, Götz von Berlichingen ; but he is also, in some sort, the erotic weakling Weislingen ; he is the dreamer Tasso, helpless to face the world. And he is at the same time Antonio, the prudent man of business ; thus in different facets of his chameleon-like personality Goethe re-creates himself.

The most uncompromising expression of Goethe's Titanism is in *Prometheus* (1774) ; it put the match to the gunpowder, as we are told in *Dichtung und Wahrheit* : Goethe's friend Fritz Jacobi showed it in manuscript to Lessing, expecting him to be shocked ; but Lessing approved of the feeling and ethics of the Ode. The meaning is simply that Prometheus—like any poet—creates human beings in his own image, and that any creator must by his very nature be a rebel against all conventional ordinance, be it of religion or of law. There is also the pantheistic rejection of a personal God : God is the good element in all that is, and thus the idea that God is outside of the individual and superior to him is absurd. ' What willst Thou do, God, if I die ? ' Rilke asked in these later days ; and the idea is that God is my own creation and therefore myself. In *Mahomets Gesang* (1772–3) we have the genius as prophet ; and the prophet is symbolized by a river flowing from source to sea ; the river as it sweeps on serves all, and is a blessing to all, until at the end of its course it flows into the bosom of the All-Father. This nature-symbolism is pantheistic ; God, the All-Father, is in all, and all flows on to and into God. Goethe's pantheism is one with his Spinozism. He had been led to Spinoza [1] by his friend FRITZ (FRIEDRICH HEINRICH) JACOBI (1743–1819)—the brother of the poet Johann Georg Jacobi (p. xxx)—whose interpretation of the Dutch-Jew philosopher was set down in *Briefe über die Lehre des Spinoza* (1875). Pantheism and Spinozism in Goethe's works blend with his worship of nature, for which he creates his own multiform

---

[1] Benedikt[us] (or—the Jewish form—Baruch) Spinoza (1632–1677), born in Amsterdam of a family of *émigrés* from Portugal, was expelled from the Jewish community because he was not orthodox in his ideas. In his *Ethics* (*Ethica ordine geometrico demonstrata*, 1677), he makes God and Nature equal ; his philosophy is therefore pantheism, as compared with the monotheism of Leibniz (p. xii). Spinozism was regarded as atheistic until Lessing, Herder, and Goethe were attracted by it and the German philosophers based their systems on it ; even Schleiermacher, a philosopher who still found it possible to preach the gospel, made his system more or less agree with that of Spinoza. Goethe remained a disciple of Spinoza all his life. Novalis described Spinoza as *ein gotttrunkener Mensch*.

mythical imagery : God is in nature, and therefore
nature is God. This—the inspiration of the *Mailied*,
of *Mahomets Gesang*—is clearest in *Ganymed* (1774) :
the poet, as the lover of nature, impassioned by the
surge of spring-time, presses close to the bosom of
Mother Earth and is raised in rapture into the embrace
of the All-Father ; embracing and embraced, he is
united with nature and is taken into the very Being
of God.

The most personal and perhaps the most allusive of
the dithyrambic odes is that addressed to Postilion
Time (*An Schwager Kronos*, 1774). Klopstock, on his
way to Karlsruhe, had broken his journey at Frankfurt
to pay the complimentary visit which it had become
the custom for notabilities to pay to the famous author
of *Götz von Berlichingen*, and Goethe had returned the
compliment by escorting the old poet as far as Mannheim. On his way home he composed this poem in the
post-chaise. Klopstock had been a disappointment ;
' *die erste Grossmacht im deutschen Geistesleben* ' was
willing to talk about riding or skating, but on literature
he was quite mum. The inspiration of the poem is
probably : anything but *this* ! The idea is : let me
rush on through life, without stop or stay ; and let me
rather die in the heat and ardour of my career than be
doomed to a slow down-hill pace and the stagnation
and apathy of toothless old age. Intensely personal,
too, is *Wanderers Sturmlied* (1771), in which the dithyrambic allusiveness runs wild ; Goethe himself, in
*Dichtung und Wahrheit*, speaks of it as *halber Unsinn*.
Because of his habit of wandering about the country
round Frankfurt—with more disturbance of mind (possibly because of his pangs of repentance over his treatment of Friederike) than in the Alsatian wanderings—
he was known as *Der Wanderer* ; ' *ich gewöhnte mich*,'
he writes in *Dichtung und Wahrheit*, ' *auf der Strasse zu
leben, und wie ein Bote zwischen dem Gebirg und dem*

*flachen Lande hin und her zu wandern.*' And so in this
poem packed with recondite meaning he wanders un-
daunted through lashing winds and driving rain,
guarded by his protecting Genius or *Schutzgeist.*

For the style and form of the dithyrambic hymns or
odes the models were Pindar and Klopstock. They
are for the most part in magnificently handled Klop-
stockian free rhythms, which admirably reproduce
every onrush and recoil of feeling, every thrust of sar-
casm or satire. They have Pindar's exultant hymning
of his heroes ; they have Klopstock's exuberant
excess of feeling—and often Klopstock's daring neo-
logisms and scorn of syntax.

The six months from May to September, 1772,
Goethe spent at Wetzlar, to extend his knowledge of
law at the Imperial Law Courts (*Reichskammergericht*),
a court where old law-suits were awaiting decision.
Here he fell in love with Charlotte Buff, the fiancée of
his friend Kestner ; he saved himself by a speedy return
home ; but the conflict he had experienced forms the
base of the novel *Die Leiden des jungen Werthers*
(1774) ; it made him famous the world over, and
served as a ferment in the beginnings of French
romanticism (' le wertherisme ').

In the winter of 1774 Goethe fell in love with
' Lili ', Elizabeth Schönemann, the seventeen-year-old
daughter of a wealthy Frankfurt banker, and in 1775
they became engaged. Her charm—and her coquetry
—stand out vividly from a handful of lovely lyrics.
Once again there was conflict, and dramatic conflict ;
this lover of open spaces, this all-weather wanderer,
was ill at ease in gilded drawing-rooms ; the more so
as Lili was given to teasing her lover, whom she led,
so we are told, by a silken string. Moreover he was
again concerned at the prospect of binding himself and
thus compromising his future. In the very first of the
Lililieder, *Neue Liebe neues Leben*, he cries out :

' *Liebe, Liebe, lass mich los!* ', and in *An Belinden* he
plaintively wonders if he was not happier dreaming in
his own moonlit room than in the glow of light at the
card-tables with ' *unerträgliche Gesichter* ' in front of
him. He sought relief from this pull of opposing
feelings in the first of his Swiss journeys (May–July,
1775), undertaken in the company of the Stolberg
brothers (p. xliii) ; in *Auf dem See*, written at Zürich,
the magic of the new free landscape—the cloud-capped
mountains, the thousand stars glimmering in the lake,
the soft mists swathing the peaks that in the far
distance rim the lake, on which the boat, fanned by
the morning breeze, moves to the sleepy rhythm of the
oars—does not banish the golden dream of love that
might be, nor the assurance that ' here, too, is love
and life '. In the poem, probably, there is something
of a fond recollection of Klopstock's poem *Der Zürchersee* ; in both poems there is the detail—perhaps acci-
dental or, in the given landscape, inevitable—of clouds
capping the silver Alps and of grape-hung vines ; in
Klopstock's poem beckoning from slope to slope of the
shore as the boatmen pass along, in Goethe's more
delicately toned picture gleaming up to the poet's
down-cast gaze, as he meditatively dreams, from the
cradling waves beneath.[1] Other Lililieder are *Vom
Berge, Herbstgefühl, Jägers Abendlied* ; they reproduce
wavering feelings, from perplexity to an illusory peace
of mind. There is no confusion of feeling in the drastic
self-irony of the long lyric *Lilis Park* : with uncompromising savagery Goethe describes those who flit
about her, her ' menagerie ' ; himself he sees as a bear
' *aus des Waldes Nacht* . . . , | *ungeleckt und ungezogen
. . . | Und mit den andern zahm gemacht* . . . , | *An*

---

[1] *die reifende Frucht* may refer to apple-trees ; ripening grapes
in June are not so likely ; but, though the poem was written in
June, we are not bound to think of June ; and the *Traubengestade*
of Klopstock's poem may be in Goethe's mind.

5

*einem Seidenfaden ihr zu Füssen.*' That in such circumstances the engagement should be broken off was
inevitable ; this happened in September, 1775. But
Goethe retained some tenderness of feeling and great
respect for Lili ; she was a great lady in the years to
come.

In 1774 Karl August, the young Duke of Saxe-
Weimar, passed through Frankfurt and renewed a
previous invitation to Goethe to visit him at Weimar.
The invitation was accepted, and in November, 1775,
he set out. He was then twenty-six years old. In
*Seefahrt* (1776) he describes his feelings as he left home :
he is the captain of a vessel steering in the face of a
darkening storm. He came as a guest ; he stayed
for the rest of his life. He was soon appointed *Lega-
tionsrat* ; he rose to be Prime Minister of the little
duchy. But he held many posts ; he was in charge
of mines and forests ; he directed education ; he was
director of the theatre. The state officials in power
when he arrived looked askance at him ; he was a
commoner (*ein Bürgerlicher*)—he was not ennobled
(given the particle of *von*) till 1782. He was at first
regarded as a court favourite ; and stories were soon
in circulation in and out of Weimar, one result of
which was that Klopstock wrote a letter to the Duke
and Goethe warning them against loose living ; ' *Ver-
schonen Sie uns in Zukunft mit solchen Briefen, lieber
Klopstock* ', Goethe replied ; and the breach thus
caused was never healed. The full story of Goethe's
comradeship with the Duke in these early years of
storm and stress—for both were still indoctrinated
with that spirit of wildness—is related and illuminated
in the poem *Ilmenau* (1783) ; what is certain is that
Goethe from the first, and ever more as the years
passed, was conscious of the high duties to which fate
had called him ; and he was determined that his
guidance of the Duke should be educative and en-

nobling. Indeed, the main purpose of Goethe's life in these ten formative years (1775–86) before he slipped away to Italy was to develop his own personality and that of the Duke to the closest possible approach to cultural perfection, to Herder's ideal of *Humanität* (' *die Heranbildung der Menschheit zur Humanität* ', the perfectability of man). Under the impact of this idea Goethe planned a great *Humanitätsdichtung*, a species of Holy Grail poem, *Die Geheimnisse*, with Humanus (i.e. Herder) as the guiding spirit ; it remained a fragment, but the dedicatory poem to it, *Zueignung*, serves as a dedication to Goethe's *Complete Works*. In this cultural striving Goethe had the help of Herder himself, whom, at Goethe's suggestion, the Duke called to Weimar in 1776 to fill the highest ecclesiastical post in the duchy.

Goethe's maturer conception of man's dependence on cosmic or heavenly laws (see pp. lxxviii ff.) shines out of noble poems of these years, such as *Harzreise im Winter* (1777), *Gesang der Geister über den Wassern* (1779), *Meine Göttin* (1780), *Grenzen der Menschheit* (1781), *Das Göttliche* (1783) ; the rebelliousness and defiant self-assertion of the *Sturm und Drang* dithyrambs have given way to a quiet and meditative submissiveness to whatever may be ordained for man's good. This acceptance and new interpretation of divine ordinance was no doubt in part due to the daily round of duties, but in so far as it reveals a growing peace of mind, it can be traced to the influence of Charlotte von Stein (the ' Lida ' of several poems), the wife of the Duke's Master of the Horse (*Oberstallmeister*). She was seven years older than the poet ; she had borne seven children, four of whom had died ; she was worn and aged before her time ; and she was inclined, at the time they met, to fits of despondency. She was not beautiful ; but Goethe had been shown her silhouette before he came to Weimar, and he had written

of it : ' *Es wäre ein herrliches Schauspiel zu sehen, wie
die Welt sich in dieser Seele spiegelt. Sie sieht die
Welt wie sie ist, und doch durchs Medium der Liebe* ' ;
in the light of what happened something in the nature
of proleptic love. She was at the lowest estimate a
distinguished and cultured lady, with a true feeling
for poetry ; and for the next ten years they were in
close and constant intellectual communion. Other-
wise their relations remain problematical ; Freiherr
von Stein had no objection to their friendship ; he
may even have been grateful to Goethe for relieving him
of the burden of marital companionship, for he was
more of a hearty eater (at the Duke's table) and a
horseman than a considerate husband. What Goethe
and Charlotte were to each other spiritually is symbolized in *Zueignung* ; she is the hovering angel to
whom he kneels : ' *Ja! rief ich aus, indem ich selig
nieder | Zur Erde sank, lang hab' ich dich gefühlt ; | Du
gabst mir Ruh, wenn durch die jungen Glieder | Die
Leidenschaft sich rastlos durchgewühlt.*' There is equal
worship in the first lyric he addressed to her, *Warum
gabst du uns die tiefen Blicke* (1776) :

> *Sag, was will das Schicksal uns bereiten?*
> *Sag, wie band es uns so rein genau?*
> *Ach, du warst in abgelebten Zeiten*
> *Meine Schwester oder meine Frau.*
>
> *Kanntest jeden Zug in meinem Wesen,*
> *Spähtest, wie die reine Nerve klingt,*
> *Konntest mich mit Einem Blicke lesen,*
> *Den so schwer ein sterblich Aug' durchdringt.*
> *Tropftest Mässigung dem heissen Blute,*
> *Richtetest den wilden, irren Lauf,*
> *Und in deinen Engelsarmen ruhte*
> *Die zerstörte Brust sich wieder auf!*

This is the general note of the poems addressed to
Frau von Stein : the poet comes to her as a man who
is the prey of whipped emotions and unsatisfied desires ;

the *Sturm und Drang* Titan is a soul tormented, and in the presence of Charlotte he learns a manly self-restraint and finds healing. It is generally agreed that Charlotte is idealized as Iphigenia ; the drama (*Iphigenia auf Tauris*) was not completed till 1787, but it had been planned and drafted in 1779. And Charlotte was to Goethe as Iphigenia was to Orestes, who comes pursued by furies, but recovers health and sanity when he finds that the vestal is his sister. The nature of Goethe's relationship to Charlotte is again idealized in *Tasso* ; she is the Princess who teaches Tasso ' *was sich ziemt* '. There are, however, indications that this love at arm's length—if such it was (only one poem, *Der Becher*, suggests the contrary) —called for a self-suppression which was at times unendurable ; this seems to emerge from the poem *Rastlose Liebe* (1776), which echoes the mood, though faintly, of *Wanderers Sturmlied*. What the poet learned from these ten years of love—but also from his self-sacrificing devotion to his official duties—was the lesson of *Entsagung*, which is the ultimate teaching of *Faust* ('*Entbehren sollst du ! sollst entbehren* '), as of so much in other works.

Frau von Stein was indeed a creative force in so far as she remoulded Goethe's seething mind to a (perhaps illusory) restfulness. In any case this, as it shows itself in the works begun at this time and later matured, was forced, and therefore in itself morbid ; it may be that when the breaking-point had been reached the change of environment, and this contact with a type of woman worlds away from the emotional explosiveness of the literary circles in which Goethe had hitherto moved, gave relief ; but the mystery remains why such a woman, intellectually mediocre so far as the evidence goes, should have taken hold of Goethe and held him so closely and so long. What she represented was the preciseness of the Age of Enlightenment, though in her case this was somewhat muddled by the maudlin sentiment of Klopstock and *La nouvelle Héloïse* ; she was at all events a pattern of restraint and propriety. Moreover, in these first Weimar years healing came, not from Frau von Stein, but from Goethe's conversion from introvert to extrovert ; or, in plainer words, by a gradually growing interest, soon to be absorbing, in the outer world and in science. The *Gefühls-Goethe*, to use Gundolf's term, was transformed into the *Gedanken-Goethe*. This must not, however, imply that his work was henceforth cerebral or subjective (*Gedankenpoesie*) ; Schiller's definition of Goethe's work as ' *naiv* ', by which he means spontaneous or objective, remains eternally true even throughout *Faust,* where a philosophical idea is pursued from its inception in a passionate fit of youthful revolt to a mature Benthamite solution. The poet's administrative duties as Minister of State were a further help ; he met practical men, and learned from them. Now began that appreciation of handicraft which he was to systematize in *Wilhelm Meisters Wanderjahre* ; in 1779 he wrote that every man should have a trade by which he could live ; and later that, whereas Plato would admit no one to his academy who was ignorant of measurement, he for his part would admit no one who was not versed in some branch of natural science. Here lies the base of his philosophy academically considered—for Goethe has his place with the philosophers, as he has with the scientists who extend the range of knowledge ; in his researches into the evolution of organic life, for instance, he was a forerunner of Darwin. Goethe's philosophy is what in Germany is called ' life-philosophy ' (*Lebensphilosophie* ; see p. lxxix).

It was in 1786—that is, ten years after he had settled in Weimar—that Goethe, tired out by his arduous official duties and longing for leisure to carry out his literary plans, obtained leave of absence from the

Duke, and spent the better part of a year in Italy. He referred to his stay in Italy as a rebirth, ' *die ihn von innen heraus umarbeitete* '. It is certain that the events and studies of these few months in the land of his longing made a new man of him, and the change appears at once in his writings : the Gothic ornamentation and extravagance of his earlier work is now replaced by chastened perfection and lofty calm. The estrangement from the Storm and Stress which had grown upon him after his arrival at Weimar was now complete.

On his return to Weimar from Italy the Duke freed Goethe from most of his official tasks ; he retained only his control of education in the State, to which was added the direction of the Weimar theatre. In Rome he had lived the life of a Bohemian with intellectual pursuits, with full satisfaction for his senses, which at Weimar had been starved. And on his return he shocked the town and alienated Frau von Stein by taking to his heart a poor and practically illiterate girl, Christiane Vulpius. She was the sister of Christian August Vulpius (1762–1827), the author of *Rinaldo Rinaldini, der Räuberhauptmann* (1798), which in spite of its absurdity was immensely popular. Goethe first met her when she waylaid him in the park with a petition on behalf of this brother, who had got into difficulties ; the manner of his finding her and of how he settled her within easy reach in the summer-house in his garden is turned into a fairy-tale that every school child knows in his poem *Gefunden*. Later she kept house for him in his mansion on the Frauenplan, but he did not marry her till 1806, five days after her presence of mind and physical courage had saved him from the imminent danger of losing his life during the plundering of Weimar by the French. He had from youth to middle age poured out his heart in immortal song to woman after woman, but he had remained unwedded. Now in these post-Roman days he is married—he calls it his ' *Gewissensehe* '—' *ich bin verheiratet*,' he says, ' *nur nicht durch Zeremonie*.'

And what all this means to him shines out from the smoothly turned hexameters and pentameters of his *Römische Elegien*, written in Weimar 1788-9 ; they appeared in Schiller's journal *Die Horen* in 1795. To the unwary reader this score of elegies will seem to record his Bohemian experiences in Rome, and in some sort no doubt they do ; certainly they aptly reflect his browsing in the old poetry of Greece and Rome, which is to show in the matter and form of the work of his remaining years. And they are defiantly erotic. But the Mädchen of his amours is not some Italian light o' love, but Christiane ; and the last of the elegies makes elegant if solemnly worded sport of the bad reputation he has earned in his home circle.

Goethe's first meeting with Schiller took place in 1788. To Goethe Schiller had been the author of raw *Sturm und Drang* tragedies, but after *Don Karlos* and the historical works which followed he had in 1789 procured his appointment as professor of history at Jena, so that when they met again at Jena in 1794 they had been neighbours for six years. Goethe had already promised to contribute to the journal *Die Horen* (1795-97), which Schiller had launched. Further meetings followed, and soon it was clear to Goethe that their views in all essentials coincided ; naturally, therefore, when in 1799 Schiller came to live in Weimar they were frequently together. Goethe had been so wrapt in his scientific studies that he was almost estranged from poetry ; Schiller restored him to himself ; ' *Sie haben mich wieder zum Dichter gemacht*,' Goethe wrote. From now on till Schiller's death they carried on a copious correspondence, which is in itself one of the classics of German literature, not merely by reason of the light it throws on their personal relationship, but for its intensive discussion of literary theories and problems.

In 1790 Goethe again visited Italy; in Venice he had to wait for the Duchess Amalie of Saxe-Weimar, who was coming up from the south. The stay was painful rather than pleasant, and his impressions form the staple of *Venezianische Epigramme* (1790). The brunt of the argument runs counter to that of the *Römische Elegien*; in Rome he had found satisfaction for the longing of years; now in Venice he pours out his contempt for canals and gondolas. But there is more solemn matter: famous is the carefully pondered tribute to Karl August, '*Klein ist unter den Fürsten Germaniens freilich der meine.*' And at the opposite pole there is Goethe's baffling dispraise of the German language as a medium for his work of writing (*Vieles hab' ich versucht*); he is deep in classical studies, his ears are attuned to the concisely phrased, clearly chiselled and pregnantly accentuated idioms of Greece and Rome; the dust flies white on Venetian quays, but the music of Italian speech rings in his ears.

*Die Horen* with its critical disquisitions proved too high-brow for a callous reading public, and the two poets avenged themselves by *Xenien*, a joint work in distiches, the first series of which appeared in a more facile type of journal, the *Musenalmanach* (p. xlii), of which Schiller as editor issued annual numbers from 1796 to 1800. It was in the second number, the *Musenalmanach für das Jahr 1797*, that the campaign began. *Xenien*, being translated, means *Gastgeschenke* or *Küchengeschenke*, presents given to guests not admitted to a Greek banquet, but, as inferiors, regaled off-side so to speak. There was praise for a few; for J. H. Voss and Kant; and nobly Lessing was remembered:

*Vormals im Leben ehrten wir dich wie einen der Götter,*
  *Nun du tot bist herrscht über die Geister dein Geist.*

Actually the *Xenien* were aimed at shallow or retrograde writers who pleased because they pandered to their public or did not rise above them. The most stinging thrusts hit the last lingering representatives of rationalism—among them Nicolai, once a friend and collaborator of Lessing, but now a hidebound Philistine. The leaders of the new Romantic movement, August Wilhelm and Friedrich Schlegel, were also the butts of ridicule. The victims were furious, but the two poet friends responded by producing masterpieces.

With these masterpieces may be reckoned the ballads the two friends wrote in the great *Balladenjahr*, 1797. Goethe in his earlier years had written some of the finest ballads in the language, dream-like, mystical, musical : *Der untreue Knabe* (1774), *Der Fischer* (1779), *Erlkönig* [1] (1782), *Der Sänger* [2] (1783), *Mignon* (1784 ; this is traditionally ranged with the ballads, though it is a pure lyric, reft of action, visionary, a sad sigh of longing) ; these early ballads, especially *Der König in Thule* (1774), are in the nature of folk-songs, lyrical in form and feeling, and they have already that sense of mystery which is again the mark of Goethe's most mature ballads. In their correspondence the two poets had discussed the nature of the genre, and now in 1797 they put precept into practice in ballad after ballad. But while Schiller delves into history for his series of dramatic ballads, which glorify the great deeds of men strong in purpose or impelled by fate, ballads which inculcate some educative moral, Goethe draws from his stored wealth of myth and legend ballads fraught with mystical meaning, poems into which are wisely inwoven his illumination of certain social problems of that time and still of today. Several of these poems

---

[1] Annette von Droste-Hülshoff's *Der Knabe im Moor* is an elaboration of the same theme ; what results is a *Schauergedicht* (p. cxix).

[2] Sung by the old harper in *Wilhelm Meisters Lehrjahre*. Since the setting is medieval, the poem tends to romanticism (p. xcviii).

*—Die Braut von Korinth, Der Gott und die Bajadere—*
he had carried about in his mind for forty years or
more, and only now does he succeed in giving them a
lyrical form which is so free from preaching that it
need not offend those who by reason of their beliefs
disagree with the lesson.

It is customary to class these 1797 poems (whether
completed then or later) as ' demonic ' (like Bürger's
ballads, but also like certain of Goethe's earlier ballads)
in the sense that the forces with which the characters
contend are superhuman, forces either of the earth
below or of the heavens above, powers devilish or
divine ; or in other words the poems symbolize the
eternal conflict of good and evil, the general lesson
being that evil (that is : social ideals and customs not
consonant with nature) triumphs over the natural needs
of mortals and their urge to union : in Goethe's show-
ing not nature is sinful, but the thwarting of nature.
These new ballads, though thematically they have
some of the elements (*naïveté* of expression, unstilled
longing) of the earlier ballads, show Schiller's influence
in so far as they may have for fundament some philosophical idea or other. Because of this thought-
content these ballads rank as ' classical ', in company
with Schiller's ballads of the period. But in Goethe's
ballads the philosophy is always secondary to the
flood of feeling which is the inspiration of the poem ;
and above all the expression of the idea is not likely to
be clear—it may indeed be so veiled that in some cases
it has taken a century of critical speculation to pierce
to the inner meaning ; it is all wrapped in symbol,
and the poetical shaping of the symbol counts more
than the thought. This return to the poetry of feeling
and symbol brought Goethe back to *Faust*, of which
the first three scenes and the pact between Faust and
Mephistopheles were now written.

The masterpieces of these years mark the heyday of

classicism or Hellenism (*die Klassik, der Klassizismus, der Hellenismus*) in German literature. This movement goes back to Winckelmann's *Geschichte der Kunst des Altertums* (p. xxv), with which Goethe busied himself again in Italy, but is more directly a reaction from *Sturm und Drang*. In place of the dithyrambic unrestraint of Storm and Stress we now have extreme precision and conciseness, plain perfection of statement, clarity of line, restraint in form and expression, simplicity and unity of theme. Moreover, in its mythopoeic functioning classicism sifts, purges and clarifies, refines reality ; that is, it is ideal. And whipped up national feeling gives way to a sense of the greatness and grandeur of Greece and Rome and of their literatures and art. In Goethe classicism was in the nature of an organic growth which gave final maturity to his mind during his Italian experiences ; it was, however, a transformation (*Wandlung*) which we see shaping itself in his great ode *Ilmenau* (1783 ; p. lxvi) ; this, written for the Duke's birthday, reveals how both Duke and poet had ' worked their way out of this Storm and Stress period to a beneficent clarity '.

Goethe's classicism is fortified by his study of the ancients in Rome and afterwards. And he joined forces with Schiller ; by different paths each had arrived at the same classical conception. There is, it is true, a distinction between Goethe's classicism and that of Schiller ; that of Goethe is native to the man, that of Schiller is acquired by thought and study ; or, to use Schiller's vivid simplification, Goethe is naïve (*Erfahrungsmensch, objektiver Idealist*), while he himself is sentimental (p. xcii ; *Ideenmensch, subjektiver Idealist*). In classicism, too, perfection of form must be matched by an intensification of the poet's inmost personal culture (*Verinnerlichung*), by his perfecting of himself more than of his form and style. For the very essence of classicism as developed in German literature at the end of the century (*Neo-Hellenismus*) is nobility of mood and mind. In classicism, therefore, there is a synthesis of the beautiful and the good (*Kalogathia*). There is no religious dogma in this Neo-Hellenism ; what Goethe in particular and repeatedly calls for is *Menschlichkeit*, a word which in the sense intended implies enhancement of all good human qualities as well as the most generous feeling for one's fellow-men, humaneness as well as humanism.

In the drama there is immediately perfection of classical form in Goethe's *Iphigenia* (1787) and *Tasso* (1789) and in Schiller's tragedies after *Don Karlos* (1787). In lyric verse the hexameters and pentameters of Goethe's *Römische Elegien* revitalize this classical metre. With the mastery of hexameters, a medium which Klopstock had handled with less suppleness if (often) with a vigour and phonetic verve consonant with his dithyrambic exuberance, goes a perfecting of blank verse, which in Lessing's *Nathan der Weise* had been bumpy and disharmonious. In Goethe's lyrical verse there is classical form—distiches [1]—in the second group of his elegies (1800) : *Alexis und Dora*, *Euphrosyne*, *Amyntas*, *Hermann und Dorothea* (there is the poem with this title as well as the epic), *Die Metamorphose der Pflanzen*. Very striking in *Die Metamorphose der Pflanzen* is the synthesis of antique metrical form with modernity of matter : the poem puts into verse what is in effect startling botanical research resulting in Goethe's conception of the *Urpflanze*. All plant life, the lesson runs, develops from the leaf (*Alles ist Blatt*), just as the body of mammals is formed by what the vertebral column throws out. A plant is thus *werdend*, as all life must be. This is the ' *geheimes Gesetz* ', the ' *heiliges Rätsel* ' of life, the principle of which is *die Einheit des Alls*. A tiny

---

[1] Mostly hexameter + pentameter. *Das Distichon*, pl. *Distichen* = *Verspaar* ; see p. xcv.

plant is thus a symbol of the universe. And there is
an erotic element in the poem : all creation, vegetable
as much as animal, is bisexual :—*die zartesten Formen,* |
*Zwiefach streben sie vor, sich zu vereinen bestimmt.*
Thus Christiane, to whom the poem is addressed, is
involved. The companion poem *Metamorphose der
Tiere* (date uncertain ; 1819 ?) works out the idea that
the vertebræ are the unifying element in mammals.

Very striking is the diversity of form and spirit
between the dithyrambic and short-lined odes, packed
with meaning, of the pre-classical phase (*Prometheus*,
1774 ; *Ganymed*, 1774 ; *Harzreise im Winter*, 1777 ;
*Grenzen der Menschheit*, 1775 or 1781 ; *Das Göttliche*,
1783) and the deeply philosophical rhymed odes with
their slower movement which are ranged with the
lyric verse of Goethe's old age : *Weltseele*, 1802 ;
*Dauer im Wechsel*, 1801 ; *Proömion*, 1816 ; *Eins und
Alles*, 1821 ; *Vermächtnis*, 1829. The theme of these
as it is of the earlier odes is, with variations of approach
and treatment, the relationship of man to the eternal.
In *Proömion, Weltseele, Eins und Alles* and *Vermächtnis*
Schelling's philosophy (*Von der Weltseele*, 1798) is
poeticized. *Grenzen der Menschheit* is built up round
the concept that the difference between gods and men
is that, while the divine spirits are infinite and eternal,
to men limits are set in space and time ; and, whereas
in the earlier odes there may be revolt and defiance,
in *Grenzen der Menschheit* there is reconciliation :
nature and the Divine are one. The poet is reconciled
because he recognizes that the gods have so placed
and endowed man that, limited as he is, progress to
higher phases is provided for. His feet must be firmly
set on earth, the sphere ordained him, and he must not
seek to strike the stars with the crown of his head.
*Das Göttliche* evolves the moral lesson that man
resembles the higher beings, for he alone on earth can
achieve the impossible ; let him then, never tiring,

create that which is just and good. Here we have
Goethe's ingrained doctrine of *Menschlichkeit*, which
alone links man with the gods. *Dauer im Wechsel* is
related in theme, but stresses those processes of
physical transformation of which the two *Metamor-
phosen* poems give concrete examples. Change, as the
title indicates, is eternal ; but so is the substance that
changes. *Sein* and *werden* are one ; and here the trend
of the argument points forward to the famous crystall-
ization of the concept in the poem *Selige Sehnsucht*
in *West-östlicher Divan* :

> *Und so lang du das nicht hast,*
> *Dieses : Stirb und werde !*
> *Bist du nur ein trüber Gast*
> *Auf der dunklen Erde.*

The lesson is : whatever lives must die ; inborn within
us there is a mystic yearning to die, like the yearning
of the moth for the flame of the candle ; but nothing
dies ; therefore yearning for death is one with yearning for rebirth beyond death. The process of life is a
burning of what is exhausted and base ; what matters
is that which comes from the burning. Not so much
the physical death of the body is meant as the extinc-
tion of our worn-out self and the rebirth of another
self—the *Wandlung* which Goethe had himself experienced. The problem of eternal flux and change is
again the theme of *Eins und Alles*, as it is of *Vermächtnis*, with its famous opening lines : *Kein Wesen
kann zu nichts zerfallen !*

Goethe's philosophy as expounded in these odes and
in the two parts of *Faust* (1808, 1832) is what in
Germany is called *Lebensphilosophie* ; broadly speaking it has the tenets of existentialism (p. lxx), so to
speak the religion of today : What is the purpose of
life except to live ? Of this philosophy Goethe is the
originator and the great exemplar. And at this stage
of history it may surely be argued that if there is a

' message ' for our times in Goethe's writings and in the example of his life, it is this creed of his that the aim of life is life itself. We must be interested in all manifestations of life ; and just as we see the plant develop from seed-leaf to flower so we ourselves should develop to the highest possibility of the life-power that is in us. Since the highest aim of life is life itself, the life and welfare of our fellow men as well is our immediate concern ; hence Faust, after exploring all the deeps and heights of life, finds the greatest good in reclaiming the waste lands round the sea. Another essential factor is that while metaphysics are abstract, inorganic, subjective, life-philosophy is concrete, organic, objective, and so closely fixed on things that experience (*Erlebnis*) rather than knowledge (*Erkenntnis*) is the aim of life. It is a biological philosophy. It is important, too, that the life-philosophers, since they develop organically stage by stage, have an aristocratic and even a markedly anti-democratic attitude towards those of their fellow men who do not develop ; their aim is man perfected to the limit of his powers (*der Vollmensch, der Übermensch*). But Goethe, though he was the first to use the term *Übermensch* (p. lxi), cannot be reckoned with Schopenhauer and Nietzsche and with those who inherit their contempt for the common man. Self-perfection, it is true, is the clearest aim of Goethe's striving ; but in him self-perfection is compatible with understanding of and sympathy for the common man and his tasks ; he is an intellectual aristocrat, but one with all possible respect for his social inferiors. And this is *Menschlichkeit* in its most simple and its deepest sense.

Chronologically considered the (1) irrationalism of *Sturm und Drang* is followed by (2) rationalism (*Aufklärung*), which tends to sanity of expression and thematically to logical criticism and to a scientific conception of life ; and (3) by Romanticism (*die Romantik*), which, as we shall see, continues the historical and international moods and forms of classicism and indeed expands its philological scholarship but allows imagination free range and, particularly in its lyric verse, has more the thrill of personal and intense feeling. The appeal of Oriental, Italian and Spanish literature comes in with a rush before the end of the century and in Goethe's verse appears in his *West-östlicher Divan* and his sonnets.

It might be shown that Goethe, though at times he turned away from literature to immerse himself in the new scientific studies of the day, was never an *Aufklärer*; for he studied his science with a poet's imagination and insight. It is indeed curious that his absorption in science keeps pace with his more and more intensive study of classical literature, and that he comes to regard science as belonging to classics. The idea is based on the ' wholeness ' of Greek culture ; in his essay on Winckelmann (1805) he says that the dualism of modern studies, ' the splitting up of the human faculties which had settled on the modern world like a disease ', was unknown to the Greeks ; since the Renaissance, he argues, the humanities—*Humaniora*—had been losing their grip on scholarship ; and that the true way to restore the integrity, or the wholeness, of culture was a return to science. He means that the true scholar is not split by ignorance on the one side of science or on the other side of literature, but is, like the scholars of the Renaissance, who strove for a full knowledge of all that was knowable, a *uomo universale*, a *Übermensch*. And this is what Goethe is ; he stands out in the history of modern times as the one well-integrated genius supreme as a poet and very eminent as a scientist ; as a scientist indeed he gains from his imagination and intuitive approach. Organically, he argues, there is no radical separation between art and science ; for the scientist

6

on the track of a discovery is undergoing the same creative process as an artist or poet in the act of creating a work of art ; the scientist is thus something of an artist, and *vice versa*. Therefore, science and art being related, the scientist will achieve nothing *total* if he does not function creatively as an artist does. For Goethe this union of art and science was possible, as it was for Leonardo da Vinci and Albrecht von Haller ; today science is so ramified that it is probably beyond the scope of the most gifted mind to achieve universality of knowledge ; Goethe was, perhaps, the last humanist.

Poems written from 1805 to 1832 we classify as Goethe's *Alterslyrik*. With the *Alterslyrik* are reckoned the sonnets, which are chronologically notable as belonging both to classicism and to romanticism. The sonnet is pre-eminently a classical form because it is so fixed and regular, and because the collection of sonnets which had served as patterns internationally through the ages is that of Petrarch. The sonnet had been introduced as early as the sixteenth century by Paulus Melissus and handled in the seventeenth century by the poets of the first Silesian school—Opitz, Logau, Gryphius ; but it was then in alexandrines of the heavy Dutch type (p. xi). The first good sonnets in German in the modern sense were written by Bürger (p. xlviii), and these were followed in 1800 by those of August Wilhelm Schlegel. Goethe heard the latter recite his sonnets at the house in Jena of the publisher Fromman, who in 1806 published Petrarch's sonnets (*Rime di Francesco Petrarca*). Petrarch's theme is his hopeless love for Laura, and something of this nature also forms the staple of Goethe's sonnets : in 1807 he had met, in Fromman's house at Jena, the publisher's foster-daughter Minna Herzlieb, a girl of eighteen, whom he had known since her childhood ; he fell in love with her, but there was no response. The sonnets, as such,

are poor, for Goethe was no sonneteer ; they have an
artificial stamp and lack that impetus which should
rise convincingly—as in the sonnets of Heredia for
instance—till the gist of the idea is gathered, to unfold
like a flower, in the final line.

Goethe's interest in the literature of the East ap-
pears in some of the work of his maturity ; e.g. *Der
Gott und die Bajadere* (1797) ; and he had followed the
growth of Oriental scholarship, which in Germany
reaches back to the poet Paul Fleming's visit to
Persia by way of Russia (1633–9) and the description
of the experiences of the party—a trade mission from
Holstein—in the *Beschreibung der neuen orientalischen
Reise* (1647) of Adam Olearius, who in his *Persianisches
Rosental* (1654) provided the first translations of
Persian poetry (Saadi), to which Goethe refers in the
voluminous *Noten und Abhandlungen* at the end of his
*West-östlicher Divan*. The immediate incentive to this
was the translation of Hafis (1812–13) by the Viennese
Orientalist Joseph von Hammer-Purgstall. Goethe's
interest had also been aroused by Sir William Jones's
translation of the Sanscrit drama *Sakontala* (translated
into German by Georg Forster), from which he had
taken a hint for the shaping of the Prologue to *Faust 1*.
An important factor, too, was Friedrich Schlegel's *Über
die Sprache und Weisheit der Indier* (1808 ; p. cxxxi).
Actually the Oriental element in the *West-östlicher
Divan* (1819) is rather pleasantly allusive than exact
and interpretative. *Divan* is Persian for ' collection ',
and what we get is a motley medley of verse, ostensibly
in Persian forms, ranging from playfulness to high
seriousness, and divided into Book (*Nameh*) this and
that. There are drinking songs (and we remember
that Goethe had written the students' songs *Ergo
bibamus ; Tischlied ; Vanitas ! vanitatum vanitas !*) ;
and there are love songs sated with tenderness and lorn
regret. The sonnets written for Minna Herzlieb had

fallen flat because the metrical form was uncongenial to the singer, whereas the stanzas and rhythms (as well as the moods) of *West-östlicher Divan* are ever varied and skilfully fitted to an alluring presentation of old Persian ways of life, wisdom, and erotic plaintiveness. These poems have the restraint and softened music of ripe old age ; Konrad Burdach speaks of their *blasser Silberton*. But the very heart of the lesson is *Schwerer Dienste tägliche Bewahrung* and the houri (*Huri*, angel) who stands guard at the gates of Paradise is hailed by the poet as he arrives : *Nicht so vieles Federlesen ! | Lass mich immer nur herein : | Denn ich bin ein Mensch gewesen, | Und das heisst ein Kämpfer sein.* And the mysticism is unfolded as that modern scientific entelechy which rings so true in one of the lines of the poem *Selige Sehnsucht : Stirb und werde* (p. lxxix). Timur persianizes the name of Napoleon, ' *der fürchterliche Weltverwüster* ', who, when he met Goethe at Erfurt in 1808, walked up to him with the words *Voilà un homme !* There are a pair of starcrossed lovers, Hatem ( = Goethe) and Suleika, that is, Marianne von Willemer. Several of the poems—and good ones—were written by Suleika, including *Ach, um deine feuchten Schwingen.* Marianne was the young wife of a Frankfurt friend with whom in these years there developed such an ' elective affinity ' as is described by Goethe in *Die Wahlverwandtschaften.*

Goethe's last love was Ulrike von Levetzow, a girl of nineteen, whom he first met at Marienbad in 1822, when he was seventy-four. Christiane had died in 1816, and marriage was contemplated, but Goethe yielded to the objections of his son and daughter-inlaw. This last passionate upheaval lives on in the poet's last great lyric work, *Trilogie der Leidenschaft* (1823–4). It is made up of three intensely personal poems : *An Werther, Elegie* (often referred to as *Marienbader Elegie*), *Aussöhnung*. The trilogy is defined by the poet himself as progressive : exposition, catastrophe, reconciliation.

His life-work was not yet finished—not till 1831 could he write down in his diary : *Das Hauptgeschäft zustande gebracht.* It was *Faust,* a work which had taken him sixty years to write. He died in 1832.

The name of FRIEDRICH SCHILLER (1759–1805) will be for ever linked with that of Goethe ; they stand side by side as they do in Rietschel's statue in Weimar, the two classical poets of Germany, facing present and future united. Schiller, a Swabian, was born in Marbach on the Neckar as the son of an army surgeon who had the rank of lieutenant in the army of Duke Karl Eugen of Württemberg (p. liv). Afterwards he lived as a recruiting officer at Lorch and later at the garrison town of Ludwigsburg, to which the Duke had transferred his court from Stuttgart ; and here, promoted captain and then major, father Schiller was in charge of the Duke's gardens at die Solitüde, his country palace near Stuttgart. Friedrich made such good progress at the *lateinische Schule* at Ludwigsburg that when he was fourteen the Duke selected him willynilly as a pupil at his military academy (*Hohe Karlsschule*), which he had got going to train the children of his officers and officials ; and here, though his dream was to be a clergyman, Schiller spent seven years at the instance of the Duke, studying law and later medicine, until in 1780 he was given a post as regimental surgeon (*Regimentsmedikus*) in Stuttgart. Here he read voraciously the literature of the day, Shakespeare in Wieland's translation, Klopstock, Rousseau, and the *Kraftgenies* of *Sturm und Drang,* in particular *Götz von Berlichingen* and *Werther.* As a result young Schiller dashed off the most revolutionary drama of Sturm und Drang, *Die Räuber.* On the title-page was a lion rampant with the motto *in tirannos* ; this was aimed directly at the Duke, who ruled his state with a rod of iron and was now keeping Schiller pinned down to iron discipline and army service at low pay. Schiller was following in the wake of another Swabian, Christian Friedrich Daniel Schubart (1739–91), who in 1774 had launched the political bi-weekly *Deutsche Chronik* (p. liv) and had aimed at the Duke the epigram : *Als Dionys von Syrakus | Aufhören muss, | Tyrann zu sein, | Da ward er ein Schulmeisterlein*, for which he was imprisoned ten years in the ducal prison die Hohenasperg. In 1782 *Die Räuber*, which had been published at Schiller's expense, was produced at Mannheim, and was a great success. The theme is the old one of *die feindlichen Brüder*, recently handled in two dramas, Maximilian Klinger's *Die Zwillinge* and Anton von Leisewitz's *Julius von Tarent*; it is the theme too of Gloucester and his two sons in *King Lear*, and Franz has the shaping of Edmund. The good brother Karl, a born *Kraftgenie*, in the belief that he has been disowned by his father, though in reality his wicked brother Franz had contrived his misfortune, takes to the woods and makes a great splash as a captain of robbers ; he rescues his father from the black hole into which Franz, who commits suicide, has cast him, and gives himself up to justice. There is the same revolutionary fervour and violence in the book of verse which follows, *Anthologie auf das Jahr 1782* ; the main influences are the dithyrambic style of Klopstock's *Odes* and thematically Rousseau's doctrine of liberty and return to nature. The place of publication is facetiously and cautiously given as Tobolsk (in Siberia). The love interest in the Laura poems (*Phantasie an Laura, Laura am Klavier, Die Entzükkung an Laura*, etc.) is curious when one considers that they are addressed to his landlady at Stuttgart, Frau Vischer, a captain's widow ripe with experience, with whom he lodged while he was serving as an army doctor, after he had earned his release from the

Academy by his final dissertation *Über den Zusammenhang der tierischen Natur des Menschen mit seiner geistigen*, which points forward to the trend of his thinking his life long (pp. xciv, lxxxix). But the coming dramatist is foreshadowed in several of the poems. *Die Kindesmörderin* is a monologue spoken on the way to execution and is dramatic in the sense that it throbs with tragic feeling at a given moment and is psychologically revealing. Taking the *Anthology* as a whole the rhymecraft is surprisingly poor and partly dialectal : short rhymes with long, *hegt* with *neckt*, *nun* with *Ton*, *fleugt* with *steigt* ; and the language may be forced and melodramatic. The flow of feeling is free and melodiously cadenced in *Brutus und Cäsar* and in *Hektors Abschied* ; in the latter and in *Der Triumph der Liebe* Greek myth and mythology, destined to play so large a part in Schiller's verse (p. xc), are for the first time tentatively used.

Forbidden by the enraged Duke to write anything in future except medical works, in 1782 Schiller saved himself by flight across the frontier to Mannheim, bringing with him his second play, *Fiesko*, a ' republican tragedy ', his first attempt at a historical play. But to the director of the theatre, Freiherr von Dalberg, Schiller was a deserter, and since there was difficulty in harbouring him the poet took refuge in Frankfurt and later in the village of Oggersheim, which lies on the Rhine opposite Mannheim. After several moves he found asylum at the country estate of Frau Henriette von Wolzogen, the mother of two of his friends at the Karlsschule, at Bauerbach near Meiningen in Thuringia, where he remained till 1783. And here he wrote his third drama, *Kabale und Liebe*, a *bürgerliches Trauerspiel*, after the manner of Lessing's *Miss Sara Sampson* and *Emilia Galotti*. In 1784 both *Fiesko* and *Kabale und Liebe* were produced ; *Fiesko* fell flat, but *Kabale und Liebe* was a great success. And when in the same

year Duke Karl August of Weimar was on a visit to the
Court at Darmstadt and Schiller by invitation read to
him the first act of his fourth drama, *Don Karlos*, the
Duke conferred on him the title of *Rat* (Councillor).
With *Kabale und Liebe* a success Schiller was now enabled to return to Mannheim, where von Dalberg
appointed him playwright (*Theaterdichter*), with the
obligation to write another drama ; but since this was
not forthcoming von Dalberg in due course cancelled
the contract, and Schiller was in financial straits and
moreover fell ill.  He attempted to gain a footing
in journalism by founding a literary journal, *Die
Rheinische Thalia,* which made no headway.  But his
fame was growing, and an admirer, Christian Gottfried
Körner (the father of the poet ; p. cxv), wrote to him
from Leipzig ;  correspondence followed, and when
Schiller's desperate financial straits were revealed
Körner invited him to visit him and his circle of
friends ;  Schiller accepted, and when the Körner family
moved to Dresden he went with them and remained
in close association with them till 1787.

*Don Karlos*, begun in Bauerbach and finished in
1787, was Schiller's first drama to be written in verse—
the decasyllabic iambic verse which was to be the
staple of his plays in the years of his prime.  The
stanchless flow of its resonant rhythm shows him now a
poet full fledged, as does too the intensity of feeling
faultlessly expressed in the great lyrics of 1784-6.  In
*Der Kampf* and *Resignation,* both written 1784, he
reveals latent urges which later he ruthlessly controlled,
and the poems rank high in his work, though the phrasing is still over-subtilized, if only because the feeling
is so deep and forceful.  In both poems the theme is
for once in his life himself and there is violent self-
assertion.  *Der Kampf* is the most erotically passionate
poem of his life ; that is, it is a ' confession ' in the
modern sense.  At Mannheim he had formed a close

friendship with Charlotte von Kalb, the wife of an officer who was mostly away on service ; in any case this gentleman had no objection to their association, and there might apparently have been at all events intimacy at arm's length such as united Goethe and Charlotte von Stein, or perhaps closer. This lady was intellectually fitted to be Schiller's mate, more so than any other woman he ever consorted with, and she was a personality of marked distinction. His feelings for her, again, find their reflex in the love of Don Karlos for Elisabeth in Schiller's fourth drama. But the poet by upbringing and strength of character had a rooted aversion to irregular relations, and in *Der Kampf*—originally *Freigeisterei der Leidenschaft*— he gives pathetic expression to the great fight he has fought against temptation. The two poems give Schiller's measure as a man : throughout life he was *integer vitae*, and all his works bear witness to his heroic conception of man's duty to his fellow-mortals and to himself. *Resignation* is the most pessimistic poem Schiller ever wrote. By comparison his dithy-rambic ode *An die Freude* (1785) is merely conventional. One might be tempted to classify it as high-flown and illusively sentimental, if one did not remember that the matter of it is incorporated in the closing chorus of Beethoven's Ninth Symphony. It should be noted as characteristic of Schiller that the inspiration of this poem of praise comes not from the love of a woman, but from friendship and the joys it brings, and it belies the grim pessimism of *Resignation*.

In July 1787 Schiller removed to Weimar. Here he devoted himself to historical work, and, though any-thing but a historian, wrote historical works which are more readable than history proper : *Geschichte des Abfalls der vereinigten Niederlande* (1788), which is closely connected with the matter of his *Don Karlos*, and *Geschichte des Dreissigjährigen Krieges* (1791-3).

In 1789, at the instigation of Goethe, he was appointed 'extraordinary' professor of history at Jena—that is, unpaid except for fees paid for individual lectures. In 1790 he married Charlotte von Lengefeld, a friend of Frau von Wolzogen.

His poem *Die Götter Griechenlands* (1788) is in this sense historical that it recapitulates in alluring images the mythology of ancient Greece, a knowledge of which is necessary for numerous allusions in Schiller's work and for the Hellenic poems (pp. xcv, xcvi) of his later years. Schiller's Greek was never more than a smattering ; he had to spell his way through texts. *Die Götter Griechenlands* is a fervent confession of faith in the religion of the ancient Greeks in so far as it symbolizes the worship of nature and the identification of beauty in nature. In Greek religion the gods, to us as symbols, but none the less real for that, represent aspects and forces of nature, whereas the religion of today, being deprived of the multiple gods the Greeks worshipped, is alienated from nature (*entgöttert*) ; the basic force of modern religion is reason, logic, and is therefore sober, while Greek religion is inspired and instinct with poetry. In all this there is some anti-Christian bias, which was of course consonant with the period of composition of the poem and a further expression of Rousseau's return to nature. *Die Künstler* (1789) is in two parts, the first philosophical and the second historical. The first part is built up on the ideas : (1) that beauty is truth visualized [1] ; (2) that all intellectual culture has proceeded from this sense of beauty and that for this reason the chief aim of cultural processes must be the perfection of art ; that is, of all imaginative creation. Since beauty is truth man owes his realization of truth to the processes of art, and art

---

[1] 'Beauty is truth, truth beauty—that is all | Ye know on earth, and all ye need to know.' Keats : *Ode on a Grecian Urn.*

can only exist and be made accessible to man by revealing truth as beauty.

In 1794 Schiller visited Tübingen and arranged with the publisher Cotta that he should edit for his firm a literary journal, *Die Horen*, to which the celebrities of the day were to contribute. The recruit to be most eagerly sought for was Goethe, and in the result there was much contact between the two poets. A first meeting had been arranged between them in 1788 by the Lengefelds, with whom Goethe had always been friendly, but neither had thus far been attracted to the other. The ice was broken when Goethe explained to Schiller his theory of the metamorphosis of plants and Schiller exclaimed : ' *Das ist keine Erfahrung, das ist eine Idee !* '

Jena, when Schiller arrived there, was the second home of Kant's philosophy, and Schiller, like those about him, plunged into the study of the Königsberg philosopher. *Kritik der reinen Vernunft* (1781) and *Kritik der praktischen Vernunft* (1788), so far as he could understand them, were not altogether acceptable to him ; he was attracted and repelled by the ' categorical imperative ' of these works, the total subordination of the senses to the mind, of sensual urges to duty, of human feeling to the moral law. Schiller was more immediately influenced by *Kritik der Urteilskraft* (1790), the first part of which deals with the critical functions of the mind and its response to urges and experience ; that is, Kant's interpretation of aesthetics, the feelings aroused in us by the beautiful and the sublime in (1) nature and (2) art, and the interrelation of these feelings. Schiller now gave a course of lectures on aesthetics, and wrote a series of essays, the most important of which are *Über Anmut und Würde* (1793) and *Über naive und sentimentalische Dichtung* (1795–6). These are based on Kant, but Fichte's criticism is probably justified that they are too clear and interesting to be true philosophy. It is the antithesis between grace and dignity which is interpreted in the essay *Über Anmut und Würde*,[1] grace being beauty in voluntary action, the mark of a Beautiful Soul, and dignity being mastery over involuntary action, the mark of a sublime spirit which has obtained moral freedom by obedience to the moral law. There is the reverse order of terms in Burke's *Essay on the Sublime and Beautiful*. What we must strive for is a synthesis.

In two important critiques, that on Bürger's poetry (1791; p. l) and that on Matthisson's poetry (1794), Schiller expounds his views on the nature of lyric verse. In the critique on Matthisson Schiller first sketched out the aesthetic principles he was to formulate more fully in *Über naive und sentimentalische Dichtung*. While painting, he says, is simultaneous, poetry is successive (p. xix). *Über naive und sentimentalische Dichtung* is essential for the comprehension and appreciation of the series of poems—classed as *Gedankenlyrik*—which followed. By *naiv* [2] he means closeness to nature and love of it; by *sentimentalisch* [3] he means reflective, moralizing on things seen, and thus not so much instinctively and by a natural urge reproducing nature, as the naïve poet does, as intellectualizing and interpreting it. The ' naïve ' poet (in Schiller's sense) reproduces directly the impressions he receives from nature, whereas the ' sentimental ' poet reflects on them. In other words, the one is objective, the other subjective ; the one is the object who is moved and moulded by nature as he beholds it, so that in his reproduction nature remains nature ; the other the

---

[1] *The Graceful and the Exalted.*

[2] *Naiv* is used by Schiller with its original sense of *natürlich, naturgetreu, einfach.*

[3] *Sentimentalisch* has not established itself and is used by Schiller in a quite different sense from that of English and German *sentimental* = *gefühlvoll, empfindsam.*

subject who places himself without his object and
forms it anew, analyses, interprets it, so that what is
reproduced is a mental fabric. (One might be tempted
to use an antithesis of today : Inspirationsdichtung
*versus* Fleissdichtung.) Thus the ancients move us
by nature as it is, the moderns move us by ideas.
Hence the ancient Greeks reproduced the finite, say
in statues, whereas modern man quests the infinite,
say in poetry. We have thus an antithesis, such as
we are to get in that of Classic and Romantic (p. xcvii).

In handling Schiller's philosophical poems (*Gedankenlyrik*) of 1795–8 one is faced with the difficulty that
so very few of them are suitable for inclusion in an
anthology. They are often too long, and they are
usually too recondite for all except philosophically
minded readers. The general reader must force himself to read these poems, with respect and even admiration, but they are likely to leave us cold. One may
quote Goethe's delicately worded verdict : they are
' *nicht zu loben, aber zu erlauben* '. These excogitated
poems of Schiller have not the ' pure poetry ' of
Klopstock's *Odes* ; these do indeed repel by their
obstinate difficulty of idiom, but they have the lyric
lift and strangeness of idiom of true verse ; in spite of
their weight of ideas they are, in Schiller's sense, *naiv*,
whereas Schiller's nobly-phrased and climaxed ideology
is, in its total effect, heavy-going to evasive minds,
or at best sacramental. He himself in a letter to
Wilhelm von Humboldt calls on his friend to read *Das
Ideal und das Leben* (which he encloses after composing
it) ' *in geweihter Stille* '. ' Pure poetry ', the argument
runs, can only be the poetry of feeling (*Gefühlslyrik*).
There is of course the contrary view ; thus C. Day
Lewis (in *The Poetic Image*, p. 133) writes the most
cogent possible defence of Schiller's *Gedankenlyrik* : ' A
poetry which excludes the searchings of reason and the
promptings of the moral sense is by so much the less

impassioned, the less various and human, the less the product of the whole man at his full imaginative height.'

Of these poems *Die Ideale*, highly personal, reviews the toils and trials through which the poet must fight his way to the heights ; in the closing stanza we are assured that he will find solace in the tasks themselves to which he devotes himself and in the love of wife and friends (he refers to the Körners). Personal too, indeed self-portraiture, is *Das Ideal und das Leben*, which is generally credited with being the very finest of these poems ; it is based on the conflict of sensual and intellectual urges (*Zwischen Sinnenglück und Seelenfrieden | Bleibt dem Menschen nur die bange Wahl*). The personality who looms through *Der Genius* is Goethe ; the poem presents genius as Schiller had defined it with such pains in the creative inspiration of *der naïve Dichter : Du nur merkst nicht den Gott, der Dir im Busen gebeut . . . | Einfach gehst du und still durch die eroberte Welt*. The poem thus contrasts with *Die Ideale*, which portrays *der sentimentalische Dichter*. Three poems broach what in these days we should regard as problems of sex. *Würde der Frauen* pays homage to woman as dowered with that synthesis of charm and dignity which Schiller expounds and extols in his essay *Über Anmut und Würde*. The theme is the contrast and conflict of man and woman ; man is pictured as the lord of creation, and there is praise which today rings antiquated for the home-keeping tasks of woman, ministering to the creature needs of her mate. *Macht des Weibes*, again, seems to imply that to a woman intellect is fatal. *Die Geschlechter* is more modern, because physical. *Der Spaziergang* with its contrast of nature and culture illuminates the lesson of *Über naïve und sentimentalische Dichtung* and is at the same time a historical survey of the onward march of man from a primitive state of existence by way of culture to a more elevated stage of nature; the poem is an epitome of the course of history. In *Das Lied von der Glocke* (1799), again, Schiller takes up the main threads of his heavily charged philosophical poems and makes them run freely in a poem of epic length which is easy to read and memorize and ranks as one of the national poems of the Germans.

With the *Gedankenlyrik* must be ranged Schiller's epigrams in the form of distiches and his *Votivtafeln* (1796); the latter derive their title from the custom in ancient Greece of those saved from some dire peril— shipwreck, &c.—dedicating votive tablets to some patron god or other; thus the first distich runs:

*Was der Gott mich gelehrt, was mir durchs Leben geholfen,*
  *Häng' ich, dankbar und fromm, hier in dem Heiligtum auf.*

The rest are wise saws neatly turned, judgments concisely couched on a multiplicity of subjects. Of the epigrams grouped as *Kleinigkeiten* (1796) one never forgets, once read, *Der epische Hexameter* with its apt definition:

*Schwindelnd trägt er dich fort auf rastlos strömenden Wogen,*
  *Hinter dir siehst du, du siehst vor dir nur Himmel und Meer.*

Nor *Das Distichon*:

*Im Hexameter steigt des Springquells flüssige Säule,*
  *Im Pentameter drauf fällt sie melodisch herab.*

For Schiller's *Xenien* and all they signify see pp. lxxiii–iv.

Schiller himself christened 1797 *das Balladenjahr* (see p. lxxiv); in the summer of this year (hence we speak also of *der Balladensommer*) were written *Der Taucher*, *Der Handschuh*, *Der Ring des Polykrates*, *Ritter Toggenburg*, *Die Kraniche des Ibykus*, *Der Gang nach dem Eisenhammer*, and thus was created a new type of didactic ballad, in which the story itself is breathlessly told and the human interest is intense and —if symbolically interpreted—psychologically true, but in which what matters is the proof that good must prevail over evil, or that ruin comes from passion uncontrolled, which is human because it is uncontrolled, but which may in the symbolical terminology of the ancients be set forth as divine intervention or the inevitability of ' Fate '. Actually these ballads—and indeed the remainder of Schiller's lyric work—were occasional productions written by way of respite at intervals while he was busy with his great dramas.

Underlying the first of these ballads, *Der Taucher*, is the Greek conception of hybris. The futility of a tyrant's arrogance and cruelty is laid bare. *Der Handschuh* (p. 220) is thematically related ; arrogance meets its reward. How differently is the identical theme treated in Browning's *The Glove !* *Ritter Toggenburg* breathes the spirit of the Minnesingers ; it is the pathetic tale of a crusader who returns from the Holy Land to find that his loved one is a nun ; he builds a hut close to her convent, clothes himself in a hairy garment, and all he lives for is to watch her window and to see her descend on her charitable errands to the village : *Und so sass er, eine Leiche, | Eines Morgens da, | Nach dem Fenster noch das bleiche, | Stille Antlitz sah.*

Schiller had been hampered in his monumental task by illness for ten years when he died in 1805, full of plans, and with his great tragedy *Demetrius* unfinished.

Summing up, one's judgment of Schiller's lyric verse must depend on one's own definition of lyric verse. There can be no denying that he was a consummate master of all metrical forms, but the final verdict may be that he was too much of an intellectual and too high-minded for lyric poetry proper ; in other words, his lyrics go to the mind, not to the heart, as does ' naïve ' poetry as he himself so brilliantly defined it.

Two poets who have no connection with the Göttinger Hainbund (p. xli) have something of their spirit but point forward to the *Naturmalerei* and the musicality of the romanticists. FRIEDRICH VON MATTHISSON (1761–1831) has something of Hölty's elegiac moods, but the soft gliding rhythm of his dreamful reveries is all his own (*Lieder*, 1781). His poem *Adelaide* is immortal in Beethoven's setting. He is a master of delicately limned vignettes (*Elegie am Genfersee*) in which the floating fancies follow aspect by aspect in linked resonance. Matthisson's friend JOHANN GAUDENZ VON SALIS-SEEWIS (1762–1834) follows him closely in his nature poetry, but he has a more masculine note (*Gedichte*, 1793).

To define exactly the meaning of romanticism is difficult. There are so many connotations. First used is the adjective *romantisch*, which takes over the sense of French ' *romantique* ' and English ' romantic ' ; and so when it begins to occur (Tieck's *Romantische Dichtungen*, 1799) it means variously related to the spirit of medieval literature or to the more fanciful or phantasmic literature of the Romance nations (*die Romanen*, the Italians, French, &c.), though the chivalric poetry of Britain also appertains. *Romantisch* is remote from the dull present ; it is strangely new, thrilling, eerie, ghostly, horrific. It turns from the clear light of day which we have in classicism to twilight moods (*Dämmerzustände*, &c.) and the dreams of night. It is filled with yearning for what is not within reach, for the unattainable, the ineffable. And therefore in the best of it there may be vagueness and shadowy outlines and glimpses of a world beyond the senses, mystery ; and in fiction a specifically romantic genre is the *Märchen*, which has some approach to the irreality of the fairy-tale. The simplest derivation of romanticism—dubious for German use, but not unhelpful—is that from *Roman* [1] ; this indicates that in

---

[1] ' *romantique, dérivé de roman = œuvre d'imagination en prose* '.

the period following the classicism of Goethe and
Schiller writers put their best effort into their novels,
whereas in the classical period the five-act tragedy with
its clear lines and logical motivation was most in
evidence. The theme is new, and the fashioning of it
as well as its substance reveals the author's mind and
its meanderings. What it actually amounts to is that,
whereas fixed form is the criterion in classicism (*die
Klassik*), in all genres of romanticism (*die Romantik*)
there is, on the face of it, formlessness. But chronologically classicism and romanticism overlap. The sub-
title of one of Schiller's tragedies, *Die Jungfrau von
Orleans* (1801), is *Eine romantische Tragödie*. There
are romantic elements in Goethe's *Wilhelm Meister*,
but this means only that this great work rambles on
and reveals psychology with the penetration of today.
The romanticists (*die Romantiker*), again, often turned
back for their themes to the Middle Ages, as Friedrich
Matthisson and Salis-Seewis did tentatively in some
of their lyric work, and reproduced these periods of
the past with dreamful longing that sang itself into a
new magic of phrasing and imagery in comparison with
which the style of the classicists (*die Klassiker*) was
cabined and confined and sometimes cold. Again,
whereas the cult of form of classicism found its ideal
in plastic art, the romanticists revelled in richness of
colouring; indeed they have colours seen with the
eye of imagination that no painter has on his palette.
But principally the romantic writer reveals his *Ich* or
ego, as the term went, following Fichte's philosophical
system as expounded in his *Wissenschaftslehre* (1794)
according to which all that is is devised by the ego.
That is: whereas the classicists had accepted Kant's
systematic philosophy, with its clear outlines of what
is knowable, the romanticists turned to the transcen-
dental philosophy of Fichte and Schelling. For the
romanticists poetry is absolute reality, not the matter

of common life. Another important aspect is that, whereas classicism looks to Greek literature for its supreme models, romanticism roves at random in all the literatures of Europe in all their periods, and indeed finds fertile fields in Asia. Goethe's *West-östlicher Divan* is thus romantic in its trend, whereas Hölderlin, though with his moods and his love-story and what he makes of it he is romantically charactered, is a Hellenist through and through and therefore a classic (one might perhaps say that he romanticizes classicism). For the student an important point is that, just because the romantics discover the treasures of medieval literature, romanticism marks the beginnings of comparative as of Germanic philology and of comparative literature. Shakespeare, translated by August Wilhelm Schlegel, is from now on a German classic, and hardly less so are the national poets of Italy and Spain. On the home front Tieck renews the *Volksbücher*, Clemens Brentano and Achim von Arnim collect the folk-songs (*Volkslieder*) of the nation in *Des Knaben Wunderhorn* (1806–8), while Uhland revives the old ballads.

Two poets are romantics of a sort, though they are not associated with the protagonists of the movement —Jean Paul and Hölderlin. JEAN PAUL (the pen name of Jean Paul Friedrich Richter, 1763–1825), hardly concerns us here, as he is a novelist ; but he was hostile to classicism and his novels have the main romantic qualities of formlessness and irony, and he has a fund of humour. See pp. lii, cv.

FRIEDRICH HÖLDERLIN (1770–1843) is root and branch a Hellenist, ' *ein nachgeborener Grieche* ', and is thus, as also by personal friendship, linked rather with the Schiller of *Die Götter Griechenlands* than with the romantics with their medieval trends. All that we can say is that he is today regarded as the greatest lyric poet of the romantic period, and that he is a romantic figure if only by reason of the love of nature which informs so much of his verse ; but he conjured into his verse that something new which the romantics strove for and which in these days is more alive and modern than it ever was. His mystic pantheism, too, relates him to the romantics ; he is romantic in his belief in the ultimate oneness of nature and man. Born at Lauffen on the Neckar he was, like Schiller, a Swabian. He studied theology at Tübingen, where he was a fellow-pupil of Hegel and Schelling ; here he read Spinoza and Kant. In 1793 Schiller, whom he met on his last visit home, recommended him to Charlotte von Kalb (p. lxxxix) at Woltershausen near Jena as tutor to her children, and he lived in her house. But her son Fritz was refractory, and in 1795 he relinquished this post and spent some time at Jena, where he was in close contact with Schiller and attended Fichte's lectures. After a period at home, busy with his novel *Hyperion*, he went to Frankfurt, where from 1796 to 1798 he was tutor to the son of Susette Gontard ; to him she was the embodiment of Greek beauty, and he fell passionately in love with her ; he expresses his feelings for her in his poem *Abbitte*. Her husband was a one-eyed business man, to whom she was just his housekeeper and the mother of his children, while Hölderlin he regarded as one of his *Domestiken*. As a native of Hamburg Susette, who was of the same age as Hölderlin, had been a friend of Klopstock ; he had been a guest at her wedding ; and with her lively interest in literature she and the poet had much in common. Hölderlin's first poems had been rhymed and in regular rhythms ; now his discussion of Klopstock brought him to rhymeless verse ; and, historically considered, the result is that Hölderlin by his free handling of rhythm is the direct continuator of Klopstock, with whom as a poet he had more in common than with Schiller. In his elegies he also handles the

hexameter paired with pentameter, a form which of
course had been used copiously by the classicists;
thus he weaves his hopeless love for Susette into an
elegiac poem of this form, *Menons Klagen um Diotima*;
it is his song of farewell to her. His odes are in the
alcaic and asclepiadic strophes; once only he uses the
sapphic strophe.

Diotima is a Greek name which is the title of one of
his *Jugendgedichte*: the singer, when in the dark days
of life he is bending down to the silent realm of shades,
is saved from despair by the vision, coming like a flash
from heaven, of a divine shape, *ein Götterbild*, Diotima;
and now he transfers this name to Susette in poems and
to the heroine of his novel *Hyperion oder der Eremit
in Griechenland*, for which Schiller had helped him to
a publisher in Cotta long before; now he finishes it;
the first volume appeared in 1796, the second in 1799.
In the lyrical prose of *Hyperion*, which is in the form
of letters, he glorifies Hellas. Hyperion is a young
Greek who takes part in 1770 in the fighting against
the Turks who have occupied his country. His loved
one, Diotima, dies; and so he turns hermit, ' *Priester
der göttlichen Natur*'. In a symbolic way the novel is
a revealing record of his development. He unfolds
what to him is religious faith: ' *Wir sind nichts, was
wir suchen ist alles.*' But it ends with *Hyperions
Schicksalslied*, which gives vivid expression to the
despair of suffering mortals—and of Hölderlin in
particular.

The poet's infatuation was discovered by Gontard in
1798 and he had to leave, though he was able to com-
municate with Susette for some time afterwards.
After leaving Frankfurt he had a period of private
teaching in Stuttgart, and then for a few months was
tutor in a merchant's family near St. Gall. At the
end of 1801 he went to Bordeaux to be tutor in the
family of the consul for Hamburg there. In May 1802

he left Bordeaux—we do not know why—and tramped home by way of Paris. He arrived home out of his mind. It was not till he reached home that he heard that Diotima had died. With his enhanced subjectivity he had been unable to adapt himself to the life of ordinary mortals about him. A friend took him to Homburg, and he was well cared for ; but his outbreaks of madness kept recurring, and finally he was found a lodging with a carpenter at Tübingen, who looked after him till he died in 1843, after forty years of lunacy.

Not alone his love-story was the cause of his breakdown. During his lifetime his poems had appeared only in almanacs and in journals (including Schiller's *Neue Thalia* and *Die Horen*). All his efforts to get his poems published in volume form were fruitless, and it was not till he was mad that he came into the forefront of interest. By 1810 he was classed by the romantics as one of the greatest of poets ; his poems were circulated in manuscript. At last in 1826 his verse was collected by the Swabian poets Ludwig Uhland and Gustav Schwab and published by Cotta. In 1846 his *Sämtliche Werke* appeared. The first *Literaturgeschichte* that mentions him is that of G. G. Gervinus (1833). The modern critical valuation of Hölderlin begins with Norbert von Hellingrath's [1] edition (1913 ff.). Judged by the standards of today he is indeed of the first rank. He has the ethereal fineness of feeling that here we ascribe to Shelley ; he was from the first influenced by Schiller's conception of the aloofness of poetry from common trends of thought. His themes—love, friendship, fatherland, nature, landscapes, heroism, freedom, the dignity of man—correspond to Schiller's ideal of the beautiful and good (*kalogathia*). Marvellously he compresses a

[1] One of the Kreis um Stefan George, who ranked Hölderlin next after Goethe.

world of feeling into short poems : ' short my song is as my happiness ' (*Die Kürze*). He asks fate (*An die Parzen*) to grant him but one summer, one autumn ' *zu reifem Gesange . . .*', until ' *das Heil'ge, das am Herzen mir liegt, | Das Gedicht, gelungen.*' And he had seven years of creative genius in the fullness of his powers. The sublimity of his diction is in the main due to his conviction that a poet is chosen and conse-crated by the gods (' *von Apollo geschlagen* '), and that as a dedicated priest of beauty and high thinking he cannot stoop to low levels. He must therefore thrill to his divine message, though it should break him, and his language must be for those worshipping in the temple. What distinguishes him from the romantics, and indeed from the classicists who preceded him, is the intensity of his feeling, the clarity of his vision, and the untrammelled flow of his rhythmic chant which often harmonically links his stanzas.

Psychiatrists in recent years have busied themselves with the cause of Hölderlin's madness. The likeliest cause is the feeling of helplessness resulting from his lifelong loneliness ; he found friends who realized his genius and did what they could to help him, but his work did not appeal to the reading public of his day, and he was forced to earn a poor living by tutoring. In his intervals of unemployment he lived in mortal fear of having to don the parson's gown, as his mother wished him to, and of having to do the preaching for which he had been trained. For a period he found a mate, Diotima, who could respond to his feelings and aspirations, but he was forced to leave her ; and his poem *Der Abschied* reveals the state of his mind at the time : as he was separated from his soul-mate so he was from the God within him and her ; he was cast out and forsaken. The world he lived in with her and without her was the ideal world of ancient Greece ; this he re-created in his beautifully imaged verse ; but a hundred years and more were to pass before he found readers who could respond to it.

Schiller (p. xcii) had defined poetry as (1) *naiv* and (2) *sentimentalisch* : (1) Greek poetry *is* nature, (2) modern poetry *strives* to be nature. FRIEDRICH SCHLEGEL (1772–1829)—fragmentary as a poet, original as a critic—now defines Greek poetry as *schön*, in the sense that it is considered with aloof appreciation (' *interesseloses Wohlgefallen* '), whereas modern poetry is individual and expressive of the writer's character and genius ; not what is beautiful in the sense of the classics must be the aim of poetry, but what is individual and characteristic ; that is, to use his word, ' *romantisch* '. This new concept ushers in a new phase of literature. Friedrich's elder brother AUGUST WILHELM SCHLEGEL (1767–1845)—they were the sons of Johann Adolf Schlegel, one of the Bremer Beiträger (p. xxv)—stands out as an essayist and translator ; of prime importance is his translation of Shakespeare (*Shakespeares dramatische Werke*, 1797–1810), in which he was helped by Tieck's daughter Dorothea and Graf Wolf Baudissin. Romanticism as a movement directly opposed to Schiller, who was at the moment in the heyday of his powers, and running contrary to classicism was thus initiated and fostered by the brothers Schlegel, together with their friends Wackenroder and Tieck. From this circle of associates with their women friends—Karoline Schlegel, the wife of August Wilhelm Schlegel (' Dame Luzifer ' as Schiller christened her) and the three brilliant Jewesses Henriette Herz, Dorothea Veit (who after her divorce married Friedrich Schlegel), Rahel Levin—was launched the literary organ of the movement, *Das Athenäum* (1798–1800), which in the first number introduced Novalis with his aphorisms *Blütenstaub* and in the second number and in later issues planned out the future for the movement with Friedrich Schlegel's *Fragmente*,

also aphorisms in which is unfolded the programme of
' *progressive Universalpoesie* ', which was to fuse poetry
and prose, art-poetry and nature-poetry, blend poetry
and philosophy (in the main that of Fichte), vitalize
poetry and with it saturate even the intercourse of
social life and with its cultural content fill every form
and phase of art.   The result was to be ' total art '.
New sources of inspiration were to be found in Shakespeare, Goethe, and the classical writers of Greece,
Spain, and Italy.   With its tendrils thus far-flung it
was indeed universal, and it was not to be tied down by
rules and even by logic ; imagination free to roam and
create was its inexhaustible well of inspiration.   In
lyric verse particularly, as the new style developed,
one salient feature was synæsthesia,[1] the use of colours
for sounds and *vice versa,* or the transfer of one
medium of sensation to another, as in Tieck's *Liebe
denkt in süssen Tönen.*   And the *Fragmente* call for
*die romantische Ironie :* the author in handling his
theme is free, he soars over his subject and can therefore change his mood, make his character critical of
himself, &c.

Thus prompted, the Romantics set out to conquer
new realms. HEINRICH WILHELM WACKENRODER
(1772–98) discovered Nuremberg and celebrated its
ancient glories in his novel *Franz Sternbalds Wanderun-
gen* (1798), which, after his death of consumption, was
completed by JOHANN LUDWIG TIECK (1773–1853),
who wrote novels and *Märchen,* renewed the old
*Volksbücher,* and translated Dante and *Don Quixote.*
His *Minnelieder aus dem schwäbischen Zeitalter* (1803),
a furbishing up of these old poems, aroused the interest
of a young student, JAKOB GRIMM (p. cxiii), and are
thus the starting-point of our medieval *Germanistik,*
for Jakob Grimm was the first great scholar in this field,

---

[1] For instance, what the French symbolists nearer our time
were to call *audition colorée,* optic for acoustic, visual for auditory.

while by his study of Sanscrit Friedrich Schlegel made a start with comparative philology.

Romanticism is divided into two stages : the first, *die Frühromantik* or *die ältere Romantik*, round the turn of the century, launched out from Berlin and centred in Jena [1] ; the second, *die jüngere Romantik* (Achim von Arnim, Clemens Brentano, Heinrich von Kleist), radiated from Heidelberg and Berlin, and had as its literary organ *Zeitung für Einsiedler*.

NOVALIS (the pen-name of Friedrich Leopold, Baron von Hardenberg ; 1772–1801) is the first poet proper of the Jena group, the first who by actual achievement realizes the poetry they dreamed of, the most romantic of the romantics ; indeed, with his symbol of *die blaue Blume* for poetry he is the very prototype and embodiment of the romantic poet ; and his life as a poet, so mysteriously inwoven with all his dreaming and thinking into his novel *Heinrich von Ofterdingen*, is itself a *Märchen*. The intensified religious faith, which is the plant and flower of his suffering and longing, and to which he gives expression both in verse and in prose that is verse transmuted, gives a halo (illusory perhaps) to the philosophy which his fellow romanticists surmise rather than define. He folds it in a phrase : ' *Nach innen geht der geheimnisvolle Weg ; in uns oder nirgends ist die Ewigkeit mit ihren Welten.*' All that *is* is the poet's inspired divination. Poetry is absolute reality (' *Die Poesie ist das echt absolut Reelle* '). And so it is Novalis who probes into his own depths and finds the infinite in the finite. Nature is spirit visible and spirit is nature unseen [2] ; what is extraneous to the thinking

---

[1] Also called Jena or Athenæum group. Friedrich Schlegel moved from Dresden to Jena in 1796. August Wilhelm Schlegel came as professor in 1798. Tieck settled in Jena in 1799. Novalis was in close touch from his post at the salt-mines not far away.

[2] ' *Die Natur soll der unsichtbare Geist, der Geist die unsichtbare Natur sein.*' Schelling.

mind is the symbol for the reality of life within. He is the poet of *Traumwirklichkeit*, to whom dream is reality and reality is a dream. And so nature and reason are a unity.

The family were members of an austere religious sect, the Moravian brothers (*Herrnhuter*). He studied law at Jena, where he attended Schiller's lectures, and then in Leipzig, where began his close friendship with Friedrich Schlegel, who recruited him for romantic doctrines, and then with Fichte and Schelling; later he was associated with Tieck. After graduating he filled a post in the civil administration at Tennstedt, near Langensalza; and here, in 1794, at the castle of a friend, he made the acquaintance of a girl of 13, Sophie von Kühn, fell in love with her, and became engaged to her in 1795. She died in 1797, and henceforth to him she is the ideal of *das Ewig-Weibliche*. His despair is inwoven in his *Hymnen an die Nacht* (written 1797–9; first printed in *Das Athenäum* in 1800). The form of the hymns is typographically new: they have the appearance of rhythmic prose, but can be metrically scanned and arranged in lines of unequal length, and they are broken at intervals by rhymed poems of regular form, which by many are reckoned as the very finest of romanticism. The sense has to be disentangled; it is veiled in a recondite mysticism. If the symbols are unravelled and interrelated the whole falls into a concord of religious and philosophic ideas which culminate in the famous poem *Sehnsucht nach dem Tode*. In the linked sense of these heterogeneous symbols Christ, death and night are now a unity and the Virgin Mary is a symbol of the lost loved one. The poet has lost his hold on life and is possessed by his feverish yearning for death. The basic concept is that night is the symbol for death, and that death here below is the womb from which a new life is born, and so it is the entrance into life eternal. Novalis had Young's *Night Thoughts* to prompt him, but the essentially Roman Catholic mystic identification of opposites is closer to the rapt symbolism of the medieval Spanish mystic Juan de la Cruz ; there is, however, no reason to think that Novalis owes a debt to anyone. In *Sehnsucht nach dem Tode* we find the Spanish mystic's version of the *unio mystica* : Jesus is the bride of the soul, Bridegroom and Bride (*amada en el amado transformada*) are one in the erotic union in the grave (*Hinunter zu der süssen Braut,* | *Zu Jesus dem Geliebten.*) Christ's own death, the sixth stanza tells us, was such a *Liebestod*, and therefore the lover's yearning for death is an *imitatio Christi*. Similarly in one of his aphorisms (*Fragmente*) Novalis says : ' In death love is sweetest ; for the lover Death is a bridal night, a sweet mystery of mysteries.' The rest of the imagery in *Sehnsucht nach dem Tode* is in equal measure hectically poetical and (to earth-bound minds) flagrantly illogical. But, historically considered, all this hymning of the *Liebestod* ushers in that morbid *Todeserotik* which was in the fullness of time to give us Wagner's *Tristan und Isolde*.

In 1799 and 1800 Novalis wrote his *Geistliche Lieder*, of which several—*Wenn ich ihn nur habe ; Was wär' ich ohne dich gewesen ?* and *Wenn alle untreu werden*— have been taken into the Protestant hymnal. These spiritual songs were directly influenced by Schleiermacher's *Reden über die Religion*.[1] The best of them

---

[1] Friedrich Ernst Daniel Schleiermacher (1768–1834), professor of theology at Halle and Berlin, remained a Christian clergyman (p. lxii). The essence of his philosophy (*Reden über die Religion an die Gebildeten unter ihren Verächtern*, 1799 ; *Monologe*, 1800) is that Thought and Being are identical and that in any Being one of two factors predominates : either the Real ( = Nature) or the Ideal ( = Spirit). God is the Unity of these two contrasting factors ; that is, He is the Absolute Unity of the Ideal and the Real (*die Ureinheit des Weltganzen*). God and the World are not identical, but each requires the other. These religious concepts greatly influenced Friedrich Schlegel, with whom Schleiermacher lodged in Berlin, and the *Athenäum* group of romanticists.

have a simple and direct appeal, and in some sort they mark a recovery from the cult of death of *Hymnen an die Nacht*. Although they are so dreamfully symbolic they have the illusion of orthodoxy because they speak in terms of the Moravian religion, which was the faith of the poet's childhood as it was of Schleiermacher; thus they sing the love of Jesus, to whom mostly they are addressed. The *Marienlieder* among them worship the Virgin in every woman, and Mary as woman is the symbol of the infinite in the finite. The seventh Song is notoriously a farrago, and taking the Songs as a whole the fleshliness of some of the imagery is repulsive to an unmystical mind. But the ' magic idealism ' of some of its nuptial eroticism is confirmed by certain of the poet's *Fragmente*—to use the second name of his *Blütenstaub*, the same as that of Friedrich Schlegel's aphorisms or *aperçus*.[1]

In his essay *Die Christenheit oder Europa* (written 1799, publication delayed by Tieck till 1826) Novalis classes Protestantism, which broke the harmony of the Middle Ages, as outlived, and he looks to Schleiermacher to found a new religion in which all sects will be united and made one. In any case a trend to Roman Catholicism is a feature of romanticism; Friedrich Schlegel, that practical mind, turned Catholic. In the later work of Novalis Roman Catholicism is the ideal religion; for it lives by images; and the loveliest image is the Virgin Mary, the symbol of purity the pure adore, the dream made visible of all that is loveliest on earth. Clearly Roman Catholicism is part and parcel of the *Gesamtkunstwerk* to which he, being duly indoctrinated, aspires.

In 1797 Novalis took a course of mineralogy at the Bergakademie under the famous professor A. G. Werner, and these studies went to the making of his

[1] Complete edition in volume form as *Fragmente* (*Blütenstaub*) (1824).

fragment of a novel *Die Lehrlinge zu Sais*, intended to be an interpretation by the medium of science of the cosmos, and of the interrelations of man and nature. His other novel, *Heinrich von Ofterdingen* (published by Tieck, 1802), in which several of his loveliest songs are interwoven, was also unfinished at his death. The period is that of the Crusades ; here we have that glorification of the Middle Ages which is to be a salient element of later romanticism. The hero of the story, Heinrich von Ofterdingen, is the fabled hero of the Middle High German poem *Der Wartburgkrieg*, which relates the contest of the Meistersingers in 1206–7 at the castle of the Wartburg. The tale was intended, as Novalis himself declared, to be an apotheosis of poetry. Heinrich is to develop not merely into a supreme poet but into poetry itself—a metamorphosis (*Wandlung*) such as Goethe had made his theme (p. lxxix)—and this was to be the prelude to the transformation of the whole world to poetry. It begins with Heinrich's dream of *die blaue Blume*, which is transformed into a maiden, whom Heinrich finds and marries ; but she dies, as Sophie had died. The novel is a strange medley of fancies and symbols ; but this one symbol of *die blaue Blume* with all its wealth of meaning, the symbol of love and poetry, has established itself.

Novalis was marked for promotion in his mining post, and was once again engaged to a charming girl, Julie von Charpentier ; but, like Wackenroder, he was consumptive, and in 1801 he died of hæmorrhage at the age of twenty-nine.

The most gifted of the Heidelberg Circle of romanticists was CLEMENS BRENTANO (1778–1842). He was born in Frankfurt as the son of a merchant of Italian birth. At the turn of the century (1797–1803) he studied in Jena and was here in touch with the Schlegels and particularly with Tieck, by whom he

was noticeably influenced later as regards style and
technique. He is thus, together with Achim von
Arnim, whom he met at Jena, the link between the
Jena Circle and the Heidelberg Circle (p. cvi). In
1804 he settled in Heidelberg, where in 1805 he was
joined by Achim von Arnim, and they lived together.
In 1811 Arnim married Brentano's sister Bettina, who
had in her time tried in vain to detach Goethe from his
wife Christiane, and after his death published her
*Briefwechsel Goethes mit einem Kinde* (1835). Brentano's first work was the novel *Godwi oder das steinerne
Bild der Mutter : ein verwilderter Roman von Maria*
(1801–2) ; it was wild and woolly indeed, but embedded
in it are poems, including his *Erntelied, Lore Lay,* and
*Die lustigen Musikanten,* which foreshadow his greatness as a lyric poet. There are all the makings of a
great achievement—he planned it as a *divina commedia,*
to rival Dante's—in his verse epic *Romanzen vom
Rosenkranz. Die Erfindung des Rosenkranzes* (1803–12).
It is in Spanish four-beat trochees, rhymed or as-
sonanced, such as Herder had introduced in *Der Cid*
(p. xli), a form henceforth very popular with the
romanticists. Actually the poem was not printed
till 1852 : Brentano at the time he wrote the poem had
lost the Roman Catholic faith of his youth, but when
he fell in love with the eighteen-year-old poetess Luise
Hensel and she brought the strayed wanderer back to
the fold (1816–17) the poem, mystic as it seems, might
have been charged with having more romantic magic
than Church doctrine, and it was held back. When in
1818 he began to record the visions of the stigmatic
nun Anna Katharina Emmerich—published as *Das
bittere Leiden unsers Herrn Jesu Christi* (1833)—Brentano lost himself more and more in what his Protestant
friend Arnim called ' his Catholic fever '. For the last
twenty-five years of his life he was dead to literature.
Brentano's best work is his lyric verse, which is

influenced by the *Volkslied* and marked by consummate mastery of the romantic devices of sound-painting and synæsthesia (p. cv). Some of his best poetry is strongly tinged with eroticism : *O lieb Mädel, wie schlecht du bist !* ; *Ich bin ein armes Waiselein* ; *Romanze.* One poem of his which has inspired other poems is the long ballad *Lore Lay* ; he takes the name of a rock, *der Lurleifels*, in the Rhine, and spins round it out of his own head the *Loreleisage*, which is therefore not, as Heine's most famous ballad might lead us to think, ' *aus uralten Zeiten* '. Eichendorff's *Waldgespräch* is from the same source.

Brentano's brother-in-law ACHIM VON ARNIM (1781–1831), a nobleman from the March of Brandenburg and a Protestant by upbringing, wrote verse, but its quality rings hard and metallic, and he ranks higher as a writer of prose tales. But Arnim is starred above all in the history of literature as the joint editor with Brentano of the collection of folk-songs *Des Knaben Wunderhorn* (3 vols., 1805–8). Herder in his essay *Von Ähnlichkeit der mittleren englischen und deutschen Dichtkunst* (1770 ; p. xxxix) had called upon the Germans to follow the example of the English and to collect the old songs of their nation, and this is what Brentano and Arnim set out to do. Arnim, too, while travelling in London, had come across Scott's *Minstrelsy of the Scottish Border* (1802) and this too pointed the way. The title of their collection is that of the first poem, which is illustrated on the title-page by a vignette representing a beautiful boy galloping along and waving an ivory horn which he is taking to King Arthur's castle ; as soon as it is touched lovely music resounds. Apart from a few original poems taken over from Brentano's novel *Godwi* (*Lore Lay*, &c.), the two editors restricted themselves to old German songs, and their collection pairs, therefore, rather with Percy's *Reliques of Ancient Poetry* (1765) than with Herder's

*Volkslieder* (p. xl), which, though it was prompted by Percy's collection, assembles folk-songs from all nations, African and American as well as European. In *Des Knaben Wunderhorn* we find the old ballad of *Tannhäuser* and many others which are a fruitful source of inspiration to the poets who follow, not to speak of texts provided for the composers of the day. From now on a distinction is made between *Volksdichtung*—produced by the somewhat mythical *Volksseele* —and *Kunstdichtung*, poetry that observes the stereotyped rules evolved from the study of the ancients and the laws of prosody. The *Volksseele* writes—or rather sings—as the spirit moves it ; it is nature upwelling —the idea is—not premeditated art.

After the *Wunderhorn* come *Die teutschen Volksbücher* (1807), collected by the founder of German ultramontanism JOSEPH GÖRRES (1776–1848), who lived in Heidelberg from 1806 to 1808 and there gave the first lectures on Old German poetry. Görres also edited the Middle High German poem *Lohengrin* (1813) and *Altdeutsche Volks- und Meisterlieder* (1817). The poets proper in their collections of ancient songs and stories were inclined to touch them up and to modernize their texts, and even to add matter of their own ; on the other hand two members of the Heidelberg group, JAKOB GRIMM (1785–1863) and WILHELM GRIMM (1786–1859), followed the principle that the original text should be respected and preserved ; their motto was ' *das Alte als Altes stehen zu lassen* '. They therefore were medievalists in the sense of today and the real founders of German philological study.

In 1809 Arnim and Brentano removed from Heidelberg to Berlin, where romanticism had actually germinated, and where the brilliant Jewesses Henriette Herz and Rahel Levin held their salons, in which the North German writers met. And now in Berlin Arnim and Brentano are joined by Fouqué, Heinrich

8

von Kleist, Chamisso, Eichendorff, and later by
Wilhelm Müller; and Heidelberg ceases to be the
centre of romanticism. In 1810 Brentano and Arnim
founded in Berlin the *Christlich Deutsche Gesellschaft*
and this carries on the patriotic fervour which had
shown itself already in *Des Knaben Wunderhorn* and
which was to inflame the youth of Germany against
Napoleon.

Now follows the poetry of the Wars of Liberation
(*Befreiungskriege*). Already in 1806 Arnim had written
war songs for the Prussians. Ernst Moritz Arndt, then
a professor in Greifswald, had to flee to Sweden after
raising his voice against Napoleon in his work *Geist
der Zeit* (1808). He returned in 1809 and wrote his
*Lied von Schill*, in praise of Major von Schill, who had
fallen after attempting a rebellion. In 1809 HEINRICH
VON KLEIST (1777–1811) wrote one of the wildest of
the war songs, *Germania an ihre Kinder*, in which he
calls upon the German patriots to make the fields white
with the bones of their foes. Friedrich Ludwig Jahn
(1778–1852), on war intent, launched a national movement for the practice of gymnastics—hence his name
Turnvater Jahn; and his book *Deutsches Volkstum*
(1810) stirred hearts and minds. In 1810 was founded
the University of Berlin, with Wilhelm von Humboldt
and Schleiermacher as professors; and the first rector
was Fichte, whose *Reden an die deutsche Nation* (1808)
written while Napoleon was investing Berlin, had
roused the temper of his countrymen. The Tyrolese
tried repeatedly to throw off the French yoke; the
name of their leader, Andreas Hofer, is great in song
and story. And at last in 1813 came the *Aufruf an
mein Volk*, the call to arms of the King of Prussia from
Breslau, and the war began that led to victory.
Fouqué made a start with his song *Frischauf zum
fröhlichen Jagen* and led his company of volunteers to
meet the King at Breslau. Jahn led a battalion of the

*Lützowsche Freischar*, Lützow's Volunteer Corps ; under him served Eichendorff and Theodor Körner. Brentano wrote what has ever since been a national song : *Am Rhein, am Rhein, da wachsen unsere Reben.*

The great mass of this war poetry is, judged as poetry and not as patriotism, poor. The rhythm is too rhetorical and the verse lacks the finesse of technique which marks the best of the romantic poetry of the period. First of the war poets in importance is ERNST MORITZ ARNDT (1769–1860), the son of a farmer from Rügen. His pamphlet *Der Rhein Deutschlands Strom, nicht Deutschlands Grenze* (1813) was as good as a battle won, so Vater Jahn said. His war poems (*Lieder für Teutsche*, 1813 ; *Bannergesänge und Wehrlieder*, 1813 ; collected in two volumes as *Gedichte*, 1818) rang out through the land ; they are remembered by their first lines rather than by their titles : *Der Gott, der Eisen wachsen liess,* | *Der wollte keine Knechte ; Was ist des Deutschen Vaterland? ; Was blasen die Trompeten? Husaren heraus!* But the nation's darling was THEODOR KÖRNER (1791–1813), the son of Schiller's friend Gottfried Körner. He is the type of the soldier poet who dies young on the battlefield. He had had some success as a dramatist, but on the outbreak of the war he joined Lützow's Volunteer Corps and fell, twenty-one years old, soon after writing his *Schwertlied*. His father published his collected verse as *Leier und Schwert* (1814) ; the songs were set to music by Karl Maria von Weber. The third in the trio, MAX VON SCHENKENDORF (1783–1817), has the softer tones of the dreamful poets, as in his *Muttersprache, Mutterlaut,* | *Wie so wonnesam, so traut!* and his *Freiheit, die ich meine* ( = *minne*). To this patriotic poetry belong also Friedrich Rückert's *Geharnischte Sonette*, which, written 1812, form part of his *Deutsche Gedichte* (1814), but his major successes lie in other fields (see p. cxxx). In any case his war poems, apart from their artificiality of form, have not the resonant, singable qualities of the true war poetry.

After the Heidelberg romanticists come the younger Berlin romanticists : de la Motte Fouqué, Chamisso, Varnhagen von Ense, and the late romanticists (*Spätromantik*) generally. They wrote in the period of reaction which followed the defeat of Napoleon, the failure of the Congress of Vienna (1814), and the suppression of freedom of thought that went with Metternich and the Holy Alliance. See, for instance, Chamisso's *Nachtwächterlied* (1826) and Uhland's *Am 18. Oktober 1816*. Significant of what happened is Arndt's dismissal, because of his upholding of free speech, from his professorship at Bonn ; he was not reinstated till 1840, when he was 71.

The historian of literature is confronted with the fact that, although several of these *Spätromantiker*—Chamisso, Wilhelm Müller, Eichendorff in particular—have always been and still are popular and beloved, critics with an acute sense of classification put them down the scale as ' *Epigonen der Romantik* ' and, most drastically of all, as *das Biedermeier*. The term *Biedermeier*, which is used both of the person (*der Biedermeier*) and of the style (*Biedermeierstil*), suffers from degrees of interpretation ; and when Eichendorff, Heine, Mörike, and Annette von Droste-Hülshoff are classed as Biedermeier pure and simple, there is good reason to dispute it. Generally speaking, the definition is chronological : it marks a transition period—from 1815 to the Paris *révolution à demi* of 1830 or to the revolution of 1848. It is a transitory period of psychic exhaustion after the over-exciting and over-fruitful periods of the French revolution, German idealism, and the Napoleonic wars. After all, it depends mathematically on one's definition of romanticism—or of Biedermeier. Critics who dispute the chronological application of the term Biedermeier point out that there is in various *Spätromantiker* a sense of the demonic (*Dämonie*), the realization that life is governed by sinister forces beyond the control of sense and reason. On the other hand, such a poem as Chamisso's *Das Kruzifix*, in which a pupil nails his master to a cross to study the revelation in his features of the agony he is suffering, may be dismissed as a crass exhibition of brutality as well as appreciated as a revelation of the death-dealing forces in art and the purification of the artist by suffering, or as a study of the psychology of crime. And certainly the sensational and over-sentimental elements in Chamisso may be classed as anti-romantic. For one thing he was by profession a scientist, and if he had a matter-of-fact way of looking at things it was natural. Friedrich Rückert again, the '*Alles-Könner und Alles-Macher*', throughout his long life moved continuously away from the real romantic nearness to nature or even heart-felt *naïveté* to sheer cult of form, learned didacticism, and exploitation of his own learning. Even his war-poems of 1813 were sonnets, scholarly and for scholars, not for marching soldiers ; that is, they were artificial. In Platen again what counts is perfection of form.

A popular Brandenburg writer was FRIEDRICH BARON DE LA MOTTE FOUQUÉ (1777–1843). He was specifically a romanticist because of his choice of medieval themes—the trilogy of dramas *Der Held des Nordens* (1810), his fantastic dramatization of the Scandinavian version of the *Nibelungenlied*, &c. His only work that lives is his Novelle *Undine* (1811), the tale of a watersprite who marries a mortal to gain a soul. It served as the text of Lortzing's *Märchenoper*.

The most talented of the later Berlin romantics and certainly one with far-flung thematic interests was ADALBERT VON CHAMISSO [1] (1781–1838). He was the one German poet in whom the Wars of Liberation

[1] His real name was Louis-Charles-Adelaïde comte de Chamisso.

aroused mixed feelings, the reason being that he was French-born and always conscious of a pull to France in his sympathies, poetical as well as national. He was born at the castle of Boncourt in the province of Champagne—his feelings for it are enshrined in one of the most famous of his poems—and his family fled to Berlin in 1790 to escape the horrors of the revolution. As a boy he was one of the queen's pages, and when the time came he entered the Prussian army. His own life-story gives the key to his Märchen *Peter Schlemihls wundersame Geschichte* (1814), the tale of a man who, to gain riches and spurious honour, sells his shadow to the devil, and, because it is seen that he is without one, is the butt of ridicule, and when the devil offers to return his shadow in return for his soul flees on seven-league boots to find refuge in the sheltering solitudes of nature—a symbol of the comfort and satisfaction he himself found in his botanical avocations in his riper years. The lost shadow is said to be the symbol—though he denied it—of his *Vaterlandslosigkeit*. He had left the Prussian army as a lieutenant, and it was while staying with Madame de Staël in Coppet on Lake Geneva that he discovered his aptitude for scientific studies. As a botanist he sailed round the world between 1815 and 1818 with a Russian scientific expedition; he described the voyage in a book which keeps its interest. It went to the making of his cycle of poems, *Salas y Gomez* (1829), and this global experience explains, apart from this Robinson Crusoe type of poem, his fondness for the South Sea Islands and primitive tribes. After his return he settled down as custodian in the Berlin Botanical Gardens. His early poems, written when he was a bilingual Prussian lieutenant with his German still shaky, had appeared in the Berlin *Grüner Almanach*, the organ of a group of young romantic poets, edited by him together with his friend KARL AUGUST VARN-

HAGEN VON ENSE (1785–1858), the husband of Rahel
Levin ; but for collected form his poems had to wait
till 1831.

He followed the Biedermeier fashion, popularized
still further by Wilhelm Müller, Uhland and Heine, in
writing ' cycles ' of lyrics, sequences of poems independent in themselves and separated by numbers or
title headings ; the cycle *Frauen-Liebe und Leben*
(1830), set to music by Robert Schumann and Karl
Löwe, is inspired by his own happy marriage ; it pairs
with his less personal cycle *Lebens-Lieder und Bilder*,
which generalizes in lyric alternation from boy—girl
to husband—wife and so on throughout life the stages
of human experience through love to parenthood and
what follows.    These cycles suffer from their excess of
middle-class (*bürgerlich*) sentiment, and the second
cycle is Biedermeier at its lowest ebb. Chamisso
reaches a much higher level in narrative poems and
ballads, in which it is the story that matters rather
than the poetical presentation of it ; in common with
the later romantics (pp. lxxiv, cxxxvii) he is fond of
sensational and gruesome themes, criminal happenings
with no psychic interest ; that is, the thrill is in the
raw happening, not in the root causes of it.    Typical
*Schauergedichte* are : *Die Löwenbraut, Die Sonne bringt
es an den Tag, Die Giftmischerin, Korsische Gastfreiheit.*
Some of these ballads, like *Salas y Gomez*, are in *terza
rima*, which Chamisso did much to popularize : *Das
Kruzifix, Die Kreuzschau, Das Mordtal.*    There is also
some treatment of social conditions, and this points
forward to the advent of realism and to the political
poetry of the forties and *Das junge Deutschland.*    The
best known of his realistic lyrics, intended to show
the sufferings of the people (*Armeleutepoesie*), is *Die
alte Waschfrau* (1833) ; it was written to help a washer-
woman in the grip of poverty to whom he passed the
money he earned by it.    These up-to-date themes he

handles (*Der Bettler und sein Hund, Das Gebet der Witwe,* &c.) in the style of Béranger, whose poems he translated together with FRANZ VON GAUDY (1800–46), he too of French extraction, who in his *Kaiserlieder* (1835) defiantly sang the praise of Napoleon. There is modern socialist feeling infolded in the playful symbolism of Chamisso's *Das Riesenspielzeug*, one of his series *Deutsche Volkssagen* (1831) ; the theme is that of Rückert's *Die Riesen und die Zwerge*. His ballads tend to be anecdotal rather than tensely dramatic, and the best of them keep their popularity by reason of their good-natured humour : *Tragische Geschichte* (the ballad of the man who turned round and round because his pigtail was hanging down behind), *Der rechte Barbier, Böser Markt, Hans im Glück*. The best known ballad is *Die Weiber von Winsperg*.

WILHELM MÜLLER (1794–1827), the father of Professor Max Müller of Oxford, was closely connected with the Berlin romanticists as well as with the Swabians. Born at Dessau, he studied philology and history in the newly founded University of Berlin, campaigned in the Wars of Liberation, in his case more with sword than pen, and settled down finally as a librarian at Dessau. His song-cycles *Die schöne Müllerin* and *Die Winterreise* are folk-songs, no doubt owing to the setting of his friend Franz Schubert as well as to the simple and direct appeal of their texts. Of these one may say, as of those of Eichendorff, Justinus Kerner and Uhland, that they are universally known by their first lines rather than by their titles : *Ich schnitt' es gern in alle Rinden ein* (*Ungeduld*) ; *Die Fenster auf, die Herzen auf* (*Frühlingseinzug*) ; *Das Wandern ist des Müllers Lust* (*Wanderschaft*) ; *Ich hört' ein Bächlein rauschen* (*Wohin ?*). Like Eichendorff he learned much from *Des Knaben Wunderhorn* and wrote with the *naïveté* of the *Volkslied*. His drinking-songs (*Meine Mus' ist gegangen in dem Schenken sein Haus* and others) found their place in the students' *Kommersbücher*. Among his most popular poems are his *Reiselieder* or *Wanderlieder*. Müller's *Wanderlust* is actual, whereas that of Eichendorff is fictional (*erträumt*), just a facet of the *Sehnsucht* which is the burden of his lyric work. Wilhelm Müller developed the *Liederzyklus* (p. cxix) to the *Rollenliederzyklus*, to which he gave its classical pattern ; the genre, very popular in late romanticism, is made up of individually independent poems strung together in epic sequence round the person of the singer, the representative of some occupation or other, who, roving around on foot, plies his trade of itinerant musician, or is a student, a sailor, an apprentice, a gipsy. The miller of the *Müllerlieder* is Müller himself singing the moods and fancies of his own love-story. His first collection of poems was *Siebenundsiebzig Gedichte aus dem hinterlassenen Papieren eines reisenden Waldhornisten* (1821 and 1824) ; this was followed by *Muscheln von der Insel Rügen* (1825) and *Lieder aus dem Meerbusen von Salerno* (1827), which together point forward to Heine's songs of the North Sea. In his own day Müller was famed far and wide for his *Lieder der Griechen* (1821) and *Neue Lieder der Griechen* (1823). The rising of the Greeks against the Turks in 1770 had gone to the making of Hölderlin's *Hyperion* (p. ci) ; the rising of 1820–9, in which Byron took part and died, was the inspiration of Müller's Greek songs, one of which is in pious commemoration of Byron. King Ludwig I of Bavaria too (1786–1868) was a poet who has his place in literature as a Philhellenist ; another was Wilhelm Waiblinger (p. cxxx) with his own *Lieder der Griechen* (1823). Actually the rhythm and diction of these fighting Greek poems are too level and trite to rival even the less stirring of those of the Wars of Liberation.

' *Der letzte Ritter der Romantik* '—to use Heine's highfalutin term—was JOSEPH FREIHERR VON

EICHENDORFF (1788–1857). More pathetic than the cognomen Heine gives him is the problem whether he was not also the last genuine romantic, those who came after him being more or less Biedermeier in the sense indicated above. In the matter of religion he was worlds away from Chamisso, who was politically a leftist and poured out his scorn for Jesuits, in that he was all his life an upholder of the established order and a staunch Roman Catholic. We have come across Eichendorff cheek by jowl with the Heidelberg romantics, and historians of literature do not forget that he too collected folk-songs for *Des Knaben Wunderhorn* and helped Görres with his *Volksbücher*. In 1813 he joined the Lützowsche Volunteer Corps. His most popular work is his short story *Aus dem Leben eines Taugenichts* (1826), which turns the free life of a vagrant with his fiddle into an idyll of *dolce far niente*. But his happy-go-lucky Novelle falls below his great wealth of lyrics, known as they are for the most part in the setting of Mendelssohn. Others of his lyrics were set to music by Hugo Wolf and Carl Maria von Weber. The burden of so many of these songs is *Sehnsucht*; just as the theme of *Aus dem Leben eines Taugenichts* is the artist's age-old yearning for Italy, so Eichendorff's yearning is for something far away even if it is ever so near, something that lives in the depths of his spirit and in the lilt of his verse but is indefinable. This is *romantische Sehnsucht* which breathes in the loveliest of Eichendorff's lyrics : *Wer hat dich, du schöner Wald . . .*; *O Täler weit, O Höhen*. In his *Wanderlieder* most of all we get yearning ; there are words which Eichendorff has invested with magic : *Waldeinsamkeit, Waldesrauschen, der Klang des Posthorns* ; we instinctively speak them with the modulation of poetry. His poem *Sehnsucht*, included among the *Wanderlieder*, gives the keynote for the intensity of this romantic longing ; all

Eichendorff is in this lyric. And, as might be expected, there are more folk-songs among his *Wanderlieder* than in any other section of his verse. In his love-songs the burden is *Schwermut*—the underlying sadness, the burdened mood of *Das zerbrochene Ringlein*, which has been a folk-song ever since it was written.

Strangely enough we find *Das zerbrochene Ringlein* ranged among Eichendorff's *Romanzen*. The general meaning of *Romanze* is 'ballad', 'narrative poem'; but there is too little of a story; and in fact Eichendorff has no power of bringing out the sharp outlines of characters in any *Romanze* where there is actually the hint of a story, as in his *Lorelei*; his *Romanzen* are all *Stimmungslieder*, not songs of action. The nearest Eichendorff can get to a ballad is *Der Reitersmann*; and this, though dramatic movement is there, is too remote from reality to be anything but a *Schauergedicht* of Chamisso's sort, but too *verschwommen* at that. What we do get in the *Romanzen* is that mysterious world which lies within us, the demonic forces (*Dämonie*) that beset us (*Der Schatzgräber*), the world of ghosts and magic; and therefore *Lorelei* is ranged among them—she is a witch. *Stimmungslieder* too are his so-called *Rollenlieder*, into which, according to the concept of the genre, the poet should weave the innermost feelings in a given situation of a representative of this or that calling (p. lxxi); but in these poems of Eichendorff, even in *Wanderlied der Prager Studenten*, it is more likely to be the mood of nature (*der grüne Wald*, etc.) round about the person or persons singing or sung about; this holds good even of *Die Spielleute*, *Der wandernde Musikant* and *Der Dichter*. In *Rollenliederzyklen* we have, no doubt, Eichendorff's personal mood as poet. Taking him all in all, Eichendorff's range is actually less than that of many of his contemporaries; that is, there is less to discuss; but all the same he is the finest lyric poet of late romanticism ; and that simply because lyric poetry is a miracle. There are no depths of thought to be probed ; he was not even a mystic like Novalis, whose Catholicity was complicated because, presumably, it was not really there. And so his *Geistliche Lieder*, as grouped in his *Collected Works*, do not all of them thrill Protestant or agnostic as well as Catholic, as do his *Mondnacht* and *Morgengebet* (*Als ging der Herr durchs stille Feld* . . .). It is when one reads Eichendorff's *Geistliche Lieder*, in which the spiritual chords, even in *Mariä Sehnsucht*, are poetical rather than Catholic, and his *Zeitlieder*, which might be expected to touch on the ethical, special, and political problems of the day, that one realizes why to some critics Eichendorff is a Biedermeier out and out : he gets no farther ; and this of course holds good of his eminently respectable life as a government official of the Biedermeierzeit. But nevertheless he is a romanticist, because of the indefinable magic of his verse with its softly gliding dreamful rhythms, and because he renders, magically still, the moods of all the seasons, with springtide and love linked in a copious section (*Frühling und Liebe*) ; the moods of dawn and morning, of night with its rustling trees and the moon over them ; and these moods are his, and he makes them ours. And above all who has sung the forest (*Waldeinsamkeit, Waldesrauschen* and all the rest) as Eichendorff has done ? And yet there is not even any metrical innovation in the facture of his verse for the prosodist to discuss ; all is in the fixed pattern of romantic verse and exceptionally simple in structure.

The Swabian poets (*die schwäbische* [*Dichter*]*schule*) have in common with the other South German romanticists the salient features of the poetry which follows that of the Heidelberg group, but share a certain sobriety of outlook and, by comparison with the fancifulness and other-worldliness of Wilhelm

Müller or Eichendorff, they show restraint and, however imaginative their theme, have a tendency to keep close to what is logically likely and possible in given circumstances. In other words they are level-headed rather than lyrically exalted ; or, more bluntly, they are nearer to the realism of the post-romantic period ; or again, as some would say, they are *bürgerlich* in their habit of mind, more or less Biedermeier. Because of their racial feeling (*Heimatliebe*) they show in their choice of themes a preference for what they find in the legendary lore and the history of Swabia—that is, Württemberg with Baden, the region of the Black Forest, the region between Bavaria and Alsace. This racial feeling is so marked with the Swabian School that the modern phase of *Heimatkunst* may be said to begin with them. They are home-loving family men ; if they leave their homeland at all they return to it ; only one of them, Wilhelm Waiblinger, feels the lure of strange lands. Another feature of the Swabian School is that there is with them no meticulous cult of form such as we find with their contemporaries Rückert and Platen ; they are satisfied with a creditable handling of established rhythmic and stanzaic forms. The same might of course be said of Eichendorff, except that in the lift and lilt of his lyric measures there is an indefinable something that some people would perhaps say is more akin to the means of music than to those of prosody. The Swabians are good craftsmen, but not more. Heine in his *Der Schwabenspiegel* (1838) made them the butt of his pungent wit, because, in his eyes, their level was low and they had the faults of decency and boredom ; but not a few of their lyrics are today just as much folk-songs and always will be as his *Lorelei*.

The acknowledged head of the Swabian School was always LUDWIG UHLAND (1787–1862). He was born in Tübingen, where his father was secretary of the

University. He entered the University as a student of law, and went to Paris in 1810 to finish off his law course; during his stay of eight months there, however, he spent most of his time in the Bibliothèque Nationale and other libraries reading medieval manuscripts, German and Romance. After his return from Paris he established himself nominally as an advocate, but in sober earnest changed over to literature, turned to Goethe, and was fascinated by Herder's *Stimmen der Völker in Liedern* and by *Des Knaben Wunderhorn*. His best poetry was written between 1807 and 1819; most of this is in his first volume of verse, *Gedichte* (1815). From 1819 to 1829 he was too absorbed in politics to write verse, but he produced a few ballads —*Bertran de Born* (1829), *Der Waller* (1829), *Das Glück von Edenhall* (1834)—in the period 1829–34, after which he wrote no more. Heine in his *Schwabenspiegel* refers to him as a dead poet who wrote no more because he knew he was dead. His *Vaterländische Gedichte* of 1816 hardly count except historically; these poems are concerned mainly with the fighting for the new constitution in Württemberg; they are the beginning of that political verse which was to aid and abet the revolutionary outbreaks of 1830 and 1848. Uhland took a vigorous personal part in this struggle for political progress when in 1819 he was elected a member of the Württemberg diet (*Landtag*). His last years were devoted to academic research in literature. As a scholar not only did he, with the Grimm brothers (p. cv), get Germanic philology going but he also, with Friedrich Diez, was the founder of Romance medieval studies: his essay *Über das altfranzösische Epos* in Fouqué's journal *Die Musen* (1812) is a landmark. His *Walther von der Vogelweide, ein altdeutscher Dichter* (1822) is the first book on this most important of Middle High German lyric poets. Still important are his *Schriften zur Geschichte der deutschen Dichtung und*

*Sage* (8 vols., not published in volume form till 1865–1873). He devoted his leisure to his collection of folk-songs, published as *Alte hoch-und niederdeutsche Volkslieder* (1844 and 1845), which, academically considered, since the texts are collated and variants given, are more valuable than *Des Knaben Wunderhorn*.

One would hardly claim great originality for Uhland, and he had not personally the poet's incalculable temperament of his friend Justinus Kerner ; he was rather a fine scholar—and above all a medievalist—with all the resources and technique of poetry at his disposal. And he had exquisite taste. He has too much of the qualities of a lawyer and of a politician to bare his secret soul in themes that can be identified with his own personality ; on the other hand, his characters are clearly defined as what the action shows them to be. One consequence of this is the wide range of his work, at all events in his ballads, which, with their wealth of themes rather than with any fund of feeling and experience, are the product of his great scholarship ; his lyrics proper are thought out and devised. Always he tells his tale attractively and in language plain and clear. Indeed, there is such a preponderance of clarity in his work that it is questionable whether Uhland belongs to romanticism at all ; he is only a romanticist in so far as what he gives us is still the motley Middle Ages ; that is, a vast variety of costume and custom, but not the stern truth of history. His handling of stanzaic and rhythmical form is perfect and severe ; but of course it is the very lack of *Formstrenge* which often gives the magic suggestiveness and the melodic thrill to the best of romantic poetry proper ; Uhland is thematically romantic, but not stylistically.

The most imposing section of Uhland's poems are classed as *Balladen und Romanzen* ; that is, if they are narrative at all they belong to this section. Classed as ballads as a rule are *Der Wirtin Töchterlein* and *Der gute Kamerad*, both written 1809 ; a more satisfactory classification of such bursts of feeling would be just folk-songs, which they have been since they were written. The finest of these *Balladen und Romanzen* were set to music by Karl Löwe. Chamisso had shown the way for Uhland, and Uhland shows the way for the ballad writers who follow him. The sources of Uhland's ballads were the Middle High German epics, old German legends generally, Scandinavian literature and medieval legendry, Saxo Grammaticus, and Old French and troubadour poetry. He is fond of Swabian themes : *Schwäbische Kunde* for instance, and—in the Nibelungen stanza—the epic cycle *Graf Eberhard der Rauschebart*. Critics find an anti-romantic element in the didacticism of the major ballads ; there is *Schuld und Sühne*, guilt is atoned for ; and for these didactic ballads a label has been found : *Gerechtigkeitsballaden*. To realize the difference all that is necessary is to compare the three stanzas of Heine's *Bertrand de Born* with Uhland's *Bertran de Born* ; both are famous, but in Heine's burst of song, since there is no retribution related, there is no lesson to be learned ; why should there be in pure poetry ? But at all events these retribution ballads have served as patterns from the late romantic days (e.g. Annette von Droste-Hülshoff's *Vergeltung*) to our own times. In his stressing of the moral lesson the story conveys Uhland is in the line of Bürger and Schiller rather than of Chamisso ; but this didactic tone or undertone also approximates him to the Biedermeier sense of what is befitting. Typical ballads of justice, in which the punishment fits the crime, are *Der blinde König*, *Die Rache*, *Der Waller*. The master ballad, perhaps, is *Taillefer*, in which there are just deeds of derring-do of the schoolboy sort. As a craftsman in verse Uhland handles with mastery not only the Nibelungen stanza, the *kurze Reimpaare* of the Middle High German court epics and the *Knüttelverse* of Hans Sachs, but also Romance forms such as Spanish trochees (p. cxix; *Rudello, Der Castellan von Couci*).

The least true to type of all the Swabians—that is, the farthest removed from Biedermeier—was JUSTINUS KERNER (1786–1862). Born at Ludwigsburg, he was apprenticed to a carpenter and was later employed in a cloth factory, but attracted the notice of the Swabian poet Karl Philipp Conz, who helped him to study medicine at Tübingen. He spent most of his life as a practising doctor at Weinsberg, where he kept open house and was visited, not only by his fellow-poets from every quarter, but by potentates—King Gustav IV of Sweden, Prinz Adalbert von Bayern. One of his guests, whom he lodged and helped generously, was the great poet Lenau. But his most famous guest—for three years—was a woman somnambulist whose visions he recorded in his book *Die Seherin von Prevorst* (1824). He tended her as Brentano tended his stigmatic nun. He studied somnambulism, magnetism, mediumism, spiritualism. The nearest as he is of the Swabians to romanticism proper he has the sensitivity of the romantics and is responsive to momentary impressions and moods. ' *Er besass im höchsten Grad,*' says Scherer, ' *das Talent, poetisch zu leben, d.h., Poetisches zu erleben und Erlebtes zu poetisieren.*' He has not the healthy common sense and the sturdy fighting spirit of Uhland and Gustav Schwab ; but his monotonous harping on misery and dissolution is relieved by roguish Swabian humour. Through all his work goes the insistent feeling that the staple of life here below is suffering (' *Schmerz ist Grundton der Natur* ') ; his staple theme is indeed pain, and death which is the release from it. He kept his coffin ready in his house. But he was unromantic in the blamelessness

9

of his life. Of his lyrics the best known is *Wanderlied* (*Wohlauf nun getrunken | Den funkelnden Wein*); it was written on a trip made with his mouth-organ on a cargo boat; it has been ever since in the students' song-books. Of his ballads *Der reichste Fürst* exemplifies that fondness for Swabian themes which he shares with the other Swabians, while *Kaiser Rudolfs Ritt zum Grabe*, *Der Geiger von Gmünd*, *Die vier wahnsinnigen Brüder* have the hall-mark of Kerner's funereal obsession.

Of the minor Swabians GUSTAV SCHWAB (1792–1850), a Protestant clergyman, was influential in the literary circles of his day as editor of Cotta's *Morgenblatt* (p. cxxxi) and as editor with Chamisso (1833–8) of *Der deutsche Musenalmanach*. He called himself Uhland's first pupil, and he did indeed go Uhland's way by putting his best strength into ballad writing. His *Gedichte* appeared in two volumes, 1828 and 1829. Still popular is his students' song *Lied eines abziehenden Burschen* (*Bemooster Bursche zieh' ich aus*), and his sensational poem *Das Gewitter* still survives in the anthologies. KARL MAYER (1786–1870) had some talent for neat nature description, while GUSTAV PFIZER (1807–90) made a reputation with his ballads. Much more alive are two poems of the popular novelist WILHELM HAUFF (1802–27): *Reiters Morgenlied* and *Soldatenliebe*. The only one of the Swabians in whom there is anything of the wandering minstrel, is WILHELM WAIBLINGER (1804–30), whose *Lieder der Griechen* have been mentioned (p. cxxi). He died in Rome of dissipation. The greatest of the Swabians is EDUARD MÖRIKE (1804–75; *Gedichte*, 1838), but he belongs to the next anthology.

FRIEDRICH RÜCKERT (1788–1866), a Franconian Protestant born at Schweinfurt am Main in Bavaria, is first and foremost a linguist and translator who did much to realize for his countrymen Goethe's dream of a *Weltliteratur*, in which all the masterpieces of the world's literature should be made available in translations or close adaptations ; geographically mapped his work ranges from English (*Hornchild*, 1818) to Chinese (*Schi-King*, 1833 ; from a Latin rendering). He is a master craftsman in a great variety of acclimatized and exotic forms : sonnet, ottava rima and Siciliane, terza rima (*Terzine*), ritornelle, and Oriental strophes : the ghasel (*das G*[*h*]*asel*, pl.-*e* or *die G*[*h*]*asele*, pl. -*n*), casside, the Persian quatrain. In 1809 he completed his studies of law and philosophy at the University of Würzburg. In 1813 appeared his *Geharnischte Sonette* ; these, as we have seen (p. cxv), hardly count—they are too scholarly in form for camp-fires and fighting men. They form part of his *Deutsche Gedichte* (1814). These made him famous, and with other activities led to his appointment in 1816 as editor of Cotta's *Morgenblatt*. In 1817 he made an intensive study of Italian literature and verse forms in Italy, and in the same year, on his return journey, made a stay in Vienna, where Josef von Hammer-Purgstall (1774-1856), whose translation of the Persian poet Hafiz (1813–14) had been the inspiration of Goethe's *West-östlicher Divan*, induced him to turn his attention to Oriental languages, in which he then specialized (Arabic, Persian, and Turkish to begin with). Though Goethe's *West-östlicher Divan* is the first milestone on the way to this orientalism, Friedrich Schlegel's study of Sanscrit and his book *Über die Sprache und Weisheit der Indier* (p. lxxxiii) had been a landmark too. In 1826 Rückert was appointed professor of Oriental languages at Erlangen, and in 1841 at Berlin. In 1848 he retired to his country estate near Coburg and spent his leisure in his literary avocations.

Rückert lives as a popular poet by one volume only —*Liebesfrühling* (1823), inspired by his own engagement. The poems are too reflective for spontaneous lyricism, and this is the general fault of Rückert's original verse. The best of the poems are still sung in Robert Schumann's setting. Certain of his poems keep their place in the anthologies; the best known is *Der alte Barbarossa* (written 1815), in which Rückert expresses his disappointment at the failure to reach political unity in Germany after the Wars of Liberation.

*Ghaselen* has historical importance if only by the fact that here Rückert introduces the ghasel into German literature. Platen's *Ghaselen* appeared in 1821 and 1823, but the first section of Rückert's *Ghaselen* had previously appeared (1821) in the *Taschenbuch für Damen*. Moreover, it was Rückert who had introduced Platen to the ghasel. The beginning portion translates the Persian poet Dschelaleddin Rumi; the form of the ghasel is not kept to throughout. The Oriental base of *Östliche Rosen* (1822) is elusive, though such a poem as *Ausgeschrieben* hints at imitation, and there is a series of 46 quatrains with the title *Stellen aus Hafisens Liedern*, 24 *Vierzeilen in persischer Form*, and 9 *Briefe des Brahmanen* in alexandrines. For the most part the poems are just exercises in simple German forms, and the thematic content, though varied, is without either depth or force of feeling. The one poem in the book which anthologists have pounced on, *Kehr' ein bei mir*, is no more than a pleasant play with words. *Die Verwandlungen des Abu Said von Serug oder die Makamen des Harari* (1826) from the Arabic relate the mad pranks of an Oriental Eulenspiegel, who dazzles his hearers by his feats in impromptu rhyming; the book is for the most part written in prose with embedded rhymes ('*Reimprosa*'). *Nal und Damajanti* (1828) is the free translation of an episode from the Indian epic of Mahâbhârata, while *Rostem und Suhrab* (1838), from Firdusi's Persian epic (1010) of *The Book of Kings*, has its rival in Matthew Arnold's poem. *Die Weisheit des Brahmanen* (1836–9) in rhymed alexandrines is an endless string in six volumes of truisms (*Sprüche*) poetically trimmed.

Another Orientalist is AUGUST GRAF VON PLATEN-HALLERMÜNDE (1796–1835), like Rückert a Franconian and a Protestant, who was born in Ansbach. After fighting as a Bavarian in the 1814 War of Liberation he studied philosophy and modern languages in Würzburg and (for seven years) in Erlangen. In Erlangen he was a pupil and friend of Schelling, whose philosophy helped to shape his mental outlook. He travelled extensively, visited Italy in 1824 and settled there in 1826 for life. He follows the lead of Rückert, whom he met in 1820, with his *Ghaselen* (1821) and *Neue Ghaselen* (1824), which show his amazing virtuosity. He handles the casside as well as the ghasel with consummate skill; there is no difference in form between the two, the difference is that of tone and contents: while the ghasel (the Persian meaning is ' flattery poem '; it is defined by Platen as ' *schelmisches Getändel* ') is jocular,—praise of wine and the boy who brings it, &c.,—the casside is serious—war songs, dirges for fallen heroes, &c. Typical cassides are Rückert's *Frühlingshymne* and Platen's address to Napoleon. It is as a master of form that Platen counts; he is one of the few German poets who shape and polish verse to the last limits of perfection, and in this respect he is the direct forerunner of the Munich school and still more of Stefan George. The danger of such intricate workmanship is that the masterpiece may seem cold or entail too much brain work to those who have not the training to seize on the subtle meanings, the finesses of diction, the delicate chiselling of the lines. Rückert was an Orientalist his life long; Platen began as such, but in his *Neue Ghaselen* the general tenor is as German as it is, say, in Rückert's *Östliche Rosen*, and Platen in his later phases is rather a Neo-Hellenist and a past master of Italian forms and

of forms developed in the classical poetry of Germany
apart from romanticism. If only because of these
affinities he can not be classed as a romantic : he is a
classicist who shares with the romanticists their love
of medieval and Oriental literatures. He has a few
ballads, which might be called romantic, but they have
their own refinement of form and diction, and, apart
from the personal imprint he gives to Oriental forms
his main strength lies in his re-creation on classical
lines of ode, hymn, eclogue, idyll, and epigram. His
verse in the later twenties is made up mostly of
Petrarchan sonnets and Neo-Hellenist genres. He
refined the Petrarchan sonnet in his *Sonette aus Venedig*
(1825) ; he follows his Italian model in using feminine
rhymes only, and this gives a falling close to his
majestic and resonant lines. There is general agreement that there are no finer sonnets in the German
language. For wealth of infolded meaning the pearl
of them all is perhaps *Venedig liegt nur noch im Land*
*der Träume* ; how vividly past and present are con-
trasted, and how delicately the tyranny of those great
old days is suggested by *Und öde feiern seines Kerkers*
*Räume* ! He marks the scansion of his Greek odes,
which he himself claimed were second only to those of
Klopstock ; his hymns are equally complex, patterned
as they are on those of Pindar. What actual popularity
Platen still has today rests on two of his early ballads :
*Der Pilgrim vor St. Just* (1819) and *Das Grab von*
*Busento* (1820) together with his lyric *Wie rafft' ich*
*mich auf in der Nacht, in der Nacht.* Important are
his two Aristophanic comedies ; quite wonderful in
their way are the parabases with which the acts end :
the chorus convey the poet's views to the audience
by way of an address. *Die verhängnisvolle Gabel* (1826)
holds the fate tragedies up to ridicule. *Der romantische*
*Ödipus* (1828) is aimed in the first place at Heine and
KARL LEBERECHT IMMERMANN (1796–1840) ; the

latter wrote mediocre verse (*Gedichte*, 1822), but had more success with his tragedies. Immerman had aimed a xenion—quoted by Heine in the second volume (*Norderney*) of his *Reisebilder*—at the Orientalists : '*Von den Früchten, die sie aus dem Gartenhain von Schiras stehlen,* | *Essen sie zu viel, die Armen, und vomieren dann Ghaselen* ', and *Der romantische Ödipus* is the counter-stroke. But in intention the sum total brands the general run of the poetry of the twenties —more or less romantic—as progressively decadent, and Platen had good grounds for setting himself up as, by this ruthless lampoon, the destroyer of romanticism. Psychology is the key to a comprehension of the currents in Platen's verse. He reveals himself in certain of his sonnets, particularly in that very fine one *Tristan*, in which he gives expression to his conviction that *ein nachgeborener Grieche* of his type is doomed to death by the very fact that his eyes have fed on beauty. But the sonnet is also given an erotic interpretation : the beauty he worships is male, and he is therefore pathologically stricken and doomed to loneliness, and to death before death is due. He reveals his own morbid psychology too in his *Tage-bücher*, which were not published till 1896–1900.

The lesson of *Der romantische Ödipus* is that in the twenties romanticism is in full decay. But does not Heine's *Buch der Lieder* (1827) belong to romanticism, and if it is decadent why is it still read and loved more than any other book of the romantic period ? It is the only book of Heine that we need deal with here, for the rest of his verse is dealt with in its place in the 1830–80 Anthology.

HEINRICH HEINE (1797–1856) is the laureate of the Jews, although in 1825 he crowned his wickedness as a university student by joining the Christian church. His Christianity of course was never even skin-deep, but neither was his Judaism ; he was a citizen of the world, and a pessimist who believed—so far as he believed anything—that the human race is hopeless, because it is congenitally immoral. But whether this state of mind was right or wrong matters little : what does matter is that he gave expression to his ideas, and still more to his feelings, in some of the finest verse the Germans have. He was born in Düsseldorf and grew up under the French occupation of the Rhineland, where he acquired his love of French culture and his admiration of Napoleon. In his teens he was sent to work in the counting-house of his rich uncle Salamon in Hamburg, with whose daughter Amalie he fell in love, but from whom he met with no response. Since he soon proved that he had no aptitude for business, Uncle Salamon provided him with the means of studying at Bonn university, where he heard Professor August Wilhelm Schlegel lecture on metrical matters and was encouraged by him to try his hand at verse-making. Then in 1821 he transferred to Göttingen, but after a few months he was relegated because he challenged an anti-Semite to a duel. He went to Berlin, where he frequented the circles of Rahel Varnhagen[1] and Elise von Hohenhausen, and here he met Chamisso and the other poets of the Berlin group. His stay in Berlin lasted three years, and many of the poems of *Buch der Lieder* were written there. In 1824 he returned to Göttingen, where he took his degree as doctor of law in 1825. The law of the land laid it down that no Jew could obtain an appointment in government service, and therefore before taking his degree Heine had turned Christian and been baptized. The step was in vain ; he obtained no post. He went for a holiday to Norderney, and on his return he made an attempt to establish himself in Hamburg as an advocate, but failed. He went travelling again, and the result was *Die Harzreise* (1826), the first volume

---

[1] Levin before her marriage; see pp. civ, cxix.

of his *Reisebilder*. The second volume, *Norderney*, appeared 1827; the success was immense. Cotta offered him the editorship of the Munich *Allgemeine politische Annalen*; he kept the post six months. He travelled in Italy and continued his *Reisebilder*; his vicious attack on Platen in one of the later volumes, *Die Bäder von Lucca*, alienated many friends; and after attempts to make a home for himself in Berlin and Hamburg, he found it convenient to settle in Paris, where he died. The French government showed their appreciation of his services to them as correspondent of German periodicals by paying him a pension between 1836 and 1848.

His books of verse *Gedichte* (1822), *Lyrisches Intermezzo* (1823), *Die Heimkehr* (1826) appeared collected with other work in *Buch der Lieder* (1827). The first section, *Junge Leiden*, is immature work; it has a good share of that *Schauerromantik* (p. cxix) which the novelist E. T. A. Hoffmann had popularized. The love poems concern his cousin Amalie. The *Romanzen* include two of the best known of all German ballads: *Belsazer* and *Die Grenadiere*, the finest possible expression of Heine's life-long worship of Napoleon. Generally speaking the first sections of *Buch der Lieder* show the influence of *Des Knaben Wunderhorn* and of Wilhelm Müller; the style is that of the folk-song, mostly in four-lined stanzas with lines alternately rhymed. But there is a group of sonnets, mostly with a personal or family interest; three addressed to A. W. von Schlegel and three to his mother. In *Junge Leiden* the imitation of his models is patent, but in the following sections Heine has reached full mastery of his craft; he invests the simplest forms with the full force of his personality and of his mood of the moment. In *Lyrisches Intermezzo*, which includes quite a number of his loveliest poems, the *Herzliebchen* referred to is still Amalie; in *Heimkehr* it is her sister Therese, with whom Heine

had fallen in love after Amalie's marriage, still without
meeting response.    There are world-famous poems such
as *Du bist wie eine Blume*.    Is any German poem more
famed and loved than the second of those in *Die
Heimkehr* : *Die Lorelei* ?    For once in a way one gives
the poem a title—which it does not have in the book
—instead of its first line (p. cxx).    Brentano's 1802
poem (p. cxi) had changed the name Lurelei to Lore
Lay, thus hiding what is suggested as the etymological
meaning : *luren* is the older form of *lauern* and *lei*
means 'rock'.[1]    There are various other versions,
including that of Eichendorff (p. cxxiii), but not one
of them has the luring magic of Heine's lyric.    In *Die
Heimkehr* there is a new note of indignation and irony :
the poet lashes himself for falling in love with Therese.
The ballad *Donna Clara*, in rhymeless Spanish trochees,
effectively    jests    at    Christians    who    deride    Jews.
Problematic and curious is a sardonic poem in rhymeless iambic, *Götterdämmerung* ; it is a vision of the evil
forces that beset us, the demons of the underworld,
giants and dwarfs, storming the skies, dethroning ' the
pale God ', and hurling to ruin all that is beautiful ;
it has been suggested [2] that Heine intended to symbolize the rise of the industrial proletariat in our own
days.    In *Die Heimkehr* too we find the first German
poems of the sea, which Heine had visited for reasons
of health and described in *Norderney*, the second volume
of his *Reisebilder* : these poems are still in quatrains
alternately rhymed ; but (after a few poems reprinted
from *Die Harzreise*) there follows the great cycle of
*Die Nordsee*, which is in free rhythms.    These, as we
have seen (pp. xxxvi, lxiv), do not constitute a new
genre ; they had long since served Klopstock, Goethe,

---

[1] Two other poems by early romanticists, Otto Heinrich Graf
von Loeben and Friedrich Förster, have as titles respectively
*Der Lurleyfels* and *Lurley*.    Lurley is the name of a steep rock
in a bend of the Rhine near St. Goarshausen.
[2] Ralph Tymms ; *German Romantic Literature*, p. 374.

and Hölderlin to produce masterpieces, but Heine miraculously fits the surge and swell, the ebb and flow of the sea to his own emotions and thus does create something new in German verse. There is a different shaping which comes from the inventiveness and suggestiveness of his imagination, his daring metaphors and images.

Taking *Buch der Lieder* in its totality there are certain difficulties in arriving at a dispassionate judgment. The loveliest poems are folk-songs known the world over in the settings of Mendelssohn, Schumann, Schubert, and Brahms. But there are certain aspects that are criticized or questioned, and they must be shortly considered.

The first thing to remember is Heine's pattern of ' romantic irony ' (p. cv), by which he expresses his contempt for all that is—especially if it is German. Heine's pattern of Friedrich Schlegel's and Tieck's romantic irony continues that of Chamisso and Brentano, but it is more drastic. It is not a mere literary device ; it would have been in Heine's verse if it had not been fixed as a feature of romanticism ; it represents Heine as he was by nature. It appears when, for instance, he calls forth a dreamful mood of tenderness or melancholy and then at the end of the poem destroys the effect by contradicting or ridiculing what he has said. A famous example is *Doktor, sind Sie des Teufels ?* at the end of *Seegespenst* (first North Sea cycle). Or, in *Die Jahre kommen und gehen* (*Die Heimkehr*), the poet protests his undying love for his lady : if only once more he could sink on his knees before her and say with his last breath : *Madame, ich liebe Sie !* The danger is that the reader of such a poem may think the poet's intention is to convey the lesson : all poetry is piffle. At all events the serious or tender mood which forms the gist of the poem is broken as it ends by a discordant note that seems to mock both the poet and the reader. More reasonable is the interpretation that behind all illusion lies reality, to which we *must* return; but the illusion, as in *Seegespenst*, may be lovely, while the return to brute reality is man's common fate. And thus this romantic irony serves to express Heine's *Weltschmerz* or pessimism, and here one has to consider how much was the fashion of the day, or in other words Byronic, and how much was inrooted in the poet. Certainly Heine's *Weltschmerz* does not amount to the deeply felt sense of hopelessness of that other great pessimist, Lenau, the Hungarian nobleman whom we have found associating with the Swabians (p. cxxix). Grillparzer's pessimism too (' *Nachdem man sterben sich gesehen,* | *Mit seiner eignen Leiche gehen* ') is the embodiment of his own despair. We must remember that it was the period when Metternich was in power and freedom of thought was being suppressed. Politically considered Heine was an exile, luckily safe in free France. And the classical philosopher of pessimism, Arthur Schopenhauer (1788–1860), whose influence on literature was to be so great, was already writing (*Die Welt als Wille und Vorstellung*, 1819).

Taking him all in all, is Heine, ' *die Spottdrossel der Romantik* ', a romanticist at all ? The earlier poems of *Buch der Lieder* are flagrantly romantic in type and feeling, but as he matures his irony, his cynicism, his sardonic and often pitiless humour intrude more and more, and in his later years he is a realist. With such a poem as *Die Weber* (but this comes late : *Zeitgedichte*, 1844), Heine, like Chamisso (p. cxix), is moving towards the revolutionary mood of 1848. *Die Weber* indeed points forward to Gerhart Hauptmann's drama *Die Weber* and thus to the break-through of socialism in our own day. In his earlier years, however, Heine is stamped as a romanticist by his subjectivity : the pronoun *ich* recurs continually in *Buch der Lieder*.

But whereas the subjectivity of Wilhelm Müller and Eichendorff makes them incapable of writing ballads, Heine, when the years have taken their toll, shows himself a master of this genre in his *Romanzero* (1851). Long before this, however, he has specifically abjured romanticism as a bastard form of art in his (for the most part) scurrilous mockery of the romantics in his treatise *Die romantische Schule* (1836). We may say then of Heine that he is the last of the romanticists because he himself, after enriching romanticism with masterpieces, tears it to pieces.

It is almost a habit with German critics to reject Heine as one unfit to be considered a German poet, while the best foreign critics on the contrary put him in the first rank, some even placing him second to Goethe. There may be some logic in Heine's contempt for the Germans because they failed to give him a respectable post and for his attacks on them as Paris correspondent of German newspapers. At all events he must be judged by his essential originality. There is no other German poet like him. He may be wicked, he is not always decent, but he is always readable.

# BARTHOLD HEINRICH BROCKES
## 1680–1747

### KIRSCHBLÜTE BEI DER NACHT

ICH sahe mit betrachtendem Gemüte
Jüngst einen Kirschbaum, welcher blühte,
In kühler Nacht beim Mondenschein;
Ich glaubt', es könne nichts von grössrer Weisse sein.
Es schien, als wär' ein Schnee gefallen;
Ein jeder, auch der kleinste Ast,
Trug gleichsam eine rechte Last
Von zierlich weissen runden Ballen.
Es ist kein Schwan so weiss, da nämlich jedes Blatt,
Indem daselbst des Mondes sanftes Licht
Selbst durch die zarten Blätter bricht,
Sogar den Schatten weiss und sonder Schwärze hat.
Unmöglich, dacht' ich, kann auf Erden
Was Weisseres gefunden werden.
Indem ich nun bald hin, bald her
Im Schatten dieses Baumes gehe,
Sah ich von ungefähr
Durch alle Blumen in die Höhe
Und ward noch einen weissern Schein,
Der tausendmal so weiss, der tausendmal so klar,
Fast halb darob erstaunt, gewahr.
Der Blüte Schnee schien schwarz zu sein
Bei diesem weissen Glanz. Es fiel mir ins Gesicht
Von einem hellen Stern ein weisses Licht,
Das mir recht in die Seele strahlte.
Wie sehr ich mich an Gott im Irdischen ergötze,
Dacht' ich, hat er dennoch weit grössre Schätze.
Die grösste Schönheit dieser Erden
Kann mit der himmlischen doch nicht verglichen
    werden.

1

### HERBSTSTIMMUNG

BLEICHE Blätter, bunte Büsche,
Gelbe Stauden, rötlichs Rohr,
Euer flüsterndes Gezische
Kommt mir wie ein Sterb-Lied vor.
Aber da ihr, wenn ihr sterbet,
(Wie in einer hellen Glut
Ein verlöschend Fünkchen tut)
Euch am allerschönsten färbet,
Wird durch euer buntes Kleid
Nicht nur Aug und Herz erfreut
Und zu Gottes Ruhm geführet,
Sondern auf besondre Weise
Durch so holden Schmuck gerühret,
Wünscht mein Herz, nicht minder schön,
Zu des Allerhöchsten Preise,
Wenn ich sterbe, zu vergehn.


# JOHANN CHRISTIAN GÜNTHER
## 1695–1723

### STUDENTENLIED

BRÜDER, lasst uns lustig sein,
Weil der Frühling währet
Und der Jugend Sonnenschein
Unser Laub verkläret;
Grab und Bahre warten nicht,
Wer die Rosen jetzo bricht,
Dem ist der Kranz bescheret.

Unsers Lebens schnelle Flucht.
Leidet keinen Zügel,
Und des Schicksals Eifersucht
Macht ihr stetig Flügel;

Zeit und Jahre fliehn davon,
Und vielleichte schnitzt man schon
An unsers Grabes Riegel.

Wo sind diese, sagt es mir,
Die vor wenig Jahren
Eben also, gleich wie wir,
Jung und fröhlich waren?
Ihre Leiber deckt der Sand,
Sie sind in ein ander Land
Aus dieser Welt gefahren.

Wer nach unsern Vätern forscht,
Mag den Kirchhof fragen;
Ihr Gebein, so längst vermorscht,
Wird ihm Antwort sagen.
Kann uns doch der Himmel bald,
Eh' die Morgenglocke schallt,
In unsre Gräber tragen.

### AM ABEND

Abermal ein Teil vom Jahre,
Abermal ein Tag vollbracht;
Abermal ein Brett zur Bahre
Und ein Schritt zur Gruft gemacht.
Also nähert sich die Zeit
Nach und nach der Ewigkeit;
Also müssen wir auf Erden
Zu dem Tode reifer werden.

## ALBRECHT VON HALLER
### 1708–1777

#### MORGENGEDANKEN

DIE Rosen öffnen sich und spiegeln an der Sonne
Des kühlen Morgens Perlentau,
Der Lilien Ambradampf belebt zu unsrer Wonne
Der zarten Blätter Atlasgrau.

O Schöpfer ! was ich seh', sind deiner Allmacht Werke !
Du bist die Seele der Natur ;
Der Sterne Lauf und Licht, der Sonne Glanz und Stärke
Sind deiner Hand Geschöpf' und Spur.

Du hast der Berge Stoff aus Ton und Staub gedrehet,
Der Schächte Erz aus Sand geschmelzt ;
Du hast das Firmament an seinen Ort erhöhet,
Der Wolken Kleid darum gewälzt.

Den Fisch, der Ströme bläst und mit dem Schwanze
    stürmet,
Hast du mit Adern ausgehöhlt ;
Du hast den Elefant aus Erden aufgetürmet
Und seinen Knochenberg beseelt.

Des weiten Himmelraums saphirene Gewölber,
Gegründet auf den leeren Ort,
Der Gottheit grosse Stadt, begrenzt nur durch sich
    selber,
Hob aus dem Nichts dein einzig Wort.

Doch, dreimal grosser Gott ! es sind erschaffne Seelen
Für deine Taten viel zu klein ;
Sie sind unendlich gross, und wer sie will erzählen,
Muss, gleich wie du, ohn Ende sein !

# FRIEDRICH VON HAGEDORN
## 1708–1754

### DER ERSTE MAI

DER erste Tag im Monat Mai
Ist mir der glücklichste von allen.
Dich sah ich und gestand dir frei,
Den ersten Tag im Monat Mai,
Dass dir mein Herz ergeben sei.
Wenn mein Geständnis dir gefallen,
So ist der erste Tag im Mai
Für mich der glücklichste von allen.


### DER MAI

DER Nachtigall reizende Lieder
Ertönen und locken schon wieder
Die fröhlichsten Stunden ins Jahr,
Nun singet die steigende Lerche,
Nun klappern die reisenden Störche,
Nun schwatzet der gaukelnde Star.


Wie munter sind Schäfer und Herde!
Wie lieblich beblümt sich die Erde!
Wie lebhaft ist jetzo die Welt!
Die Tauben verdoppeln die Küsse,
Der Entrich besuchet die Flüsse,
Der lustige Sperling sein Feld.


Nun heben sich Binsen und Keime,
Nun kleiden die Blätter die Bäume,
Nun schwindet des Winters Gestalt;
Nun rauschen lebendige Quellen
Und tränken mit spielenden Wellen
Die Triften, den Anger, den Wald.

Wie buhlerisch, wie so gelinde
Erwärmen die westlichen Winde
Das Ufer, den Hügel, die Gruft!
Die jugendlich scherzende Liebe
Empfindet die Reizung der Triebe,
Empfindet die schmeichelnde Lust.

### DIE ROSE

Siehst du jene Rose blühen?
Schönste, so erkenne dich.
Siehst du Bienen zu ihr fliehen,
Phyllis, so gedenk an mich.


Deine Blüte lockt die Triebe
Auf den Reichtum der Natur
Und der Jugend süsse Liebe
Raubt dir nichts und nährt sich nur.

### DER WUNSCH

Du holder Gott der süss'sten Lust auf Erden,
    Der schönsten Göttin schöner Sohn!
Komm, lehre mich die Kunst, geliebt zu werden;
    Die leichte Kunst zu lieben weiss ich schon.


Komm ebenfalls und bilde Phyllis' Lachen,
    Zythere! gib ihr Unterricht;
Denn Phyllis weiss die Kunst, verliebt zu machen;
    Die leichte Kunst zu lieben weiss sie nicht.

## CHRISTIAN FÜRCHTEGOTT GELLERT
### 1715–1769

#### DER ZEISIG

EIN Zeisig war's und eine Nachtigall,
Die einst zu gleicher Zeit vor Damons Fenster hingen.
Die Nachtigall fing an, ihr göttlich Lied zu singen,
Und Damons kleinem Sohn gefiel der süsse Schall.
„ Ach, welcher singt von beiden doch so schön ?
Den Vogel möcht' ich wirklich sehn ! "
Der Vater macht ihm diese Freude,
Er nimmt die Vögel gleich herein.
„ Hier," spricht er, „ sind sie alle beide ;
Doch welcher wird der schöne Sänger sein ?
Getraust du dich, mir das zu sagen ? "
Der Sohn lässt sich nicht zweimal fragen,
Schnell weist er auf den Zeisig hin.
„ Der," spricht er, „ muss es sein, so wahr ich ehrlich
      bin.
Wie schön und gelb ist sein Gefieder !
Drum singt er auch so schöne Lieder ;
Dem andern sieht man's gleich an seinen Federn an,
Dass er nichts Kluges singen kann."

#### DER TANZBÄR

EIN Bär, der lange Zeit sein Brot ertanzen müssen,
Entrann und wählte sich den ersten Aufenthalt.
Die Bären grüssten ihn mit brüderlichen Küssen
Und brummten freudig durch den Wald.
Und wo ein Bär den andern sah,
So hiess es : „ Petz ist wieder da ! "
Der Bär erzählte drauf, was er in fremden Landen
Für Abenteuer ausgestanden,
Was er gesehn, gehört, getan,

Und fing, da er vom Tanzen red'te,
Als ging' er noch an seiner Kette,
Auf polnisch schön zu tanzen an.
Die Brüder, die ihn tanzen sahn,
Bewunderten die Wendung seiner Glieder,
Und gleich versuchten es die Brüder.
Allein anstatt wie er zu gehn,
So konnten sie kaum aufrecht stehn,
Und mancher fiel die Länge lang danieder.
Um desto mehr liess sich der Tänzer sehn;
Doch seine Kunst verdross den ganzen Haufen.
,, Fort ! ", schrieen alle, ,, fort mit dir !
Du Narr willst klüger sein als wir ? "
Man zwang den Petz, davonzulaufen.

### DIE BEIDEN MÄDCHEN

Zwo junge Mädchen hofften beide,
Worauf ?  Gewiss auf einen Mann ;
Denn dies ist doch die grösste Freude,
Auf die ein Mädchen hoffen kann.
Die jüngste Schwester, Philippine,
War nicht unordentlich gebaut ;
Sie hatt' ein rund Gesicht und eine zarte Haut ;
Doch eine sehr gezwungne Miene.
So fest geschnürt sie immer ging,
So viel sie Schmuck ins Ohr und vor den Busen hing,
So ward sie doch bei alledem,
Je mehr man sah, dass sie gefallen wollte,
Um desto minder angenehm.


Die andre Schwester, Karoline,
War im Gesichte nicht so zart ;
Doch frei und reizend in der Miene
Und liebreich mit gelassner Art.

Und wenn man auf den heitern Wangen
Gleich kleine Sommerflecken fand:
Ward ihrem Reiz doch nichts dadurch entwandt,
Und selbst ihr Reiz schien solche zu verlangen.
Sie putzte sich nicht mühsam aus,
Sie prahlte nicht mit teuren Kostbarkeiten.
Ein artig Band, ein frischer Strauss,
Die über ihren Ort, den sie erlangt, sich freuten,
Und eine nach dem Leib wohl abgemessne Tracht,
War Karolinens ganze Pracht.

Ein Freier kam; man wies ihm Philippinen;
Er sah sie an, erstaunt, und hiess sie schön;
Allein sein Herz blieb frei, er wollte wieder gehn.
Kaum aber sah er Karolinen:
So blieb er vor Entzückung stehn.

\*

Im Bilde dieser Frauenzimmer
Zeigt sich die Kunst und die Natur;
Die erste prahlt mit weit gesuchtem Schimmer,
Sie fesselt nicht; sie blendet nur.
Die andre sucht durch Einfalt zu gefallen,
Lässt sich bescheiden sehn; und so gefällt sie allen.


# EWALD CHRISTIAN VON KLEIST
## 1715–1759

### DITHYRAMBE

FREUND, versäume nicht zu leben:
Denn die Jahre fliehn,
Und es wird der Saft der Reben
Uns nicht lange glühn!

Lach' der Ärzt' und ihrer Ränke!
Tod und Krankheit laurt,
Wenn man bei dem Froschgetränke
Seine Zeit vertraurt.


Moslerwein, der Sorgenbrecher,
Schafft gesundes Blut!
Trink aus dem bekränzten Becher
Glück und frohen Mut.


So! — Noch eins! — Siehst du Lyäen
Und die Freude nun?
Bald wirst du auch Amorn sehen,
Und auf Rosen ruhn.


### LIED EINES LAPPLÄNDERS

KOMM, Zama, komm, lass deinen Unmut fahren!
O du, der Preis
Der Schönen, komm! In den zerstörten Haaren
Hängt mir schon Eis.


Du zürnst umsonst. Mir gibt die Liebe Flügel.
Nichts hält mich auf;
Kein tiefer Schnee, kein Sumpf, kein Tal, kein Hügel
Hemmt meinen Lauf.


Ich will im Wald auf hohe Bäume klimmen,
Dich auszuspähn,
Und durch die Flut der tiefsten Ströme schwimmen,
Um dich zu sehn.


Das dürre Laub will ich vom Strauche pflücken,
Der dich verdeckt,
Und auf der Wies' ein jedes Rohr zerknicken,
Das dich versteckt.

Und solltest du weit übers Meer, in Wüsten
Verborgen sein,
So will ich bald an Grönlands weiten Küsten
Nach Zama schrein.

Die lange Nacht kommt schon.  Still' mein Verlangen
Und eil' zurück !
Du kommst, mein Licht, du kommst, mich zu umfangen !
O, welch ein Glück !


## JOHANN WILHELM LUDWIG GLEIM
### 1719–1803

#### AN LEUKON

ROSEN pflücke, Rosen blühn,
Morgen ist nicht heut !
Keine Stunde lass entfliehn,
Flüchtig ist die Zeit !

Trinke, küsse !  Sieh, es ist
Heut Gelegenheit ;
Weisst du, wo du morgen bist ?
Flüchtig ist die Zeit !

Aufschub einer guten Tat
Hat schon oft gereut —
Hurtig leben ist mein Rat,
Flüchtig ist die Zeit !


#### PFLICHT ZU VERLIEBTEN GESPRÄCHEN

IN den lauten Nachtigallen
Lockt und schlägt und jauchzt die Liebe ;
In der Lerche unterm Himmel
Lobt und tiriliert die Liebe ;

In dem Enter auf dem Wasser
Schwimmt und schnattert nichts als Liebe;
In den Schwalben unterm Dache
Zwitschert, baut und spricht die Liebe;
In den Spatzen vor dem Fenster
Lauscht und ruft und hüpft die Liebe;
In dem Täuber, in der Taube
Girrt und lockt und lacht die Liebe;
In den Tönen meiner Laute
Klingt und lobt und scherzt die Liebe;
In dem Kind auf meinem Schosse
Hüpft und scherzt und singt die Liebe;
Alles Wild im freien Felde,
Alle Vögel unterm Himmel
Haben Stimmen zu der Liebe;
Alles scherzt und spricht vom Lieben,
Soll ich denn davon nicht sprechen?


# JOHANN PETER UZ

## 1720–1796

### DER VERLORNE AMOR

Amor hat sich jüngst verloren;
Und nun will, die ihn geboren,
Ihren Flüchtling wieder küssen,
Den wir alle suchen müssen.
In dem Schatten dunkler Linden,
Wo wir Dichter Amorn finden,
Unter froher Dichter Myrten,
In den Städten, bei den Hirten,
Kann man nichts von ihm erfragen.
Mädchen, wollt ihr mir's nicht sagen?
Denn ihr hegt den Gott der Sorgen:
Hat er sich bei euch verborgen?
In den Rosen eurer Wangen,

Die mit frischer Jugend prangen ?
Oder auf den Lilienhügeln,
Wo der Gott mit leisen Flügeln
Sich schon öfters hingestohlen ?
Darf ich suchen und ihn holen ?


## JOHANN NIKOLAUS GÖTZ
### 1721–1781

#### DAS LEBEN

WIE ein Gewölk so schnelle,
So schnell wie deine Welle
Entflieht die Zeit, beliebter Bach !
Ein Tor allein sieht ihr mit Wehmut nach.
Nur der sie nutzt,
Kann, fleucht sie gleich den Winden,
So sehr sie stutzt,
Ihr ihre regen Flügel binden.
Ist unser Leben nur ein kurzer Weg,
Ist unser Leben nur ein schmaler Steg,
So lasst uns diesen kurzen Weg
Und schmalen Steg,
So lang wir noch im Frieden drüber gehen,
Mit Rosen übersäen.


## FRIEDRICH GOTTLIEB KLOPSTOCK
### 1724–1803

#### DAS ROSENBAND

IM Frühlingsschatten fand ich sie,
Da band ich sie mit Rosenbändern :
Sie fühlt' es nicht und schlummerte.

Ich sah sie an; mein Leben hing
Mit diesem Blick an ihrem Leben:
Ich fühlt' es wohl und wusst' es nicht.


Doch lispelt' ich ihr sprachlos zu
Und rauschte mit den Rosenbändern:
Da wachte sie vom Schlummer auf.


Sie sah mich an; ihr Leben hing
Mit diesem Blick an meinem Leben,
Und um uns ward's Elysium.


### DER EISLAUF

VERGRABEN ist in ewige Nacht
Der Erfinder grosser Name zu oft!
  Was ihr Geist grübelnd entdeckt, nutzen wir;
    Aber belohnt Ehre sie auch?


Wer nannte dir den kühneren Mann,
Der zuerst am Maste Segel erhob?
  Ach, verging selber der Ruhm dessen nicht,
    Welcher dem Fuss Flügel erfand!


Und sollte der unsterblich nicht sein,
Der Gesundheit uns und Freuden erfand,
  Die das Ross, mutig im Lauf, niemals gab,
    Welche der Reih'n selber nicht hat?


Unsterblich ist mein Name dereinst!
Ich erfinde noch dem schlüpfenden Stahl
  Seinen Tanz! Leichteres Schwungs fliegt er hin,
    Kreiset umher, schöner zu sehn.

Du kennest jeden reizenden Ton
Der Musik, drum gib dem Tanz Melodie!
  Mond und Wald höre den Schall ihres Horns,
    Wenn sie des Flugs Eile gebeut.

O Jüngling, der den Wasserkothurn
Zu beseelen weiss und flüchtiger tanzt,
  Lass der Stadt ihren Kamin! Komm mit mir,
    Wo des Kristalls Ebne dir winkt!

Sein Licht hat er in Düfte gehüllt;
Wie erhellt des Winters werdender Tag
  Sanft den See! Glänzenden Reif, Sternen gleich,
    Streute die Nacht über ihn aus!

Wie schweigt um uns das weisse Gefild!
Wie ertönt vom jungen Froste die Bahn!
  Fern verrät deines Kothurns Schall dich mir,
    Wenn du dem Blick, Flüchtling, enteilst.

Wir haben doch zum Schmause genug
Von des Halmes Frucht? und Freuden des Weins?
  Winterluft reizt die Begier nach dem Mahl;
    Flügel am Fuss reizen sie mehr!

Zur Linken wende du dich, ich will
Zu der Rechten hin halbkreisend mich drehn;
  Nimm den Schwung, wie du mich ihn nehmen siehst:
    Also! nun fleug schnell mir vorbei!

So gehen wir den schlängelnden Gang
An dem langen Ufer schwebend hinab.
  Künstle nicht! Stellung, wie die, lieb' ich nicht,
    Zeichnet dir auch Preisler nicht nach.

Was horchst du nach der Insel hinauf?
Unerfahrne Läufer tönen dort her.
  Huf und Last gingen noch nicht übers Eis,
  Netze noch nicht unter ihm fort.


Sonst späht dein Ohr ja alles; vernimm,
Wie der Todeston wehklagt auf der Flut!
  O wie tönt's anders! wie hallt's, wenn der Frost
  Meilen hinab spaltet den See!


Zurück! lass nicht die schimmernde Bahn
Dich verführen, weg vom Ufer zu gehn!
  Denn wo dort Tiefen sie deckt, strömt's vielleicht,
  Sprudeln vielleicht Quellen empor.


Den ungehörten Wogen entströmt,
Dem geheimen Quell entrieselt der Tod!
  Glittst du auch leicht, wie dies Laub, ach dorthin,
  Sänkest du doch, Jüngling, und stürbst!


### DEM ERLÖSER

DER Seraph stammelt, und die Unendlichkeit
Bebt durch den Umkreis ihrer Gefilde nach
  Dein hohes Lob, o Sohn! Wer bin ich,
  Dass ich mich auch in die Jubel dränge?


Vom Staube Staub! Doch wohnt ein Unsterblicher
Von hoher Abkunft in den Verwesungen!
  Und denkt Gedanken, dass Entzückung
  Durch die erschütterte Nerve schauert!


Auch du wirst einmal mehr als Verwesung sein,
Der Seele Schatten, Hütte von Erd erbaut,
  Und andre Schauer von Trunkenheiten
  Werden dich dort, wo du schlummerst, wecken!

Der Leben Schauplatz, Feld, wo wir schlummerten,
Wo Adams Enkel wird, was sein Vater war,
    Als er sich jetzt der Schöpfung Armen
        Jauchzend entriss, und ein Leben dastand!

O Feld, vom Aufgang bis wo sie untergeht,
Der Sonnen letzte, heiliger Toten voll,
    Wann seh' ich dich? Wann weint mein Auge
        Unter den tausendmal tausend Tränen?

Des Schlafes Stunden oder Jahrhunderte,
Fliesst schnell vorüber, fliesst, dass ich aufersteh'!
    Allein sie säumen, und ich bin noch
        Diesseits am Grabe! O helle Stunde,

Der Ruh' Gespielin, Stunde des Todes, komm!
O du Gefilde, wo zur Unsterblichkeit
    Dies Leben reift, noch nie besuchte
        Ruhestatt meines Gebeins, wo bist du?

Lass mich dort hingehn, dass ich die Stätte seh',
Mit hingesenktem trunkenem Blick sie seh'!
    Der Ernte Blumen drüber streue,
        Unter die Blumen mich leg' und sterbe!

Wunsch grosser Aussicht, aber nur Glücklichen!
Wenn du, die süsse Stunde Seligkeit,
    Da wir dich wünschen, kämst: wer gliche
        Dem, der alsdann mit dem Tode ränge?

Doch ich will leben, dass ich des Todes wert
Entschlummre, dass ich, wenn es gesungen ist,
    Das Lied vom Sohne, triumphierend
        Über das Grab den erhabenen Weg geh'!

O Du, mein Meister, der Du gewaltiger
Die Gottheit lehrtest! zeige die Stufen mir,

Wo du hinaufstiegst, wo die Seher,
    Die dich verkündigten, Palmen tragen.


Dort ist es himmlisch! Ach, aus der Ferne Nacht
Folg' ich der Spur nach, welche Du wandeltest,
    Doch fällt von Deiner Strahlenhöhe
        Schimmer herab, und mein Auge sieht ihn.


Dann hebt mein Geist sich, dürstet nach Ewigkeit,
Nicht jener kurzen, die auf der Erde bleibt;
    Nach Palmen ringt er, die der Seraph
        Um des Unsterblichen Schläfe windet!


Zeig' mir die Laufbahn, wo an dem fernen Ziel
Die Krone schimmert! Meinen erhabensten
    Gedanken, lehr' ihn Hoheit, führ' ihm
        Wahrheiten zu, die es ewig bleiben!


Dass ich den Nachhall derer, die ewig sind,
Den Menschen singe! dass mein geweihter Arm
    Vom Altar Gottes Flammen nehme,
        Flammen ins Herz der Erlösten ströme!


### DIE FRÜHEN GRÄBER

WILLKOMMEN, o silberner Mond,
Schöner, stiller Gefährt' der Nacht!
Du entfliehst? Eile nicht, bleib, Gedankenfreund!
Sehet, er bleibt, das Gewölk wallte nur hin.


Des Maies Erwachen ist nur
Schöner noch wie die Sommernacht,
Wenn ihm Tau, hell wie Licht, aus der Locke träuft,
Und zu dem Hügel herauf rötlich er kommt.

Ihr Edleren, ach es bewächst
Eure Male schon ernstes Moos!
O wie war glücklich ich, als ich noch mit euch
Sahe sich röten den Tag, schimmern die Nacht!

### DAS EPIGRAMM

BALD ist das Epigramm ein Pfeil,
Trifft mit der Spitze;
Ist bald ein Schwert,
Trifft mit der Schärfe;
Ist manchmal auch — die Griechen liebten's so —
Ein klein Gemäld', ein Strahl, gesandt
Zum Brennen nicht, nur zum Erleuchten.

## SALOMON GESSNER
### 1730–1788

### DIE NELKE

EIN Nelkenstock ist in Daphnens Garten, am Zaun.
Im Garten ging sie, trat zum Nelkenstock; eine Nelke,
rotgestreift, blühte da frisch auf. Jetzt bog sie lächelnd
die Blume zu ihrem schönen Gesicht und freute sich
des süssen Geruches; die Blume schmiegte sich an
ihre Lippen. Warme Röte stieg auf meine Wangen;
denn ich dachte: Könnt', o könnt' ich so die süssen
Lippen berühren! Weg ging jetzt Daphne; da trat
ich an den Zaun. Soll ich, soll ich die Nelke brechen,
die ihre Lippen berührten? Mehr würd' ihr Geruch
mich erquicken, als Tau die Blumen erquickt. Begie-
rig langt' ich nach ihr: Nein, so sprach ich, sollt' ich
die Nelke rauben, die sie liebt? Nein, an ihren Busen
wird Daphne sie pflanzen; dann werden ihre süssen
Gerüche zum schönen Gesicht aufduften, wie ein
süsser Geruch zum Olymp aufsteigt, wenn man der
Göttin der Schönheit opfert.

11

## MORITZ AUGUST VON THÜMMEL
### 1738–1817

#### DER VOGELSTELLER

Die Liebe und der Vogelfang
Sind ziemlich einerlei,
Es lockt der männliche Gesang,
Er lockt — er lockt
Vögel und Mädchen herbei.

Sie achten ihre Schwäche nicht,
Denn ihre Herzen sind
In jugendlicher Zuversicht
Betäubt — betäubt,
Liebevoll, fröhlich und blind.

Zwar bei dem ersten Ausflug ist
Das Vögelchen verzagt,
Hält jeden Laut für Hinterlist,
Wohin, wohin
Es seine Flügelchen wagt.

Doch hüpft es bei dem zweiten Flug
Mit jubelndem Geschwätz
Von Baum zu Baum und dünkt sich klug
Und hüpft, und hüpft
Dem Vogelsteller ins Netz.

## JOHANN GEORG JACOBI
### 1740–1814

#### ABENDS

DER Himmel, ich bitte,
Von Wölkchen wie leer,
Der Mond in der Mitte,
Die Sternlein umher!

Komm, Liebchen, es neigen
Die Wälder sich dir,
Und alles mit Schweigen
Erwartet dich hier.

Der Himmel im glatten,
Umdämmerten Quell!
Dies Plätzchen im Schatten,
Das andre so hell!

Im Schatten: der Liebe
Dich lockendes Glück,
Dir flüsternd: es bliebe
Noch vieles zurück.

Es blieben der süssen
Geheimnisse viel,
So festes Umschliessen,
So wonniges Spiel!

Da rauscht es! Da wanken
Auf jeglichem Baum
Die Äste; da schwanken
Die Vöglein im Traum.

Dies Wanken, dies Zittern
Der Blätter im Teich —
O Liebe, dein Wittern!
O Liebe, dein Reich!

### ERINNERUNG

GLÜCK der Engel! Wo geblieben?
Wo geblieben, schöner Tag,
Als mit unbesorgtem Lieben
Ihre Hand auf meinem Herzen lag?

Oh, sie fühlte jeden Schlag,
Und in jedem lauter Lieben!
Wo geblieben,
Glück der Engel, schöner Tag?


## MATTHIAS CLAUDIUS
### 1740–1815

#### EIN LIED
*hinterm Ofen zu singen*

DER Winter ist ein rechter Mann,
Kernfest und auf die Dauer;
Sein Fleisch fühlt sich wie Eisen an
Und scheut nicht Süss noch Sauer.

War je ein Mann gesund, ist er's;
Er krankt und kränkelt nimmer,
Weiss nichts von Nachtschweiss und Vapeurs
Und schläft im kalten Zimmer.

Er zieht sein Hemd im Freien an
Und lässt's vorher nicht wärmen;
Und spottet über Fluss im Zahn
Und Kolik in Gedärmen.

Aus Blumen und aus Vogelsang
Weiss er sich nichts zu machen,
Hasst warmen Drang und warmen Klang
Und alle warmen Sachen.

Doch wenn die Füchse bellen sehr,
Wenn 's Holz im Ofen knittert,
Und um den Ofen Knecht und Herr
Die Hände reibt und zittert;

Wenn Stein und Bein von Frost zerbricht
Und Teich' und Seen krachen —
Das klingt ihm gut, das hasst er nicht,
Dann will er tot sich lachen. —

Sein Schloss von Eis liegt ganz hinaus
Beim Nordpol an dem Strande;
Doch hat er auch ein Sommerhaus
Im lieben Schweizerlande.

Da ist er denn bald dort bald hier,
Gut Regiment zu führen.
Und wenn er durchzieht, stehen wir
Und sehn ihn an und frieren.


### RHEINWEINLIED

BEKRÄNZT mit Laub den lieben, vollen Becher,
Und trinkt ihn fröhlich leer!
In ganz Europia, ihr Herren Zecher!
Ist solch ein Wein nicht mehr.

Er kommt nicht her aus Ungarn noch aus Polen,
Noch wo man franzmänn'sch spricht;
Da mag Sankt Veit, der Ritter, Wein sich holen,
Wir holen ihn da nicht.

Ihn bringt das Vaterland aus seiner Fülle;
Wie wär' er sonst so gut?
Wie wär' er sonst so edel, wäre stille
Und doch voll Kraft und Mut?

Er wächst nicht überall im deutschen Reiche;
Und viele Berge, hört,
Sind, wie die weiland Krater, faule Bäuche
Und nicht der Stelle wert.

Thüringens Berge zum Exempel bringen
Gewächs, sieht aus wie Wein;
Ist's aber nicht: man kann dabei nicht singen,
Dabei nicht fröhlich sein.

Im Erzgebirge dürft ihr auch nicht suchen,
Wenn ihr Wein finden wollt;
Das bringt nur Silbererz und Kobaltkuchen
Und etwas Lausegold.

Der Blocksberg ist der lange Herr Philister,
Er macht nur Wind, wie der;
Drum tanzen auch der Kuckuck und sein Küster
Auf ihm die Kreuz und Quer.

Am Rhein, am Rhein, da wachsen unsre Reben;
Gesegnet sei der Rhein!
Da wachsen sie am Ufer hin und geben
Uns diesen Labewein.

So trinkt ihn denn und lasst uns allewege
Uns freun und fröhlich sein!
Und wüssten wir, wo jemand traurig läge,
Wir gäben ihm den Wein.

### ABENDLIED

Der Mond ist aufgegangen,
Die goldnen Sternlein prangen
Am Himmel hell und klar;
Der Wald steht schwarz und schweiget,
Und aus den Wiesen steiget
Der weisse Nebel wunderbar.

Wie ist die Welt so stille
Und in der Dämmrung Hülle
So traulich und so hold!

Als eine stille Kammer,
Wo ihr des Tages Jammer
Verschlafen und vergessen sollt.

Seht ihr den Mond dort stehen?
Er ist nur halb zu sehen
Und ist doch rund und schön.
So sind wohl manche Sachen,
Die wir getrost belachen,
Weil unsre Augen sie nicht sehn.

Wir stolze Menschenkinder
Sind eitel arme Sünder
Und wissen gar nicht viel;
Wir spinnen Luftgespinste
Und suchen viele Künste
Und kommen weiter von dem Ziel.

Gott, lass uns Dein Heil schauen,
Auf nichts Vergänglichs trauen,
Nicht Eitelkeit uns freun!
Lass uns einfältig werden
Und vor Dir hier auf Erden
Wie Kinder fromm und fröhlich sein!

Wollst endlich sonder Grämen
Aus dieser Welt uns nehmen
Durch einen sanften Tod!
Und wenn Du uns genommen,
Lass uns in Himmel kommen,
Du unser Herr und unser Gott!

So legt euch denn, ihr Brüder,
In Gottes Namen nieder;
Kalt ist der Abendhauch.
Verschon uns, Gott, mit Strafen,
Und lass uns ruhig schlafen,
Und unsern kranken Nachbar auch!

### DIE LIEBE

DIE Liebe hemmet nichts; sie kennt nicht Tür noch
    Riegel
Und dringt durch alles sich;
Sie ist ohn Anbeginn, schlug ewig ihre Flügel
Und schlägt sie ewiglich.

### DIE STERNSEHERIN

Ich sehe oft um Mitternacht,
Wenn ich mein Werk getan
Und niemand mehr im Hause wacht,
Die Stern' am Himmel an.

Sie gehn da, hin und her zerstreut,
Als Lämmer auf der Flur;
In Rudeln auch, und aufgereiht
Wie Perlen an der Schnur;

Und funkeln alle weit und breit
Und funkeln rein und schön.
Ich seh' die grosse Herrlichkeit
Und kann nicht satt mich sehn.

Dann saget unterm Himmelszelt
Mein Herz mir in der Brust:
,, Es gibt was Bessers in der Welt
Als all ihr Schmerz und Lust.''

Ich werf' mich auf mein Lager hin
Und liege lange wach,
Und suche es in meinem Sinn
Und sehne mich darnach.

### BEI DEM GRABE MEINES VATERS

FRIEDE sei um diesen Grabstein her !
Sanfter Friede Gottes ! Ach, sie haben
Einen guten Mann begraben,
    Und mir war er mehr.


Träufte mir von Segen, dieser Mann,
Wie ein milder Stern aus bessern Welten ;
Und ich kann's ihm nicht vergelten,
    Was er mir getan.


Er entschlief ; sie gruben hier ihn ein.
Leiser, süsser Trost, von Gott gegeben,
Und ein Ahnden von dem ew'gen ·Leben
    Düft' um sein Gebein !


Bis ihn Jesus Christus, gross und hehr,
Freundlich wird erwecken. — Ach, sie haben
Einen guten Mann begraben,
    Und mir war er mehr.


### DER SÄEMANN SÄET

DER Säemann säet den Samen,
Die Erd' empfängt ihn, und über ein kleines
Keimet die Blume herauf.


Du liebtest sie. Was auch dies Leben
Sonst für Gewinn hat, war klein dir geachtet,
Und sie entschlummerte dir.


Was weinest du neben dem Grabe
Und hebst die Hände zur Wolke des Todes
Und der Verwesung empor ?

Wie Gras auf dem Felde sind Menschen
Dahin, wie Blätter! nur wenige Tage
Gehn wir verkleidet einher.

Der Adler besuchet die Erde,
Doch säumt nicht, schüttelt vom Flügel den
  Staub und
Kehret zur Sonne zurück.

DER TOD UND DAS MÄDCHEN

*Das Mädchen :*

VORÜBER, ach vorüber
Geh, wilder Knochenmann!
Ich bin noch jung! Geh, Lieber,
Und rühre mich nicht an!

*Der Tod :*

Gib deine Hand, du schön und zart Gebild!
Bin Freund und komme nicht zu strafen.
Sei gutes Muts! Ich bin nicht wild!
Sollst sanft in meinen Armen schlafen!

DER TOD

Ach, es ist so dunkel in des Todes Kammer,
  Tönt so traurig, wenn er sich bewegt
Und nun aufhebt seinen schweren Hammer
  Und die Stunde schlägt.

## JOHANN GOTTFRIED HERDER
### 1744–1803

ERLKÖNIGS TOCHTER

HERR Oluf reitet spät und weit,
Zu bieten auf seine Hochzeitleut'.

Da tanzen die Elfen auf grünem Land,
Erlkönigs Tochter reicht ihm die Hand.

„ Willkommen, Herr Oluf ! Was eilst von hier ?
Tritt her in den Reihen und tanz' mit mir ! " —

„ Ich darf nicht tanzen, nicht tanzen ich mag :
Frühmorgen ist mein Hochzeittag." —

„ Hör' an, Herr Oluf, tritt tanzen mit mir !
Zwei güldne Sporne schenk' ich dir.

Ein Hemd von Seide so weiss und fein,
Meine Mutter bleicht's mit Mondenschein." —

„ Ich darf nicht tanzen, nicht tanzen ich mag :
Frühmorgen ist mein Hochzeittag." —

„ Hör' an, Herr Oluf, tritt tanzen mit mir !
Einen Haufen Goldes schenk' ich dir." —

„ Einen Haufen Goldes nähm' ich wohl,
Doch tanzen ich nicht darf noch soll." —

„ Und willst, Herr Oluf, nicht tanzen mit mir,
Soll Seuch' und Krankheit folgen dir."

Sie tät einen Schlag ihm auf sein Herz,
Noch nimmer fühlt' er solchen Schmerz.

Sie hob ihn bleichend auf sein Pferd :
„ Reit heim nun zu deinem Fräulein wert ! "

Und als er kam vor Hauses Tür,
Seine Mutter zitternd stand dafür.

„ Hör' an, mein Sohn, sag an mir gleich,
Wie ist deine Farbe blass und bleich ? " —

,, Und sollt' sie nicht sein blass und bleich ?
Ich traf in Erlenkönigs Reich ! " —

,, Hör' an, mein Sohn, so lieb und traut,
Was soll ich nun sagen deiner Braut ? " —

,, Sagt ihr, ich sei im Wald zur Stund',
Zu proben da mein Pferd und Hund."

Frühmorgen und als es Tag kaum war,
Da kam die Braut mit der Hochzeitschar.

Sie schenkten Met, sie schenkten Wein :
,, Wo ist Herr Oluf, der Bräut'gam mein ? " —

,, Herr Oluf, er ritt in Wald zur Stund',
Er probt allda sein Pferd und Hund."

Die Braut hob auf den Scharlach rot —
Da lag Herr Oluf, und er war tot.

### DIE FAHRT ZUR GELIEBTEN
#### Lappländisch

SONNE, wirf den hellesten Strahl auf den Orrasee !
Ich möchte steigen auf jeden Fichtengipfel,
Wüsst' ich nur, ich sähe den Orrasee.

Ich stieg' auf ihn und blickte nach meiner Lieben,
Wo unter Blumen sie itzo sei.

Ich schnitt' ihm ab die Zweige, die jungen, frischen
    Zweige,
Alle Ästchen schnitt' ich ihm ab, die grünen Ästchen.

Hätt' ich Flügel, zu dir zu fliegen, Krähenflügel,
Dem Laufe der Wolken folgt' ich, ziehend zum Orrasee.

Aber mir fehlen die Flügel, Entenflügel,
Füsse, rudernde Füsse der Gänse, die mich trügen zu
    dir.

Lange g'nug hast du gewartet, so viel Tage,
Deine schönsten Tage,
Mit deinen lieblichen Augen, mit deinem freundlichem
    Herzen.

Und wolltest du mir auch weit entfliehn
Ich holte dich schnell ein.

Was ist stärker und fester als Eisenketten, als gewundne
    Flechten ?
So flicht die Lieb' uns unsern Sinn um
Und ändert Will' und Gedanken.

Knabenwille ist Windeswille,
Jünglings Gedanken lange Gedanken.

Wollt' ich alle sie hören, alle —
Ich irrte ab vom Wege, dem rechten Wege.

Einen Schluss hab' ich, dem will ich folgen ;
So weiss ich, ich finde den rechten Weg.

### DER AUGENBLICK

WARUM denn währt des Lebens Glück
Nur Einen Augenblick ?
Die zartestete der Freuden
Stirbt wie ein Schmetterling,
Der, hangend an der Blume,
Verging, verging.

Wir ahnen, wir geniessen kaum
Des Lebens kurzen Traum.
Nur im unsel'gen Leiden
Wird unser Herzeleid
In einer bangen Stunde
Zur Ewigkeit.

### DAS LICHT

So wie die Flamme des Lichts auch umgewendet
  hinaufstrahlt,
      So vom Schicksal gebeugt, strebet das Gute
      empor.

## GOTTFRIED AUGUST BÜRGER

### 1747–1794

#### DIE SCHATZGRÄBER

Ein Winzer, der am Tode lag,
Rief seine Kinder an und sprach:
„ In unserm Weinberg liegt ein Schatz;
Grabt nur danach! " — „ An welchem Platz ? "
Schrie alles laut den Vater an.
„ Grabt nur ! "  O weh ! da starb der Mann.

Kaum war der Alte beigeschafft,
So grub man nach aus Leibeskraft.
Mit Hacke, Karst und Spaten ward
Der Weinberg um und um gescharrt.
Da war kein Kloss, der ruhig blieb;
Man warf die Erde gar durchs Sieb
Und zog die Harken kreuz und quer
Nach jedem Steinchen hin und her.
Allein da ward kein Schatz verspürt,
Und jeder hielt sich angeführt.

Doch kaum erschien das nächste Jahr,
So nahm man mit Erstaunen wahr,
Dass jede Rebe dreifach trug.
Da wurden erst die Söhne klug
Und gruben nun jahrein, jahraus
Des Schatzes immer mehr heraus.


### DER BAUER

*An seinen Durchlauchtigen Tyrannen*

WER bist du, Fürst, dass ohne Scheu
Zerrollen mich dein Wagenrad,
Zerschlagen darf dein Ross?

Wer bist du, Fürst, dass in mein Fleisch
Dein Freund, dein Jagdhund, ungebleut
Darf Klau' und Rachen hau'n?

Wer bist du, dass, durch Saat und Forst,
Das Hurra deiner Jagd mich treibt,
Entatmet, wie das Wild?

Die Saat, so deine Jagd zertritt,
Was Ross, und Hund, und du verschlingst,
Das Brot, du Fürst, ist mein.

Du Fürst hast nicht, bei Egg' und Pflug,
Hast nicht den Erntetag durchschwitzt.
Mein, mein ist Fleiss und Brot!

Ha! du wärst Obrigkeit von Gott?
Gott spendet Segen aus; du raubst!
Du nicht von Gott, Tyrann!

## MUTTERTÄNDELEI

### *Für meine Dorette*

SEHT mir doch mein schönes Kind,
Mit den goldnen Zottellöckchen,
Blauen Augen, roten Bäckchen!
Leutchen, habt ihr auch so eins? —
Leutchen, nein ihr habet keins!

Seht mir doch mein süsses Kind!
Fetter als ein fettes Schneckchen,
Süsser als ein Zuckerweckchen!
Leutchen, habt ihr auch so eins? —
Leutchen, nein ihr habet keins!

Seht mir doch mein holdes Kind!
Nicht zu mürrisch, nicht zu wählig!
Immer freundlich, immer fröhlich!
Leutchen, habt ihr auch so eins? —
Leutchen, nein ihr habet keins!

Seht mir doch mein frommes Kind!
Keine bitterböse Sieben
Würd' ihr Mütterchen so lieben.
Leutchen, möchtet ihr so eins? —
O ihr kriegt gewiss nicht meins!

Komm' einmal ein Kaufmann her!
Hunderttausend blanke Taler,
Alles Gold der Erde zahl' er!
O er kriegt gewiss nicht meins!
Kauf' er sich woanders eins!

### DAS MÄDEL, DAS ICH MEINE [1]

O, was in tausend Liebespracht
Das Mädel, das ich meine, lacht!
Nun sing, o Lied, und sag' mir an!
Wer hat das Wunder aufgetan:
Dass so in tausend Liebespracht
Das Mädel, des ich meine, lacht?

Wer hat, wie Paradieseswelt,
Des Mädels blaues Aug' erhellt?
Der liebe Gott! der hat's getan,
Der's Firmament erleuchten kann
Der hat wie Paradieseswelt
Des Mädels blaues Aug' erhellt.

Wer hat das Rot auf Weiss gemalt,
Das von des Mädels Wange strahlt?
Der liebe Gott! der hat's getan,
Der Pfirsichblüten malen kann;
Der hat das Rot auf Weiss gemalt,
Das von des Mädels Wange strahlt.

Wer schuf des Mädels Purpurmund
So würzig, süss und lieb und rund?
Der liebe Gott! der hat's getan,
Der Nelk' und Erdbeer' würzen kann,
Der schuf des Mädels Purpurmund
So würzig, süss und lieb und rund.

Wer liess vom Nacken, blond und schön,
Des Mädels seidne Locken wehn?
Der liebe Gott! der gute Geist!
Der goldne Saaten reifen heisst;
Der liess vom Nacken, blond und schön,
Des Mädels seidne Locken wehn.

---

[1] Zu Mollys 18. Geburtstag (24 Aug. 1776).

Wer gab, zu Liebesred' und Sang,
Dem Mädel holder Stimme Klang?
Der liebe, liebe Gott tat dies,
Der Nachtigallen flöten hiess;
Der gab zu Liebesred' und Sang
Dem Mädel holder Stimme Klang.

Wer hat, zur Fülle süsser Lust,
Gewölbt des Mädels weisse Brust?
Der liebe Gott hat's auch getan,
Der stolz die Schwäne kleiden kann;
Der hat, zur Fülle süsser Lust,
Gewölbt des Mädels weisse Brust.

Durch welches Bildners Hände ward
Des Mädels Wuchs so schlank und zart?
Das hat die Meisterhand getan,
Die alle Schönheit bilden kann;
Durch Gott, den höchsten Bildner, ward
Des Mädels Wuchs so schlank und zart.

Wer blies so lichthell, schön und rein,
Die fromme Seel' dem Mädel ein?
Wer anders hat's als Er getan,
Der Seraphim erschaffen kann;
Der blies so lichthell, schön und rein
Die Engelseel' dem Mädel ein.

Lob sei, o Bildner, deiner Kunst!
Und hoher Dank für deine Gunst!
Dass du dein Wunder ausstaffiert
Mit allem, was die Schöpfung ziert.
Lob sei, o Bildner, deiner Kunst!
Und hoher Dank für deine Gunst!

Doch ach! für wen auf Erden lacht
Das Mädel so in Liebespracht?

O Gott! bei deinem Sonnenschein!
Bald möcht' ich nie geboren sein,
Wenn nie in solcher Liebespracht
Dies Mädel mir auf Erden lacht.


### LIEBESZAUBER

Mädel, schau' mir ins Gesicht!
Schelmenauge, blinzle nicht!
Mädel, merke, was ich sage!
Gib mir Rede, wenn ich frage!
Holla hoch, mir ins Gesicht!
Schelmenauge, blinzle nicht!


Bist nicht hässlich, das ist wahr;
Äuglein hast du, blau und klar;
Wang' und Mund sind süsse Feigen;
Ach! vom Busen lass mich schweigen!
Reizend, Liebchen, das ist wahr,
Reizend bist du offenbar.


Aber reizend her und hin!
Bist ja doch nicht Kaiserin;
Nicht die Kaiserin der Schönen,
Wer wird dich allein nur krönen?
Reizend her und reizend hin!
Fehlt noch viel zur Kaiserin.


Hundert Schönen sicherlich,
Hundert, hundert! fänden sich,
Die vor Eifer würden lodern,
Dich auf Schönheit 'rauszufodern,
Hundert Schönen fänden sich;
Hundert siegten über dich.

Dennoch hegst du Kaiserrecht
Über deinen treuen Knecht:
Kaiserrecht in seinem Herzen,
Bald zu Wonne, bald zu Schmerzen,
Tod und Leben, Kaiserrecht,
Nimmt von dir der treue Knecht!

Hundert ist wohl grosse Zahl;
Aber, Liebchen, lass es 'mal
Hunderttausend Schönen wagen,
Dich von Thron und Reich zu jagen!
Hunderttausend! Welche Zahl!
Sie verlören allzumal.

Schelmenauge, Schelmenmund,
Sieh mich an und tu mir's kund:
He, warum bist du die Meine?
Du allein und anders keine?
Sieh mich an und tu mir's kund,
Schelmenauge, Schelmenmund!

Sinnig forsch' ich auf und ab:
Was so ganz dir hin mich gab? —
Ha! durch nichts mich so zu zwingen,
Geht nicht zu mit rechten Dingen.
Zaubermädel, auf und ab,
Sprich, wo ist dein Zauberstab?

### MOLLYS WERT

Ach, könnt' ich Molly kaufen
Für Gold und Edelstein,
Und hätte grosse Haufen:
Die sollten mich nicht reu'n.

Zwar wühlt sich's hübsch im Golde;
Wohl dem, der wühlen kann! —
Doch ohne sie, die Holde,
Was hätt' ich Frohes dran?


Ja, wenn ich der Regente
Von ganz Europa wär',
Und Molly kaufen könnte:
So gäb' ich alles her.
Vor Städten, Schlössern, Thronen,
Und mancher fetten Flur
Wählt' ich, mit ihr zu wohnen,
Ein Gartenhüttchen nur.


Mein liebes Leben enden
Darf nur der Herr der Welt.
Doch dürft' ich es verspenden,
Sowie mein Gut und Geld:
So gäb' ich gern, ich schwöre,
Für jeden Tag ein Jahr,
Dass sie mein eigen wäre,
Mein eigen ganz und gar.


### DIE EINE

Nicht selten hüpft, dem Finken gleich im Haine,
Der Flattersinn mir keck vors Angesicht:
,, Warum, warum bist du so denn auf Eine,
Auf Eine nur bei Tag und Nacht erpicht?


Ha! Glaubst du denn, weil diese dir gebricht,
Dass Liebe dich mit keiner mehr vereine?
Der Gram um sie beflort dein Augenlicht;
Und freilich glänzt durch diesen Flor dir keine.

Die Welt ist gross, und in der grossen Welt
Blühn schön und süss viel Mädchen noch und Frauen.
Du kannst dich ja in manches Herz noch bauen." —

Ach, alles wahr! Vom Rhein an bis zum Belt
Blüht Reiz genug auf allen deutschen Auen.
Was hilft es mir, dem Molly nur gefällt?

### FÜR SIE MEIN EINS UND ALLES

Nicht zum Fürsten hat mich das Geschick,
Nicht zum Grafen, noch zum Herrn geboren,
Und fürwahr, nicht Hellers Wert verloren
Hat an mich das goldbeschwerte Glück.

Günstig hat auch keines Wesirs Blick
Mich im Staat zu hoher Würd' erkoren.
Alles stösst, wie gegen mich verschworen,
Jeden Wunsch mir unerhört zurück.

Von der Wieg' an, bis zu meinem Grabe,
Ist ein wohl ersungnes Lorbeerreis
Meine Ehr' und meine ganze Habe.

Dennoch auch dies eine, so ich weiss,
Spendet' ich mit Lust zur Opfergabe,
Wär', o Molly, dein Besitz der Preis.

### TROST

Wenn dich die Lästerzunge sticht,
So lass dir dies zum Troste sagen:
Die schlechtsten Früchte sind es nicht,
Woran die Wespen nagen.

# LUDWIG HÖLTY
## 1748–1776

### AUFMUNTERUNG ZUR FREUDE

WER wollte sich mit Grillen plagen,
So lang uns Lenz und Jugend blühn?
Wer wollt', in seinen Blütentagen,
Die Stirn in düstre Falten ziehn?

Die Freude winkt auf allen Wegen,
Die durch dies Pilgerleben gehn;
Sie bringt uns selbst den Kranz entgegen,
Wenn wir am Scheidewege stehn.

Noch rinnt und rauscht die Wiesenquelle,
Noch ist die Laube kühl und grün;
Noch scheint der liebe Mond so helle,
Wie er durch Adams Bäume schien.

Noch macht der Saft der Purpurtraube
Des Menschen krankes Herz gesund;
Noch schmecket, in der Abendlaube,
Der Kuss auf einen roten Mund.

Noch tönt der Busch voll Nachtigallen
Dem Jüngling süsse Fühlung zu;
Noch strömt, wenn ihre Lieder schallen,
Selbst in zerrissne Seelen Ruh.

O wunderschön ist Gottes Erde
Und wert, darauf vergnügt zu sein;
Drum will ich, bis ich Asche werde,
Mich dieser schönen Erde freun.

### LEBENSPFLICHTEN

Rosen auf den Weg gestreut,
Und des Harms vergessen!
Eine kleine Spanne Zeit
Ward uns zugemessen.

Heute hüpft im Frühlingstanz
Noch der frohe Knabe;
Morgen weht der Totenkranz
Schon auf seinem Grabe.

Wonne führt die junge Braut
Heute zum Altare;
Eh' die Abendwolke taut,
Ruht sie auf der Bahre.

Ungewisser, kurzer Dau'r
Ist dies Erdeleben;
Und zur Freude, nicht zur Trau'r
Uns von Gott gegeben.

Gebet Harm und Grillenfang,
Gebet ihn den Winden;
Ruht bei frohem Becherklang
Unter grünen Linden.

Lasset keine Nachtigall
Unbehorcht verstummen,
Keine Bien' im Frühlingstal
Unbelauschet summen.

Fühlt, so lang es Gott erlaubt,
Kuss und süsse Trauben,
Bis der Tod, der alles raubt,
Kommt, sie euch zu rauben.

Unser schlummerndes Gebein,
In die Gruft gesäet,
Fühlet nicht den Rosenhain,
Der das Grab umwehet;

Fühlet nicht den Wonneklang
Angestossner Becher,
Nicht den frohen Rundgesang
Weingelehrter Zecher.

### DIE MAINACHT

WENN der silberne Mond durch die Gesträuche blickt
Und sein schlummerndes Licht über den Rasen geusst,
    Und die Nachtigall flötet,
        Wandl' ich traurig von Busch zu Busch.

Überhüllet von Laub, girret ein Taubenpaar
Sein Entzücken mir vor; aber ich wende mich;
    Suche dunklere Schatten,
        Und die einsame Träne rinnt.

Wann, o lächelndes Bild, welches wie Morgenrot
Durch die Seele mir strahlt, find' ich auf Erden dich?
    Und die einsame Träne
        Bebt mir heisser die Wang' herab!

### DIE LIEBE

EINE Schale des Harms, eine der Freude wog
Gott dem Menschengeschlecht; aber der lastende
    Kummer senket die Schale,
        Immer hebet die andre sich.

Irren, traurigen Tritts wanken wir unsern Weg
Durch das Leben hinab, bis sich die Liebe naht,
    Eine Fülle der Freuden
        In die steigende Schale geusst.


Wie dem Pilger der Quell silbern entgegenrinnt,
Wie der Regen des Mais über die Blüten träuft,
    Naht die Liebe ; des Jünglings
        Seele zittert, und huldigt ihr !


Nähm' er Kronen und Gold, misste der Liebe ?  Gold
Ist ihm fliegende Spreu ;  Kronen ein Flittertand ;
    Alle Hoheit der Erde,
        Sonder herzliche Liebe, Staub.


Los der Engel !  Kein Sturm düstert die Seelenruh
Des Beglückten !  Der Tag hüllt sich in lichtes Blau ;
    Kuss und Flüstern und Lächeln
        Flügelt Stunden an Stunden fort.


Herrscher neideten ihn, kosteten sie des Glücks,
Das dem Liebenden ward, würfen den Königsstab
    Aus den Händen und suchten
        Sich ein friedliches Hüttendach.


Unter Rosengesträuch spielet ein Quell und mischt
Dem begegnenden Bach Silber.  So strömen flugs
    Seel' und Seele zusammen,
        Wann allmächtige Liebe naht.


### DER ALTE LANDSMANN AN SEINEN SOHN

        Üb' immer Treu' und Redlichkeit
        Bis an dein kühles Grab
        Und weiche keinen Finger breit
        Von Gottes Wegen ab !

Dann wirst du wie auf grünen Aun
Durchs Pilgerleben gehn,
Dann kannst du sonder Furcht und Graun
Dem Tod ins Antlitz sehn.

Dann wird die Sichel und der Pflug
In deiner Hand so leicht;
Dann singest du beim Wasserkrug,
Als wär' dir Wein gereicht.
Dem Bösewicht wird alles schwer,
Er tue, was er tu';
Der Teufel treibt ihn hin und her
Und lässt ihm keine Ruh.

Der schöne Frühling lacht ihm nicht,
Ihm lacht kein Ährenfeld;
Er ist auf Lug und Trug erpicht
Und wünscht sich nichts als Geld.
Der Wind im Hain, das Laub am Baum
Saust ihm Entsetzen zu;
Er findet nach des Lebens Raum
Im Grabe keine Ruh.

Üb' immer Treu' und Redlichkeit
Bis an dein kühles Grab,
Und weiche keinen Finger breit
Von Gottes Wegen ab!
Dann suchen Enkel deine Gruft
Und weinen Tränen drauf,
Und Sommerblumen, voll von Duft,
Blühn aus den Tränen auf.

### DER TOD

Wann, Friedensbote, der du das Paradies
Dem müden Erdenpilger entschliessest, Tod,
    Wann führst du mich mit deinem goldnen
        Stabe gen Himmel, zu meiner Heimat?

O Wasserblase, Leben, zerfleug nur bald!
Du gabest wenig lächelnde Stunden mir
   Und viele Tränen, Qualenmutter
      Warest du mir, seit der Kindheit Knospe

Zur Blume wurde. Pflücke sie weg, o Tod,
Die dunkle Blume! Sinke, du Staubgebein,
   Zur Erde, deiner Mutter, sinke
      Zu den verschwisterten Erdgewürmen!

Dem Geïste winden Engel den Palmenkranz
Der Überwinder. Rufet, o Freunde, mich
   Nicht wieder auf das Meer, wo Trümmer,
      Türmende Trümmer das Ufer decken!

Wir sehn uns, Teure, wieder, umarmen uns,
Wie Engel sich umarmen, in Licht gehüllt,
   Am Throne Gottes, Ewigkeiten
      Lieben wir uns, wie sich Engel lieben.

### AUFTRAG

IHR Freunde, hänget, wann ich gestorben bin,
Die kleine Harfe hinter dem Altar auf,
   Wo an der Wand die Totenkränze
      Manches verstorbenen Mädchens schimmern.

Der Küster zeigt dann freundlich dem Reisenden
Die kleine Harfe, rauscht mit dem roten Band,
   Das, an der Harfe festgeschlagen,
      Unter den goldenen Saiten flattert.

„ Oft ", sagt er staunend, „ tönen im Abendrot
Von selbst die Saiten leise wie Bienenton ;
   Die Kinder, hergelockt vom Kirchhof,
      Hörten's, und sahn, wie die Kränze bebten."

## LEOPOLD FRIEDRICH GÜNTHER VON GÖCKINGK
### 1748–1828

#### ALS DER ERSTE SCHNEE FIEL

GLEICH einem König, der in seine Staaten
Zurück als Sieger kehrt, empfängt ein Jubel dich!
Der Knabe balgt um deine Flocken sich
Wie bei der Krönung um Dukaten.

Selbst mir, obschon ein Mädchen und der Rute
Lang' nicht mehr untertan, bist du ein lieber Gast;
Denn siehst du nicht, seit du die Erde hast
So weich belegt, wie ich mich spute?

Zu fahren, ohne Segel, ohne Räder,
Auf einer Muschel hin durch deinen weissen Flor,
So sanft und doch so leicht, so schnell, wie vor
Dem Westwind eine Flaumenfeder.

Aus allen Fenstern und aus allen Türen
Sieht mir der bleiche Neid aus hohlen Augen nach;
Selbst die Matrone wird ein leises Ach
Und einen Wunsch um mich verlieren.

Denn der, um den wir Mädchen oft uns stritten,
Wird hinter mir, so schlank wie eine Tanne, stehn
Und sonst auf nichts mit seinen Augen sehn
Als auf das Mädchen in dem Schlitten.

## JOHANN WOLFGANG VON GOETHE
### 1749–1832

#### MIT EINEM GEMALTEN BAND

KLEINE Blumen, kleine Blätter
Streuen mir mit leichter Hand
Gute junge Frühlingsgötter
Tändelnd auf ein luftig Band.

Zephyr, nimm's auf deine Flügel,
Schling's um meiner Liebsten Kleid!
Und so tritt sie vor den Spiegel
All in ihrer Munterkeit.

Sieht mit Rosen sich umgeben,
Selbst wie eine Rose jung.
Einen Blick, geliebtes Leben!
Und ich bin belohnt genung.

Fühle, was dies Herz empfindet,
Reiche frei mir deine Hand,
Und das Band, das uns verbindet,
Sei kein schwaches Rosenband!

#### MAILIED

WIE herrlich leuchtet
Mir die Natur!
Wie glänzt die Sonne!
Wie lacht die Flur!

Es dringen Blüten
Aus jedem Zweig
Und tausend Stimmen
Aus dem Gesträuch,

Und Freud' und Wonne
Aus jeder Brust.
O Erd', o Sonne!
O Glück, o Lust!

O Lieb', o Liebe!
So golden schön,
Wie Morgenwolken
Auf jenen Höhn!

Du segnest herrlich
Das frische Feld,
Im Blütendampfe
Die volle Welt.

O Mädchen, Mädchen,
Wie lieb' ich dich!
Wie blinkt dein Auge
Wie liebst du mich!

So liebt die Lerche
Gesang und Luft,
Und Morgenblumen
Den Himmelsduft,

Wie ich dich liebe
Mit warmem Blut,
Die du mir Jugend
Und Freud' und Mut

Zu neuen Liedern
Und Tänzen gibst.
Sei ewig glücklich,
Wie du mich liebst!

## NACHTGESANG

O, GIEB vom weichen Pfühle,
Träumend, ein halb Gehör!
Bei meinem Saitenspiele
Schlafe! was willst du mehr?

Bei meinem Saitenspiele
Segnet der Sterne Heer
Die ewigen Gefühle;
Schlafe! was willst du mehr?

Die ewigen Gefühle
Heben mich, hoch und hehr,
Aus irdischem Gewühle;
Schlafe! was willst du mehr?

Vom irdischen Gewühle
Trennst du mich nur zu sehr,
Bannst mich in diese Kühle;
Schlafe! was willst du mehr?

Bannst mich in diese Kühle;
Giebst nur im Traum Gehör.
Ach, auf dem weichen Pfühle
Schlafe! was willst du mehr?

## WILLKOMMEN UND ABSCHIED

Es schlug mein Herz, geschwind zu Pferde
Es war getan fast eh' gedacht;
Der Abend wiegte schon die Erde,
Und an den Bergen hing die Nacht;
Schon stand im Nebelkleid die Eiche
Ein aufgetürmter Riese da,
Wo Finsternis aus dem Gesträuche
Mit hundert schwarzen Augen sah.

Der Mond von einem Wolkenhügel
Sah kläglich aus dem Duft hervor;
Die Winde schwangen leise Flügel,
Umsausten schauerlich mein Ohr;
Die Nacht schuf tausend Ungeheuer,
Doch frisch und fröhlich war mein Mut;
In meinen Adern welches Feuer!
In meinem Herzen welche Glut!

Dich sah ich, und die milde Freude
Floss von dem süssen Blick auf mich
Ganz war mein Herz an deiner Seite,
Und jeder Atemzug für dich.
Ein rosenfarbnes Frühlingswetter
Umgab das liebliche Gesicht,
Und Zärtlichkeit für mich — ihr Götter!
Ich hofft' es, ich verdient' es nicht!

Doch ach, schon mit der Morgensonne
Verengt der Abschied mir das Herz:
In deinen Küssen welche Wonne!
In deinem Auge welcher Schmerz!
Ich ging, du standst und sahst zur Erden
Und sahst mir nach mit nassem Blick;
Und doch, welch Glück, geliebt zu werden!
Und lieben, Götter, welch ein Glück!

### HEIDENRÖSLEIN

Sah ein Knab' ein Röslein stehn,
Röslein auf der Heiden,
War so jung und morgenschön,
Lief er schnell es nah zu sehn,
Sah's mit vielen Freuden.
Röslein, Röslein, Röslein rot,
Röslein auf der Heiden.

13

Knabe sprach : „ Ich breche dich,
Röslein auf der Heiden ! "
Röslein sprach : „ Ich steche dich,
Dass du ewig denkst an mich,
Und ich will's nicht leiden."
Röslein, Röslein, Röslein rot,
Röslein auf der Heiden.

Und der wilde Knabe brach
's Röslein auf der Heiden ;
Röslein wehrte sich und stach,
Half ihm doch kein Weh und Ach,
Musst' es eben leiden.
Röslein, Röslein, Röslein rot,
Röslein auf der Heiden.


### PROMETHEUS

BEDECKE deinen Himmel, Zeus,
Mit Wolkendunst,
Und übe, dem Knaben gleich,
Der Disteln köpft,
An Eichen dich und Bergeshöhn ;
Musst mir meine Erde
Doch lassen stehn,
Und meine Hütte, die du nicht gebaut,
Und meinen Herd,
Um dessen Glut
Du mich beneidest.

Ich kenne nichts Ärmeres
Unter der Sonn' als euch, Götter !
Ihr nähret kümmerlich
Von Opfersteuern
Und Gebetshauch
Eure Majestät,

Und darbtet, wären
Nicht Kinder und Bettler
Hoffnungsvolle Toren.

Da ich ein Kind war,
Nicht wusste, wo aus noch ein,
Kehrt' ich mein verirrtes Auge
Zur Sonne, als wenn drüber wär'
Ein Ohr, zu hören meine Klage,
Ein Herz, wie mein's,
Sich des Bedrängten zu erbarmen.

Wer half mir
Wider der Titanen Übermut?
Wer rettete vom Tode mich,
Von Sklaverei?
Hast du nicht alles selbst vollendet,
Heilig glühend Herz?
Und glühtest jung und gut,
Betrogen, Rettungsdank
Dem Schlafenden da droben?

Ich dich ehren? Wofür?
Hast du die Schmerzen gelindert
Je des Beladenen?
Hast du die Tränen gestillet
Je des Geängsteten?
Hat nicht mich zum Manne geschmiedet
Die allmächtige Zeit
Und das ewige Schicksal,
Meine Herrn und deine?

Wähntest du etwa,
Ich sollte das Leben hassen,
In Wüsten fliehen,
Weil nicht alle
Blütenträume reiften?

Hier sitz' ich, forme Menschen
Nach meinem Bilde,
Ein Geschlecht, das mir gleich sei,
Zu leiden, zu weinen,
Zu geniessen und zu freuen sich,
Und dein nicht zu achten,
Wie ich !

### NEUE LIEBE NEUES LEBEN

HERZ, mein Herz, was soll das geben ?
Was bedränget dich so sehr ?
Welch ein fremdes, neues Leben !
Ich erkenne dich nicht mehr.
Weg ist alles, was du liebtest,
Weg, warum du dich betrübtest,
Weg dein Fleiss und deine Ruh —
Ach, wie kamst du nur dazu !

Fesselt dich die Jugendblüte,
Diese liebliche Gestalt,
Dieser Blick voll Treu' und Güte
Mit unendlicher Gewalt ?
Will ich rasch mich ihr entziehen,
Mich ermannen, ihr entfliehen,
Führet mich im Augenblick,
Ach, mein Weg zu ihr zurück.

Und an diesem Zauberfädchen,
Das sich nicht zerreissen lässt,
Hält das liebe, lose Mädchen
Mich so wider Willen fest ;
Muss in ihrem Zauberkreise
Leben nun auf ihre Weise.
Die Verändrung, ach, wie gross !
Liebe ! Liebe ! lass mich los !

### AN BELINDEN

WARUM ziehst du mich unwiderstehlich,
Ach, in jene Pracht ?
War ich guter Junge nicht so selig
In der öden Nacht ?

Heimlich in mein Zimmerchen verschlossen,
Lag im Mondenschein,
Ganz von seinem Schauerlicht umflossen,
Und ich dämmert' ein ;

Träumte da von vollen goldnen Stunden
Ungemischter Lust,
Hatte schon dein liebes Bild empfunden
Tief in meiner Brust.

Bin ich's noch, den du bei so viel Lichtern
An dem Spieltisch hältst ?
Oft so unerträglichen Gesichtern
Gegenüber stellst ?

Reizender ist mir des Frühlings Blüte
Nun nicht auf der Flur ;
Wo du, Engel, bist, ist Lieb' und Güte,
Wo du bist, Natur.

### RASTLOSE LIEBE

DEM Schnee, dem Regen,
Dem Wind entgegen,
Im Dampf der Klüfte,
Durch Nebeldüfte,
Immer zu ! Immer zu !
Ohne Rast und Ruh !

Lieber durch Leiden
Möcht' ich mich schlagen,
Als so viel Freuden
Des Lebens ertragen.
Alle das Neigen
Von Herzen zu Herzen,
Ach, wie so eigen
Schaffet das Schmerzen !

Wie soll ich fliehen ?
Wälderwärts ziehen ?
Alles vergebens !
Krone des Lebens,
Glück ohne Ruh,
Liebe, bist du !

### AN LIDA

Den Einzigen, Lida, welchen du lieben kannst,
Forderst du ganz für dich, und mit Recht.
Auch ist er einzig dein ;
Denn, seit ich von dir bin,
Scheint mir des schnellsten Lebens
Lärmende Bewegung
Nur ein leichter Flor, durch den ich deine Gestalt
Immerfort wie in Wolken erblicke :
Sie leuchtet mir freundlich und treu,
Wie durch des Nordlichts bewegliche Strahlen
Ewige Sterne schimmern.

### GEFUNDEN

Ich ging im Walde
So für mich hin,
Und nichts zu suchen,
Das war mein Sinn.

Im Schatten sah ich
Ein Blümchen stehn,
Wie Sterne leuchtend,
Wie Äuglein schön.

Ich wollt' es brechen,
Da sagt' es fein :
Soll ich zum Welken
Gebrochen sein ?

Ich grub's mit allen
Den Würzlein aus,
Zum Garten trug ich's
Am hübschen Haus.

Und pflanzt' es wieder
Am stillen Ort ;
Nun zweigt es immer
Und blüht so fort.


VENEZIANISCHE EPIGRAMME
29

VIELES hab' ich versucht, gezeichnet, in Kupfer
    gestochen,
Öl gemalt, in Ton hab' ich auch manches gedruckt,
Unbeständig jedoch, und nichts gelernt noch geleistet ;
    Nur ein einzig Talent bracht' ich der Meisterschaft
    nah :
Deutsch zu schreiben.   Und so verderb' ich unglück-
    licher Dichter
    In dem schlechtesten Stoff leider nun Leben und
    Kunst.

35

KLEIN ist unter den Fürsten Germaniens freilich der
    meine ;
    Kurz und schmal ist sein Land, mässig nur, was er
    vermag.

Aber so wende nach innen, so wende nach aussen die
  Kräfte
  Jeder ;  da wär' es ein Fest, Deutscher mit Deutschen
  zu sein.
Doch  was  priesest  du  Ihn,  den  Taten  und  Werke
  verkünden ?
  Und bestochen erschien deine Verehrung vielleicht ;
Denn mir hat er gegeben, was Grosse selten gewähren,
  Neigung, Musse, Vertraun, Felder und Garten und
  Haus.
Niemand braucht' ich zu danken als Ihm, und manches
  bedurft' ich,
  Der  ich  mich  auf  den  Erwerb  schlecht,  als  ein
  Dichter, verstand.
Hat mich Europa gelobt, was hat mir Europa gegeben ?
  Nichts !  Ich  habe,  wie  schwer !  meine  Gedichte
  bezahlt.
Deutschland ahmte mich nach, und Frankreich mochte
  mich lesen ;
  England ! freundlich empfingst du den zerrütteten
  Gast.
Doch, was fördert es mich, dass auch sogar der Chinese
  Malet mit ängstlicher Hand Werthern und Lotten
  auf Glas ?
Niemals frug ein Kaiser nach mir, es hat sich kein
  König
  Um mich bekümmert, und Er war mir August und
  Mäzen.


### GRENZEN DER MENSCHHEIT

    Wenn der uralte
    Heilige Vater
    Mit gelassener Hand
    Aus rollenden Wolken
    Segnende Blitze

Über die Erde sät,
Küss' ich den letzten
Saum seines Kleides,
Kindliche Schauer
Treu in der Brust.

Denn mit Göttern
Soll sich nicht messen
Irgend ein Mensch.
Hebt er sich aufwärts,
Und berührt
Mit dem Scheitel die Sterne,
Nirgends haften dann
Die unsichern Sohlen,
Und mit ihm spielen
Wolken und Winde.

Steht er mit festen
Markigen Knochen
Auf der wohlgegründeten,
Dauernden Erde,
Reicht er nicht auf,
Nur mit der Eiche
Oder der Rebe
Sich zu vergleichen.

Was unterscheidet
Götter von Menschen?
Dass viele Wellen
Vor jenen wandeln,
Ein ewiger Strom:
Uns hebt die Welle,
Verschlingt die Welle,
Und wir versinken.

Ein kleiner Ring
Begrenzt unser Leben,

Und viele Geschlechter
Reihen sich dauernd
An ihres Daseins
Unendliche Kette.

## DAS GÖTTLICHE

EDEL sei der Mensch,
Hilfreich und gut!
Denn das allein
Unterscheidet ihn
Von allen Wesen,
Die wir kennen.

Heil den unbekannten
Höhern Wesen,
Die wir ahnen!
Ihnen gleiche der Mensch,
Sein Beispiel lehr' uns
Jene glauben.

Denn unfühlend
Ist die Natur:
Es leuchtet die Sonne
Über Bös' und Gute,
Und dem Verbrecher
Glänzen, wie dem Besten,
Der Mond und die Sterne.

Wind und Ströme,
Donner und Hagel
Rauschen ihren Weg,
Und ergreifen,
Vorübereilend,
Einen um den andern.

Auch so das Glück
Tappt unter die Menge,
Fasst bald des Knaben
Lockige Unschuld,
Bald auch den kahlen
Schuldigen Scheitel.

Nach ewigen, ehrnen,
Grossen Gesetzen
Müssen wir alle
Unseres Daseins
Kreise vollenden.

Nur allein der Mensch
Vermag das Unmögliche :
Er unterscheidet,
Wählet und richtet ;
Er kann dem Augenblick
Dauer verleihen.

Er allein darf
Den Guten lohnen,
Den Bösen strafen,
Heilen und retten,
Alles Irrende, Schweifende
Nützlich verbinden.

Und wir verehren
Die Unsterblichen,
Als wären sie Menschen,
Täten im Grossen
Was der Beste im Kleinen
Tut oder möchte.

Der edle Mensch
Sei hilfreich und gut !

Unermüdet schaff' er
Das Nützliche, Rechte,
Sei uns ein Vorbild
Jener geahneten Wesen!


### NÄHE DES GELIEBTEN

Ich denke dein, wenn mir der Sonne Schimmer
 Vom Meere strahlt;
Ich denke dein, wenn sich des Mondes Flimmer
 In Quellen malt.

Ich sehe dich, wenn auf dem fernen Wege
 Der Staub sich hebt;
In tiefer Nacht, wenn auf dem schmalen Stege
 Der Wandrer bebt.

Ich höre dich, wenn dort mit dumpfem Rauschen
 Die Welle steigt.
Im stillen Haine geh' ich oft zu lauschen,
 Wenn alles schweigt.

Ich bin bei dir, du seist auch noch so ferne,
 Du bist mir nah!
Die Sonne sinkt, bald leuchten mir die Sterne.
 O wärst du da!


### DER SCHÄFER PUTZTE SICH ZUM TANZ

Der Schäfer putzte sich zum Tanz,
Mit bunter Jacke, Band und Kranz,
Schmuck war er angezogen.
Schon um die Linde war es voll,
Und alles tanzte schon wie toll.
Juchhe! Juchhe!
Juchheisa! Heisa! He!
So ging der Fiedelbogen.

Er drückte hastig sich heran,
Da stiess er an ein Mädchen an
Mit seinem Ellenbogen ;
Die frische Dirne kehrt' sich um
Und sagte : „ Nun, das find' ich dumm ! "
Juchhe ! Juchhe !
Juchheisa ! Heisa ! He !
„ Seid nicht so ungezogen."

Doch hurtig in dem Kreise ging's,
Sie tanzten rechts, sie tanzten links,
Und alle Röcke flogen.
Sie wurden rot, sie wurden warm
Und ruhten atmend Arm in Arm —
Juchhe ! Juchhe !
Juchheisa ! Heisa ! He !
Und Hüft' an Ellenbogen.

„ Und tu' mir doch nicht so vertraut !
Wie mancher hat nicht seine Braut
Belogen und betrogen ! "
Er schmeichelte sie doch beiseit',
Und von der Linde scholl es weit :
Juchhe ! Juchhe !
Juchheisa ! Heisa ! He !
Geschrei und Fiedelbogen.

### DER KÖNIG IN THULE

Es war ein König in Thule,
Gar treu bis an das Grab,
Dem sterbend seine Buhle
Einen goldnen Becher gab.

Es ging ihm nichts darüber,
Er leert' ihn jeden Schmaus ;
Die Augen gingen ihm über,
So oft er trank daraus.

Und als er kam zu sterben,
Zählt' er seine Städt' im Reich,
Gönnt' alles seinem Erben,
Den Becher nicht zugleich.

Er sass beim Königsmahle,
Die Ritter um ihn her,
Auf hohem Vätersaale
Dort auf dem Schloss am Meer.

Dort stand der alte Zecher,
Trank letzte Lebensglut
Und warf den heil'gen Becher
Hinunter in die Flut.

Er sah ihn stürzen, trinken
Und sinken tief ins Meer.
Die Augen täten ihm sinken;
Trank nie einen Tropfen mehr.

### MEINE RUH IST HIN

MEINE Ruh ist hin,
Mein Herz ist schwer;
Ich finde sie nimmer
Und nimmermehr.

Wo ich ihn nicht hab',
Ist mir das Grab,
Die ganze Welt
Ist mir vergällt.

Mein armer Kopf
Ist mir verrückt,
Mein ganzer Sinn
Ist mir zerstückt.

Meine Ruh ist hin,
Mein Herz ist schwer ;
Ich finde sie nimmer
Und nimmermehr.

Nach ihm nur schau' ich
Zum Fenster hinaus,
Nach ihm nur geh' ich
Aus dem Haus.

Sein hoher Gang,
Sein' edle Gestalt,
Seines Mundes Lächeln,
Seiner Augen Gewalt,

Und seiner Rede
Zauberfluss,
Sein Händedruck,
Und ach, sein Kuss !

Meine Ruh ist hin,
Mein Herz ist schwer ;
Ich finde sie nimmer
Und nimmermehr.

Mein Busen drängt
Sich nach ihm hin ;
Ach dürft' ich fassen
Und halten ihn

Und küssen ihn,
So wie ich wollt',
An seinen Küssen
Vergehen sollt' !

### DER FISCHER

Das Wasser rauscht', das Wasser schwoll,
Ein Fischer sass daran,
Sah nach dem Angel ruhevoll,
Kühl bis ans Herz hinan.
Und wie er sitzt und wie er lauscht,
Teilt sich die Flut empor;
Aus dem bewegten Wasser rauscht
Ein feuchtes Weib hervor.

Sie sang zu ihm, sie sprach zu ihm:
,, Was lockst du meine Brut
Mit Menschenwitz und Menschenlist
Hinauf in Todesglut?
Ach, wüsstest du, wie's Fischlein ist
So wohlig auf dem Grund,
Du stiegst herunter, wie du bist,
Und würdest erst gesund.

Labt sich die liebe Sonne nicht,
Der Mond sich nicht im Meer?
Kehrt wellenatmend ihr Gesicht
Nicht doppelt schöner her?
Lockt dich der tiefe Himmel nicht,
Das feuchtverklärte Blau?
Lockt dich dein eigen Angesicht
Nicht her in ew'gen Tau? "

Das Wasser rauscht', das Wasser schwoll,
Netzt' ihm den nackten Fuss;
Sein Herz wuchs ihm so sehnsuchtsvoll
Wie bei der Liebsten Gruss.
Sie sprach zu ihm, sie sang zu ihm;
Da war's um ihn geschehn:
Halb zog sie ihn, halb sank er hin
Und ward nicht mehr gesehn.

### DER SÄNGER

„ Was hör' ich draussen vor dem Tor,
Was auf der Brücke schallen ?
Lass den Gesang vor unserm Ohr
Im Saale widerhallen ! "
Der König sprach's, der Page lief ;
Der Knabe kam, der König rief :
„ Lasst mir herein den Alten ! "

„ Gegrüsset seid mir, edle Herrn,
Gegrüsst ihr, schöne Damen !
Welch reicher Himmel ! Stern bei Stern !
Wer kennet ihre Namen ?
Im Saal voll Pracht und Herrlichkeit
Schliesst, Augen, euch ; hier ist nicht Zeit,
Sich staunend zu ergötzen."

Der Sänger drückt' die Augen ein
Und schlug in vollen Tönen ;
Die Ritter schauten mutig drein,
Und in den Schoss die Schönen.
Der König, dem das Lied gefiel,
Liess, ihn zu ehren für sein Spiel,
Eine goldne Kette holen.

„ Die goldne Kette gib mir nicht,
Die Kette gib den Rittern,
Vor deren kühnem Angesicht
Der Feinde Lanzen splittern !
Gib sie dem Kanzler, den du hast,
Und lass ihn noch die goldne Last
Zu andern Lasten tragen !

Ich singe, wie der Vogel singt,
Der in den Zweigen wohnet ;
Das Lied, das aus der Kehle dringt,
Ist Lohn, der reichlich lohnet.

Doch darf ich bitten, bitt' ich eins:
Lass mir den besten Becher Weins
In purem Golde reichen!"

Er setzt' ihn an, er trank ihn aus:
,, O Trank voll süsser Labe!
O wohl dem hochbeglückten Haus,
Wo das ist kleine Gabe!
Ergeht's euch wohl, so denkt an mich,
Und danket Gott so warm, als ich
Für diesen Trunk euch danke."

### ERLKÖNIG

WER reitet so spät durch Nacht und Wind?
Es ist der Vater mit seinem Kind;
Er hat den Knaben wohl in dem Arm,
Er fasst ihn sicher, er hält ihn warm.

Mein Sohn, was birgst du so bang dein Gesicht? —
Siehst, Vater, du den Erlkönig nicht?
Den Erlenkönig mit Kron' und Schweif? —
Mein Sohn, es ist ein Nebelstreif. —

,, Du liebes Kind, komm, geh mit mir!
Gar schöne Spiele spiel' ich mit dir,
Manch bunte Blumen sind an dem Strand,
Meine Mutter hat manch gülden Gewand."

Mein Vater, mein Vater, und hörest du nicht,
Was Erlenkönig mir leise verspricht? —
Sei ruhig, bleibe ruhig, mein Kind:
In dürren Blättern säuselt der Wind. —

,, Willst, feiner Knabe, du mit mir gehn?
Meine Töchter sollen dich warten schön;

Meine Töchter führen den nächtlichen Reihn
Und wiegen und tanzen und singen dich ein." —

Mein Vater, mein Vater, und siehst du nicht dort
Erlkönigs Töchter am düstern Ort ? —
Mein Sohn, mein Sohn, ich seh' es genau :
Es scheinen die alten Weiden so grau. —

,, Ich liebe dich, mich reizt deine schöne Gestalt ;
Und bist du nicht willig, so brauch' ich Gewalt." —
Mein Vater, mein Vater, jetzt fasst er mich an !
Erlkönig hat mir ein Leids getan ! —

Dem Vater grauset's, er reitet geschwind,
Er hält in Armen das ächzende Kind,
Erreicht den Hof mit Mühe und Not ;
In seinen Armen das Kind war tot.

### DER SCHATZGRÄBER

ARM am Beutel, krank am Herzen
Schleppt' ich meine langen Tage.
Armut ist die grösste Plage,
Reichtum ist das höchste Gut !
Und zu enden meine Schmerzen,
Ging ich einen Schatz zu graben.
,, Meine Seele sollst du haben ! "
Schrieb ich hin mit eignem Blut.

Und so zog ich Kreis' um Kreise,
Stellte wunderbare Flammen,
Kraut und Knochenwerk zusammen
Die Beschwörung war vollbracht.
Und auf die gelernte Weise
Grub ich nach dem alten Schatze
Auf dem angezeigten Platze.
Schwarz und stürmisch war die Nacht.

Und ich sah ein Licht von weiten;
Und es kam gleich einem Sterne
Hinten aus der fernsten Ferne,
Eben als es zwölfe schlug.
Und da galt kein Vorbereiten:
Heller ward's mit einem Male
Von dem Glanz der vollen Schale,
Die ein schöner Knabe trug.

Holde Augen sah ich blinken
Unter dichtem Blumenkranze;
In des Trankes Himmelsglanze
Trat er in den Kreis herein.
Und er hiess mich freundlich trinken;
Und ich dacht': ,, Es kann der Knabe
Mit der schönen lichten Gabe
Wahrlich nicht der Böse sein."

,, Trinke Mut des reinen Lebens!
Dann verstehst du die Belehrung,
Kommst mit ängstlicher Beschwörung
Nicht zurück an diesen Ort.
Grabe hier nicht mehr vergebens!
Tages Arbeit, abends Gäste!
Saure Wochen, frohe Feste!
Sei dein künftig Zauberwort! "

### MIGNONS LIEDER

*Aus 'Wilhelm Meister'*

#### I

KENNST du das Land, wo die Zitronen blühn,
Im dunkeln Laub die Gold-Orangen glühn,
Ein sanfter Wind vom blauen Himmel weht,
Die Myrte still und hoch der Lorbeer steht?

Kennst du es wohl?
>Dahin! Dahin
Möcht' ich mit dir, o mein Geliebter, ziehn.


Kennst du das Haus? Auf Säulen ruht sein Dach,
Es glänzt der Saal, es schimmert das Gemach,
Und Marmorbilder stehn und sehn mich an:
Was hat man dir, du armes Kind, getan?
Kennst du es wohl?
>Dahin! Dahin
Möcht' ich mit dir, o mein Beschützer, ziehn.


Kennst du den Berg und seinen Wolkensteg?
Das Maultier sucht im Nebel seinen Weg;
In Höhlen wohnt der Drachen alte Brut;
Es stürzt der Fels und über ihn die Flut.
Kennst du es wohl?
>Dahin! Dahin
Geht unser Weg! o Vater, lass uns ziehn!


## II

Nur wer die Sehsucht kennt,
Weiss, was ich leide!
Allein und abgetrennt
Von aller Freude
Seh' ich ans Firmament
Nach jener Seite.
Ach! der mich liebt und kennt,
Ist in der Weite.
Es schwindelt mir, es brennt
Mein Eingeweide.
Nur wer die Sehnsucht kennt,
Weiss, was ich leide!

### KOPHTISCHES LIED

GEH ! gehorche meinen Winken,
Nutze deine jungen Tage,
Lerne zeitig klüger sein.
Auf des Glückes grosser Wage
Steht die Zunge selten ein.
Du musst steigen oder sinken,
Du musst herrschen und gewinnen,
Oder dienen und verlieren,
Leiden oder triumphieren,
Amboss oder Hammer sein.

### LEGENDE VOM HUFEISEN

ALS noch, verkannt und sehr gering,
Unser Herr auf der Erde ging
Und viele Jünger sich zu ihm fanden,
Die sehr selten sein Wort verstanden,
Liebt' er sich gar über die Massen,
Seinen Hof zu halten auf der Strassen,
Weil unter des Himmels Angesicht
Man immer besser und freier spricht.
Er liess sie da die höchsten Lehren
Aus seinem heiligen Munde hören ;
Besonders durch Gleichnis und Exempel
Macht' er einen jeden Markt zum Tempel.

So schlendert' er in Geistes Ruh
Mit ihnen einst einem Städtchen zu,
Sah etwas blinken auf der Strass',
Das ein zerbrochen Hufeisen was.
Er sagte zu Sankt Peter drauf :
,, Heb doch einmal das Eisen auf ! "
Sankt Peter war nicht aufgeräumt,
Er hatte soeben im Gehen geträumt
So was vom Regiment der Welt,

Was einem jeden wohlgefällt;
Denn im Kopf hat das keine Schranken;
Das waren so seine liebsten Gedanken.
Nun war der Fund ihm viel zu klein,
Hätte müssen Kron' und Zepter sein;
Aber wie sollt' er seinen Rücken
Nach einem halben Hufeisen bücken?
Er also sich zur Seite kehrt
Und tut, als hätt' er's nicht gehört.

Der Herr, nach seiner Langmut, drauf
Hebt selber das Hufeisen auf
Und tut auch weiter nicht dergleichen.
Als sie nun bald die Stadt erreichen,
Geht er vor eines Schmiedes Tür,
Nimmt von dem Mann drei Pfennig dafür.
Und als sie über den Markt nun gehen,
Sieht er daselbst schöne Kirschen stehen,
Kauft ihrer so wenig oder so viel,
Als man für einen Dreier geben will,
Die er sodann nach seiner Art
Ruhig im Ärmel aufbewahrt.

Nun ging's zum andern Tor hinaus,
Durch Wies' und Felder ohne Haus,
Auch war der Weg von Bäumen bloss;
Die Sonne schien, die Hitz' war gross,
So dass man viel an solcher Stätt'
Für einen Trunk Wasser gegeben hätt'.
Der Herr geht immer voraus vor allen,
Lässt unversehens eine Kirsche fallen.
Sankt Peter war gleich dahinter her,
Als wenn es ein goldner Apfel wär';
Das Beerlein schmeckte seinem Gaum.
Der Herr nach einem kleinen Raum
Ein ander Kirschlein zur Erde schickt,
Wornach Sankt Peter schnell sich bückt.

So lässt der Herr ihn seinen Rücken
Gar vielmal nach den Kirschen bücken.
Das dauert eine ganze Zeit;
Dann sprach der Herr mit Heiterkeit:
,, Tätst du zur rechten Zeit dich regen,
Hättst du's bequemer haben mögen.
Wer geringe Ding' wenig acht't,
Sich um geringere Mühe macht ".

### WANDRERS NACHTLIED

DER du von dem Himmel bist,
Alles Leid und Schmerzen stillest,
Den, der doppelt elend ist,
Doppelt mit Erquickung füllest,
Ach, ich bin des Treibens müde!
Was soll all der Schmerz und Lüst?
Süsser Friede,
Komm, ach komm in meine Brust!

### ÜBER ALLEN GIPFELN

ÜBER allen Gipfeln
Ist Ruh,
In allen Wipfeln
Spürest du
Kaum einen Hauch;
Die Vögelein schweigen im Walde.
Warte nur, balde
Ruhest du auch.

### GOTT UND WELT

*Proömion*

IM Namen Dessen, der Sich selbst erschuf,
Von Ewigkeit in schaffendem Beruf;
In Seinem Namen, der den Glauben schafft,

Vertrauen, Liebe, Tätigkeit und Kraft;
In Jenes Namen, der, so oft genannt,
Dem Wesen nach blieb immer unbekannt:

So weit das Ohr, so weit das Auge reicht,
Du findest nur Bekanntes, das Ihm gleicht,
Und deines Geistes höchster Feuerflug
Hat schon am Gleichnis, hat am Bild genug;
Es zieht dich an, es reisst dich heiter fort,
Und wo du wandelst, schmückt sich Weg und Ort;
Du zählst nicht mehr, berechnest keine Zeit,
Und jeder Schritt ist Unermesslichkeit.

Was wär' ein Gott, der nur von aussen stiesse,
Im Kreis das All am Finger laufen liesse!
Ihm ziemt's, die Welt im Innern zu bewegen,
Natur in Sich, Sich in Natur zu hegen,
So dass, was in Ihm lebt und webt und ist,
Nie Seine Kraft, nie Seinen Geist vermisst.

Im Innern ist ein Universum auch;
Daher der Völker löblicher Gebrauch,
Dass jeglicher das Beste, was er kennt,
Er Gott, ja, seinen Gott benennt,
Ihm Himmel und Erden übergibt,
Ihn fürchtet, und wo möglich liebt.

### GESANG DER GEISTER ÜBER DEN WASSERN

Des Menschen Seele
Gleicht dem Wasser:
Vom Himmel kommt es,
Zum Himmel steigt es,
Und wieder nieder
Zur Erde muss es,
Ewig wechselnd.

Strömt von der hohen
Steilen Felswand
Der reine Strahl,
Dann stäubt er lieblich
In Wolkenwellen
Zum glatten Fels,
Und leicht empfangen,
Wallt er verschleiernd,
Leisrauschend,
Zur Tiefe nieder.

Ragen Klippen
Dem Sturz entgegen,
Schäumt er unmutig
Stufenweise
Zum Abgrund.

Im flachen Bette
Schleicht er das Wiesental hin,
Und in dem glatten See
Weiden ihr Antlitz
Alle Gestirne.

Wind ist der Welle
Lieblicher Buhler;
Wind mischt vom Grund aus
Schäumende Wogen.

Seele des Menschen,
Wie gleichst du dem Wasser!
Schicksal des Menschen,
Wie gleichst du dem Wind!

### SPRÜCHE

#### *Freisinn*

Lasst mich nur auf meinem Sattel gelten!
Bleibt in euren Hütten, euren Zelten!
Und ich reite froh in alle Ferne,
Über meiner Mütze nur die Sterne.

#### *Noch ist es Tag*

Noch ist es Tag, da rühre sich der Mann!
Die Nacht tritt ein, wo niemand wirken kann.

#### *Mein Erbteil*

Mein Erbteil wie herrlich, weit und breit!
Die Zeit ist mein Besitz, mein Acker ist die Zeit!

#### *Dilettant*

Weil ein Vers dir gelingt in einer gebildeten Sprache,
Die für dich dichtet und denkt, glaubst du schon
    Dichter zu sein?

#### *Das Naturgesetz*

So war's immer, mein Freund, und so wird's bleiben,
    die Ohnmacht
Hat die Regel für sich, aber die Kraft den Erfolg.


### LYNCEUS DER TÜRMER

Zum Sehen geboren,
Zum Schauen bestellt,
Dem Turme geschworen,
Gefällt mir die Welt.
Ich blick' in die Ferne,
Ich seh' in die Näh,
Den Mond und die Sterne,
Den Wald und das Reh.

So seh' ich in allen
Die ewige Zier,
Und wie mir's gefallen,
Gefall' ich auch mir.
Ihr glücklichen Augen,
Was je ihr gesehn,
Es sei wie es wolle,
Es war doch so schön!

### GEDICHTE

GEDICHTE sind gemalte Fensterscheiben!
Sieht man vom Markt in die Kirche hinein,
Da ist alles dunkel, und düster;
Und so sieht's auch der Herr Philister:
Der mag denn wohl verdriesslich sein
Und lebenslang verdriesslich bleiben.

Kommt aber nun einmal herein!
Begrüsst die heilige Kapelle;
Da ist's auf einmal farbig helle,
Geschicht' und Zierat glänzt in Schnelle,
Bedeutend wirkt ein edler Schein;
Dies wird euch Kindern Gottes taugen,
Erbaut euch und ergötzt die Augen!

## JOHANN HEINRICH VOSS
### 1751–1826

#### DER LANDMANN

IHR Städter, sucht ihr Freude,
So kommt aufs Land heraus.
Seht, Garten, Feld und Weide
Umgrünt hier jedes Haus.

Kein reicher Mann verbauet
Uns Mond und Sonnenschein;
Und abends überschauet
Man jedes Sternelein.

Wenn früh des Dorfes Wecker
Aus leichtem Schlaf uns kräht,
Durchjauchzt man rasch die Äcker
Mit blankem Feldgerät.
Das Weib indes treibt singend
Die Milchküh' aus dem Stall;
Laut folgen sie und springend
Des Hirtenhornes Schall.

Wir sehn, wie Gott den Segen
Aus milden Händen streut,
Wie Frühlingssonn' und Regen
Uns Wald und Flur erneut.
Uns blühn des Gartens Bäume,
Uns wallt das grüne Korn;
Uns schwärmt nach Honigseime
Die Bien' um Blum' und Born.

Uns singt das Vöglein Lieder;
Uns rauscht die blaue Flut;
Uns schwirrt des Hofs Gefieder,
Umpiept von junger Brut;
Uns blöken rings und brüllen
Die Herden durch die Au'n;
Uns tanzt das schlanke Füllen
Und gaffet übern Zaun.

Die Arbeit aber würzet
Dem Landmann seine Kost,
Und Mut und Freude kürzet
Die Müh' in Hitz' und Frost.

Sein Weib begrüsst ihn schmeichelnd,
Wenn er vom Felde kehrt
Und, seine Kindlein streichelnd,
Sich setzt am hellen Herd.

Die Bursch' und Mägde strotzen
Von Jugendreiz und Mark;
Ja, selbst die Greise trotzen
Dem Alter, frisch und stark.
Und heisst der Tod uns wandern,
Wir gehn, wie über Feld,
Aus einer Welt zur andern
Und schönern Gotteswelt.

Ihr armen Städter trauert
Und kränkelt in der Stadt,
Die euch wie eingemauert
In dumpfe Kerker hat.
O! wollt ihr Freude schauen,
So wandelt Hand in Hand,
Ihr Männer und ihr Frauen,
Und kommt zu uns aufs Land.

### STAND UND WÜRDE

#### *Der adelige Rat*

Mein Vater war ein Reichsbaron!
Und Ihrer war, ich meine —

#### *Der bürgerliche Rat*

So niedrig, dass, mein Herr Baron,
Ich glaube, wären Sie sein Sohn,
Sie hüteten die Schweine.

# FRIEDRICH VON SCHILLER
## 1759–1805

### POESIE [1]

Mich hält kein Band, mich fesselt keine Schranke,
Frei schwing' ich mich durch alle Räume fort,
Mein unermesslich Reich ist der Gedanke,
Und mein geflügelt Werkzeug ist das Wort.
Was sich bewegt im Himmel und auf Erden,
Was die Natur tief im Verborgnen schafft,
Muss mir entschleiert und entsiegelt werden,
Denn nichts beschränkt die freie Dichterkraft;
Doch Schön'res find' ich nichts, wie lang' ich wähle,
Als in der schönen Form — die schöne Seele.

### DAS MÄDCHEN AUS DER FREMDE

In einem Tal bei armen Hirten
Erschien mit jedem jungen Jahr,
Sobald die ersten Lerchen schwirrten,
Ein Mädchen schön und wunderbar.

Sie war nicht in dem Tal geboren,
Man wusste nicht, woher sie kam,
Und schnell war ihre Spur verloren,
Sobald das Mädchen Abschied nahm.

Beseligend war ihre Nähe,
Und alle Herzen wurden weit;
Doch eine Würde, eine Höhe
Entfernte die Vertraulichkeit.

Sie brachte Blumen mit und Früchte,
Gereift auf einer andern Flur,
In einem andern Sonnenlichte,
In einer glücklichern Natur.

[1] Spoken by *Poesie* in *Die Huldigung der Künste*.

Und teilte jedem eine Gabe,
Dem Früchte, jenem Blumen aus;
Der Jüngling und der Greis am Stabe,
Ein jeder ging beschenkt nach Haus.

Willkommen waren alle Gäste;
Doch nahte sich ein liebend Paar,
Dem reichte sie der Gaben beste,
Der Blumen allerschönste dar.


### DIE DEUTSCHE MUSE

KEIN Augustisch Alter blühte,
Keines Medicäers Güte
Lächelte der deutschen Kunst;
Sie ward nicht gepflegt vom Ruhme,
Sie entfaltete die Blume
Nicht am Strahl der Fürstengunst.

Von dem grössten deutschen Sohne,
Von des grossen Friedrichs Throne
Ging sie schutzlos, ungeehrt.
Rühmend darf's der Deutsche sagen,
Höher darf das Herz ihm schlagen:
Selbst erschuf er sich den Wert.

Darum steigt in höherm Bogen,
Darum strömt in vollern Wogen
Deutscher Barden Hochgesang;
Und in eigner Fülle schwellend
Und aus Herzens Tiefen quellend,
Spottet er der Regeln Zwang.

### DIE GÖTTER GRIECHENLANDS

Da ihr noch die schöne Welt regieret,
An der Freude leichtem Gängelband,
Selige Geschlechter noch geführet,
Schöne Wesen aus dem Fabelland!
Ach, da euer Wonnedienst noch glänzte,
Wie ganz anders, anders war es da!
Da man deine Tempel noch bekränzte,
Venus Amathusia!

Da der Dichtung zauberische Hülle
Sich noch lieblich um die Wahrheit wand —
Durch die Schöpfung floss da Lebensfülle,
Und was nie empfinden wird, empfand.
An der Liebe Busen sie zu drücken,
Gab man höhern Adel der Natur,
Alles wies den eingeweihten Blicken,
Alles eines Gottes Spur.

Wo jetzt nur, wie unsre Weisen sagen,
Seelenlos ein Feuerball sich dreht,
Lenkte damals seinen goldnen Wagen
Helios in stiller Majestät.
Diese Höhen füllten Oreaden,
Eine Dryas lebt' in jenem Baum,
Aus den Urnen lieblicher Najaden
Sprang der Ströme Silberschaum.

Jener Lorbeer wand sich einst um Hilfe,
Tantals Tochter schweigt in diesem Stein,
Syrinx' Klage tönt aus jenem Schilfe,
Philomelas Schmerz aus diesem Hain;
Jener Bach empfing Demeters Zähre,
Die sie um Persephonen geweint,
Und von diesem Hügel rief Zythere,
Ach, umsonst! dem schönen Freund.

Zu Deukalions Geschlechte stiegen
Damals noch die Himmlischen herab;
Pyrrhas schöne Töchter zu besiegen,
Nahm der Leto Sohn den Hirtenstab.
Zwischen Menschen, Göttern und Heroen
Knüpfte Amor einen schönen Bund,
Sterbliche mit Göttern und Heroen
Huldigten in Amathunt.

Finstrer Ernst und trauriges Entsagen
War aus eurem heitern Dienst verbannt;
Glücklich sollten alle Herzen schlagen,
Denn euch war der Glückliche verwandt.
Damals war nichts heilig als das Schöne,
Keiner Freude schämte sich der Gott,
Wo die keusch errötende Kamöne,
Wo die Grazie gebot.

Eure Tempel lachten gleich Palästen,
Euch verherrlichte das Heldenspiel
An des Isthmus kronenreichen Festen,
Und die Wagen donnerten zum Ziel.
Schön geschlung'ne, seelenvolle Tänze
Kreisten um den prangenden Altar,
Eure Schläfe schmückten Siegeskränze,
Kronen euer duftend Haar.

Das Evoe muntrer Thyrsusschwinger
Und der Panther prächtiges Gespann
Meldeten den grossen Freudebringer,
Faun und Satyr taumeln ihm voran;
Um ihn springen rasende Mänaden,
Ihre Tänze loben seinen Wein,
Und des Wirtes braune Wangen laden
Lustig zu dem Becher ein.

Damals trat kein grässliches Gerippe
Vor das Bett des Sterbenden. Ein Kuss
Nahm das letzte Leben von der Lippe,
Seine Fackel senkt' ein Genius.
Selbst des Orkus strenge Richterwage
Hielt der Enkel einer Sterblichen,
Und des Thrakers seelenvolle Klage
Rührte die Erinnyen.


Seine Freuden traf der frohe Schatten
In Elysiens Hainen wieder an,
Treue Liebe fand den treuen Gatten
Und der Wagenlenker seine Bahn;
Linus' Spiel tönt die gewohnten Lieder,
In Alcestens Arme sinkt Admet,
Seinen Freund erkennt Orestes wieder,
Seine Pfeile Philoktet.


Höh're Preise stärkten da den Ringer
Auf der Tugend arbeitvoller Bahn,
Grosser Taten herrliche Vollbringer
Klimmten zu den Seligen hinan;
Vor dem Wiederfoderer der Toten
Neigte sich der Götter stille Schar;
Durch die Fluten leuchtet dem Piloten
Vom Olymp das Zwillingspaar.


Schöne Welt, wo bist du? Kehre wieder,
Holdes Blütenalter der Natur!
Ach, nur in dem Feenland der Lieder
Lebt noch deine fabelhafte Spur.
Ausgestorben trauert das Gefilde,
Keine Gottheit zeigt sich meinem Blick,
Ach, von jenem lebenswarmen Bilde
Blieb der Schatten nur zurück.

Alle jene Blüten sind gefallen
Von des Nordes schauerlichem Wehn;
Einen zu bereichern unter allen,
Musste diese Götterwelt vergehn.
Traurig such' ich an dem Sternenbogen,
Dich, Selene, find' ich dort nicht mehr,
Durch die Wälder ruf' ich, durch die Wogen,
Ach, sie widerhallen leer!

Unbewusst der Freuden, die sie schenket,
Nie entzückt von ihrer Herrlichkeit,
Nie gewahr des Geistes, der sie lenket,
Sel'ger nie durch meine Seligkeit,
Fühllos selbst für ihres Künstlers Ehre,
Gleich dem toten Schlag der Pendeluhr,
Dient sie knechtisch dem Gesetz der Schwere,
Die entgötterte Natur.

Morgen wieder neu sich zu entbinden,
Wühlt sie heute sich ihr eignes Grab,
Und an ewig gleicher Spindel winden
Sich von selbst die Monde auf und ab.
Müssig kehrten zu dem Dichterlande
Heim die Götter, unnütz einer Welt,
Die, entwachsen ihrem Gängelbande,
Sich durch eignes Schweben hält.

Ja, sie kehrten heim, und alles Schöne,
Alles Hohe nahmen sie mit fort,
Alle Farben, alle Lebenstöne,
Und uns blieb nur das entseelte Wort.
Aus der Zeitflut weggerissen schweben
Sie gerettet auf des Pindus Höhn:
Was unsterblich im Gesang soll leben,
Muss im Leben untergehn.

### HEKTORS ABSCHIED

*Andromache*

WILL sich Hektor ewig von mir wenden,
Wo Achill mit den unnahbar'n Händen
Dem Patroklus schrecklich Opfer bringt?
Wer wird künftig deinen Kleinen lehren
Speere werfen und die Götter ehren,
Wenn der finstre Orkus dich verschlingt?


*Hektor*

Teures Weib, gebiete deinen Tränen!
Nach der Feldschlacht ist mein feurig Sehnen,
Diese Arme schützen Pergamus.
Kämpfend für den heil'gen Herd der Götter
Fall' ich, und des Vaterlandes Retter
Steig' ich nieder zu dem styg'schen Fluss.


*Andromache*

Nimmer lausch' ich deiner Waffen Schalle,
Müssig liegt dein Eisen in der Halle,
Priams grosser Heldenstamm verdirbt.
Du wirst hingehn, wo kein Tag mehr scheinet,
Der Kozytus durch die Wüsten weinet,
Deine Liebe in dem Lethe stirbt.


*Hektor*

All mein Sehnen will ich, all mein Denken
In des Lethe stillen Strom versenken,
Aber meine Liebe nicht.
Horch! der Wilde tobt schon an den Mauern,
Gürte mir das Schwert um, lass das Trauern!
Hektors Liebe stirbt im Lethe nicht.

### DIE TEILUNG DER ERDE

,, Nehmt hin die Welt! " rief Zeus von seinen Höhen
Den Menschen zu.　,, Nehmt, sie soll euer sein !
Euch schenk' ich sie zum Erb' und ew'gen Lehen —
Doch teilt euch brüderlich darein ! "

Da eilt, was Hände hat, sich einzurichten,
Es regte sich geschäftig jung und alt.
Der Ackermann griff nach des Feldes Früchten,
Der Junker birschte durch den Wald.

Der Kaufmann nimmt, was seine Speicher fassen,
Der Abt wählt sich den edeln Firnewein,
Der König sperrt die Brücken und die Strassen
Und sprach :　,, Der Zehente ist mein."

Ganz spät, nachdem die Teilung längst geschehen,
Naht der Poet, er kam aus weiter Fern' ;
Ach ! da war überall nichts mehr zu sehen,
Und alles hatte seinen Herrn.

,, Weh mir ! so soll denn ich allein von allen
Vergessen sein, ich, dein getreuster Sohn ? "
So liess er laut der Klage Ruf erschallen
Und warf sich hin vor Jovis Thron.

,, Wenn du im Land der Träume dich verweilet,"
Versetzt der Gott, ,, so hadre nicht mit mir.
Wo warst du denn, als man die Welt geteilet ? " —
,, Ich war," sprach der Poet, ,, bei dir.

Mein Auge hing an deinem Angesichte,
An deines Himmels Harmonie mein Ohr ;
Verzeih' dem Geiste, der, von deinem Lichte
Berauscht, das Irdische verlor ! "

„ Was tun ? “ spricht Zeus. „ Die Welt ist weg-
    gegeben ;
Der Herbst, die Jagd, der Markt ist nicht mehr mein.
Willst du im Himmel mit mir leben :
So oft du kommst, er soll dir offen sein.“

### HOFFNUNG

Es reden und träumen die Menschen viel
Von bessern künftigen Tagen,
Nach einem glücklichen, goldenen Ziel
Sieht man sie rennen und jagen.
Die Welt wird alt und wird wieder jung,
Doch der Mensch hofft immer Verbesserung.

Die Hoffnung führt ihn ins Leben ein,
Sie umflattert den fröhlichen Knaben,
Den Jüngling begeistert ihr Zauberschein,
Sie wird mit dem Greis nicht begraben ;
Denn beschliesst er im Grabe den müden Lauf,
Noch am Grabe pflanzt er — die Hoffnung auf.

Es ist kein leerer schmeichelnder Wahn,
Erzeugt im Gehirne des Toren,
Im Herzen kündet es laut sich an :
Zu was Besserm sind wir geboren.
Und was die innere Stimme spricht,
Das täuscht die hoffende Seele nicht.

### SEHNSUCHT

Ach, aus dieses Tales Gründen,
Die der kalte Nebel drückt,
Könnt’ ich doch den Ausgang finden,
Ach, wie fühlt’ ich mich beglückt !

Dort erblick' ich schöne Hügel,
Ewig jung und ewig grün!
Hätt' ich Schwingen, hätt' ich Flügel,
Nach den Hügeln zög' ich hin.

Harmonien hör' ich klingen,
Töne süsser Himmelsruh,
Und die leichten Winde bringen
Mir der Düfte Balsam zu.
Goldne Früchte seh' ich glühen,
Winkend zwischen dunkelm Laub,
Und die Blumen, die dort blühen,
Werden keines Winters Raub.

Ach, wie schön muss sich's ergehen
Dort im ew'gen Sonnenschein,
Und die Luft auf jenen Höhen,
O wie labend muss sie sein!
Doch mir wehrt des Stromes Toben,
Der ergrimmt dazwischen braust,
Seine Wellen sind gehoben,
Dass die Seele mir ergraust.

Einen Nachen seh' ich schwanken,
Aber ach! der Fährmann fehlt!
Frisch hinein und ohne Wanken!
Seine Segel sind beseelt.
Du musst glauben, du musst wagen,
Denn die Götter leihn kein Pfand;
Nur ein Wunder kann dich tragen
In das schöne Wunderland.

### MACHT DES WEIBES

MÄCHTIG seid ihr, ihr seid's durch der Gegenwart
    ruhigen Zauber;
  Was die Stille nicht wirkt, wirket die Rauschende
    nie.

Kraft erwart' ich vom Mann, des Gesetzes Würde
    behaupt' er,
    Aber durch Anmut allein herrschet und herrsche
      das Weib.
Manche zwar haben geherrscht durch des Geistes
    Macht und der Taten,
    Aber dann haben sie dich, höchste der Kronen,
      entbehrt.
Wahre Königin ist nur des Weibes weibliche Schönheit :
    Wo sie sich zeige, sie herrscht, herrschet doch,
      weil sie sich zeigt.

### AN DIE FREUDE

FREUDE, schöner Götterfunken,
Tochter aus Elysium,
Wir betreten feuertrunken,
Himmlische, dein Eigentum.
Deine Zauber binden wieder,
Was die Mode streng geteilt :
Alle Menschen werden Brüder,
Wo dein sanfter Flügel weilt.
    Seid umschlungen, Millionen !
    Diesen Kuss der ganzen Welt !
    Brüder — überm Sternenzelt
    Muss ein lieber Vater wohnen.

Wem der grosse Wurf gelungen,
Eines Freundes Freund zu sein,
Wer ein holdes Weib errungen,
Mische seinen Jubel ein !
Ja, wer auch nur eine Seele
Sein nennt auf dem Erdenrund !
Und wer's nie gekonnt, der stehle
Weinend sich aus diesem Bund !

Was den grossen Ring bewohnet,
Huldige der Sympathie!
Zu den Sternen leitet sie,
Wo der Unbekannte thronet.

Freude trinken alle Wesen
An den Brüsten der Natur,
Alle Guten, alle Bösen
Folgen ihrer Rosenspur.
Küsse gab sie uns und Reben,
Einen Freund, geprüft im Tod;
Wollust ward dem Wurm gegeben,
Und der Cherub steht vor Gott.
  Ihr stürzt nieder, Millionen?
  Ahnest du den Schöpfer, Welt?
  Such' ihn überm Sternenzelt!
  Über Sternen muss er wohnen.

Freude heisst die starke Feder
In der ewigen Natur.
Freude, Freude treibt die Räder
In der grossen Weltenuhr.
Blumen lockt sie aus den Keimen,
Sonnen aus dem Firmament,
Sphären rollt sie in den Räumen,
Die des Sehers Rohr nicht kennt.
  Froh, wie seine Sonnen fliegen
  Durch des Himmels prächt'gen Plan,
  Wandelt, Brüder, ihre Bahn,
  Freudig, wie ein Held zum Siegen!

Aus der Wahrheit Feuerspiegel
Lächelt sie den Forscher an.
Zu der Tugend steilem Hügel
Leitet sie des Dulders Bahn.
Auf des Glaubens Sonnenberge
Sieht man ihre Fahnen wehn,

Durch den Riss gesprengter Särge
Sie im Chor der Engel stehn.
  Duldet mutig, Millionen!
  Duldet für die bess're Welt!
  Drüben überm Sternenzelt
  Wird ein grosser Gott belohnen.

Göttern kann man nicht vergelten,
Schön ist's, ihnen gleich zu sein.
Gram und Armut soll sich melden,
Mit den Frohen sich erfreun.
Groll und Rache sei vergessen,
Unserm Todfeind sei verziehn,
Keine Träne soll ihn pressen,
Keine Reue nage ihn.
  Unser Schuldbuch sei vernichtet!
  Ausgesöhnt die ganze Welt!
  Brüder — überm Sternenzelt
  Richtet Gott, wie wir gerichtet.

Freude sprudelt in Pokalen,
In der Traube goldnem Blut
Trinken Sanftmut Kannibalen,
Die Verzweiflung Heldenmut.
Brüder, fliegt von euren Sitzen,
Wenn der volle Römer kreist,
Lasst den Schaum zum Himmel spritzen:
Dieses Glas dem guten Geist!
  Den der Sterne Wirbel loben,
  Den des Seraphs Hymne preist,
  Dieses Glas dem guten Geist
  Überm Sternenzelt dort oben!

Festen Mut in schwerem Leiden,
Hilfe, wo die Unschuld weint,
Ewigkeit geschwor'nen Eiden,
Wahrheit gegen Freund und Feind,

Männerstolz vor Königsthronen, —
Brüder, gält' es Gut und Blut!
Dem Verdienste seine Kronen,
Untergang der Lügenbrut!
  Schliesst den heil'gen Zirkel dichter,
  Schwört bei diesem goldnen Wein,
  Dem Gelübde treu zu sein,
  Schwört es bei dem Sternenrichter!


### BREITE UND TIEFE

Es glänzen viele in der Welt,
Sie wissen von allem zu sagen,
Und wo was reizet und wo was gefällt,
Man kann es bei ihnen erfragen;
Man dächte, hört man sie reden laut,
Sie hätten wirklich erobert die Braut.

Doch gehn sie aus der Welt ganz still,
Ihr Leben war verloren.
Wer etwas Treffliches leisten will,
Hätt' gern was Grosses geboren,
Der sammle still und unerschlafft
Im kleinsten Punkte die höchste Kraft.

Der Stamm erhebt sich in die Luft
Mit üppig prangenden Zweigen,
Die Blätter glänzen und hauchen Duft,
Doch können sie Früchte nicht zeugen;
Der Kern allein im schmalen Raum
Verbirgt den Stolz des Waldes, den Baum.


### NÄNIE

AUCH das Schöne muss sterben!  Das Menschen und
    Götter bezwinget,
  Nicht die eherne Brust rührt es des stygischen Zeus.

Einmal nur erweichte die Liebe den Schattenbeherr-
    scher,
    Und an der Schwelle noch, streng, rief er zurück
    sein Geschenk.
Nicht stillt Aphrodite dem schönen Knaben die Wunde,
    Die in den zierlichen Leib grausam der Eber geritzt.
Nicht errettet den göttlichen Held die unsterbliche
    Mutter,
    Wann er, am skäischen Tor fallend, sein Schicksal
    erfüllt.
Aber sie steigt aus dem Meer mit allen Töchtern des
    Nereus,
    Und die Klage hebt an um den verherrlichten Sohn.
Siehe, da weinen die Götter, es weinen die Göttinnen
    alle,
    Dass das Schöne vergeht, dass das Vollkommene
    stirbt.
Auch ein Klaglied zu sein im Mund der Geliebten ist
    herrlich,
    Denn das Gemeine geht klanglos zum Orkus hinab.


AUS „ WILHELM TELL "

### 1. *Lied des Fischerknaben*

Es lächelt zum See, er ladet zum Bade,
Der Knabe schlief ein am grünen Gestade,
Da hört er ein Klingen
Wie Flöten so süss,
Wie Stimmen der Engel
Im Paradies.

Und wie er erwachet in seliger Lust,
Da spülen die Wasser ihm um die Brust,
Und es ruft aus den Tiefen :
„ Lieb Knabe, bist mein !
Ich locke den Schläfer,
Ich zieh' ihn herein."

## 2.   *Lied des Hirten*

IHR Matten, lebt wohl,
Ihr sonnigen Weiden!
Der Senne muss scheiden,
Der Sommer ist hin.

Wir fahren zu Berg, wir kommen wieder,
Wenn der Kuckuck ruft, wenn erwachen die Lieder,
Wenn mit Blumen die Erde sich kleidet neu,
Wenn die Brünnlein fliessen im lieblichen Mai.

Ihr Matten, lebt wohl,
Ihr sonnigen Weiden!
Der Senne muss scheiden,
Der Sommer ist hin.

## 3.   *Lied des Alpenjägers*

Es donnern die Höhen, es zittert der Steg,
Nicht grauet dem Schützen auf schwindlichtem Weg,
Er schreitet verwegen
Auf Feldern von Eis,
Da pranget kein Frühling,
Da grünet kein Reis.

Und unter den Füssen ein neblichtes Meer,
Erkennt er die Städte der Menschen nicht mehr,
Durch den Riss nur der Wolken
Erblickt er die Welt,
Tief unter den Wassern
Das grünende Feld.

## 4.   *Jägerliedchen*

MIT dem Pfeil, dem Bogen
Durch Gebirg und Tal

Kommt der Schütz' gezogen
Früh im Morgenstrahl.

Wie im Reich der Lüfte
König ist der Weih,
Durch Gebirg und Klüfte
Herrscht der Schütze frei.

Ihm gehört das Weite,
Was sein Pfeil erreicht,
Das ist seine Beute,
Was da fleugt und kreucht.

### DER ALPENJÄGER

„ WILLST du nicht das Lämmlein hüten ?
Lämmlein ist so fromm und sanft,
Nährt sich von des Grases Blüten,
Spielend an des Baches Ranft." —
„ Mutter, Mutter, lass mich gehen
Jagen nach des Berges Höhen ! " —

„ Willst du nicht die Herde locken
Mit des Hornes munterm Klang ?
Lieblich tönt der Ton der Glocken
In des Waldes Lustgesang." —
„ Mutter, Mutter, lass mich gehen,
Schweifen auf den wilden Höhen ! "

„ Willst du nicht der Blümlein warten,
Die im Beete freundlich stehn ?
Draussen ladet dich dein Garten ;
Wild ist's auf den wilden Höh'n ! " —
„ Lass die Blümlein, lass sie blühen !
Mutter, Mutter, lass mich ziehen ! "

Und der Knabe ging zu jagen,
Und es treibt und reisst ihn fort,
Rastlos fort mit blindem Wagen
An des Berges finstern Ort;
Vor ihm her mit Windesschnelle
Flieht die zitternde Gazelle.


Auf der Felsen nackte Rippen
Klettert sie mit leichtem Schwung,
Durch den Riss geborstner Klippen
Trägt sie der gewagte Sprung;
Aber hinter ihr verwogen
Folgt er mit dem Todesbogen.


Jetzo auf den schroffen Zinken
Hängt sie, auf dem höchsten Grat,
Wo die Felsen jäh versinken
Und verschwunden ist der Pfad,
Unter sich die steile Höhe,
Hinter sich des Feindes Nähe.


Mit des Jammers stummen Blicken
Fleht sie zu dem harten Mann,
Fleht umsonst, denn loszudrücken
Legt er schon den Bogen an.
Plötzlich aus der Felsenspalte
Tritt der Geist, der Bergesalte.


Und mit seinen Götterhänden
Schützt er das gequälte Tier.
,, Musst du Tod und Jammer senden ",
Ruft er, ,, bis herauf zu mir?
Raum für alle hat die Erde,
Was verfolgst du meine Herde? "

### DER HANDSCHUH

Vor seinem Löwengarten,
Das Kampfspiel zu erwarten,
Sass König Franz,
Und um ihn die Grossen der Krone
Und rings auf hohem Balkone
Die Damen in schönem Kranz.


Und wie er winkt mit dem Finger,
Auf tut sich der weite Zwinger,
Und hinein mit bedächtigem Schritt
Ein Löwe tritt;
Und sieht sich stumm
Rings um
Mit langem Gähnen
Und schüttelt die Mähnen
Und streckt die Glieder
Und legt sich nieder.


Und der König winkt wieder —
Da öffnet sich behend'
Ein zweites Tor,
Daraus rennt
Mit wildem Sprunge
Ein Tiger hervor.
Wie der den Löwen erschaut,
Brüllt er laut,
Schlägt mit dem Schweif
Einen furchtbaren Reif
Und recket die Zunge,
Und im Kreise scheu
Umgeht er den Leu,
Grimmig schnurrend;
Drauf streckt er sich murrend
Zur Seite nieder.

Und der König winkt wieder —
Da speit das doppelt geöffnete Haus
Zwei Leoparden auf einmal aus.
Die stürzen mit mutiger Kampfbegier
Auf das Tigertier ;
Das packt sie mit seinen grimmigen Tatzen,
Und der Leu mit Gebrüll
Richtet sich auf — da wird's still,
Und herum im Kreis,
Von Mordsucht heiss,
Lagern die greulichen Katzen.


Da fällt von des Altans Rand
Ein Handschuh von schöner Hand
Zwischen den Tiger und den Leun
Mitten hinein.


Und zu Ritter Delorges, spottender Weis',
Wendet sich Fräulein Kunigund' ;
„ Herr Ritter, ist Eure Lieb' so heiss,
Wie Ihr mir's schwört zu jeder Stund',
Ei, so hebt mir den Handschuh auf! "


Und der Ritter in schnellem Lauf
Steigt hinab in den furchtbaren Zwinger
Mit festem Schritte,
Und aus der Ungeheuer Mitte
Nimmt er den Handschuh mit keckem Finger.


Und mit Erstaunen und mit Grauen
Sehen's die Ritter und Edelfrauen,
Und gelassen bringt er den Handschuh zurück.
Da schallt ihm sein Lob aus jedem Munde,
Aber mit zärtlichem Liebesblick —

Er verheisst ihm sein nahes Glück —
Empfängt ihn Fräulein Kunigunde.
Und er wirft ihr den Handschuh ins Gesicht:
,, Den Dank, Dame, begehr' ich nicht ! ''
Und verlässt sie zur selben Stunde.

### NADOWESSIERS TOTENLIED

SEHT, da sitzt er auf der Matte,
    Aufrecht sitzt er da,
Mit dem Anstand, den er hatte,
    Als er's Licht noch sah.

Doch wo ist die Kraft der Fäuste,
    Wo des Atems Hauch,
Der noch jüngst zum grossen Geiste
    Blies der Pfeife Rauch ?

Wo die Augen, falkenhelle,
    Die des Renntiers Spur
Zählten auf des Grases Welle,
    Auf dem Tau der Flur ?

Diese Schenkel, die behender
    Flohen durch den Schnee,
Als der Hirsch, der Zwanzigender,
    Als des Berges Reh ?

Diese Arme, die den Bogen
    Spannten streng und straff ?
Seht, das Leben ist entflogen !
    Seht, sie hängen schlaff !

Wohl ihm, er ist hingegangen,
    Wo kein Schnee mehr ist,
Wo mit Mais die Felder prangen,
    Der von selber spriesst,

Wo mit Vögeln alle Sträuche,
   Wo der Wald mit Wild,
Wo mit Fischen alle Teiche
   Lustig sind gefüllt.

Mit den Geistern speist er droben,
   Liess uns hier allein,
Dass wir seine Taten loben
   Und ihn scharren ein.

Bringet her die letzten Gaben,
   Stimmt die Totenklag'!
Alles sei mit ihm begraben,
   Was ihn freuen mag.

Legt ihm unterm Haupt die Beile,
   Die er tapfer schwang,
Auch des Bären fette Keule,
   Denn der Weg ist lang;

Auch das Messer scharf geschliffen,
   Das vom Feindeskopf
Rasch mit drei geschickten Griffen
   Schälte Haut und Schopf;

Farben auch, den Leib zu malen,
   Steckt ihm in die Hand,
Das er rötlich möge strahlen
   In der Seelen Land.

### SPRUCH DES KONFUZIUS

DREIFACH ist des Raumes Mass,
Rastlos fort ohn' Unterlass
Strebt die Länge fort ins Weite,
 Endlos giesset sich die Breite,
 Grundlos senkt die Tiefe sich.

Dir ein Bild sind sie gegeben :
Rastlos vorwärts musst du streben,
Nie ermüdet stille stehn,
Willst du die Vollendung sehn ;
Musst ins Breite dich entfalten,
Soll sich dir die Welt gestalten ;
In die Tiefe musst du steigen,
Soll sich dir das Wesen zeigen.


Nur Beharrung führt zum Ziel,
Nur die Fülle führt zur Klarheit,
Und im Abgrund wohnt die Wahrheit.


## KOLUMBUS

Steure, mutiger Segler ! Es mag der Witz dich verhöhnen,
  Und der Schiffer am Steu'r senken die lässige Hand.
Immer, immer nach West ! Dort muss die Küste sich zeigen,
  Liegt sie doch deutlich und liegt schimmernd vor deinem Verstand.
Traue dem leitenden Gott und folge dem schweigenden Weltmeer !
  Wär' sie noch nicht, sie stieg' jetzt aus den Fluten empor.
Mit dem Genius steht die Natur in ewigem Bunde :
  Was der eine verspricht, leistet die andre gewiss.


## UNTERSCHIED DER STÄNDE

Adel ist auch in der sittlichen Welt. Gemeine Naturen
  Zahlen mit dem, was sie tun, edle mit dem, was sie sind.

### PFLICHT FÜR JEDEN

IMMER strebe zum Ganzen, und kannst du selber kei
   Ganzes
    Werden, als dienendes Glied schliess' an ein Ganze
    dich an !

### WEISHEIT UND KLUGHEIT

WILLST du, Freund, die erhabensten Höh'n der Weishei
   erfliegen,
    Wag' es auf die Gefahr, dass dich die Klughei
    verlacht.
Die Kurzsichtige sieht nur das Ufer, das dir zurück
   flieht,
    Jenes nicht, wo dereinst landet dein mutiger Flug

### DER MEISTER

JEDEN anderen Meister erkennt man an dem, was e
   ausspricht ;
    Was er weise verschweigt, zeigt mir den Meiste
    des Stils.

### DAS NATURGESETZ

So war's immer, mein Freund, und so wird's bleiben
   die Ohnmacht
    Hat die Regel für sich, aber die Kraft den Erfolg

### TONKUNST

LEBEN atme die bildende Kunst, Geist fodr' ich von
   Dichter ;
    Aber die Seele spricht nur Polyhymnia aus.

## WISSENSCHAFT

Einem ist sie die hohe, die himmlische Göttin, dem
    andern
Eine tüchtige Kuh, die ihn mit Butter versorgt.

# FRIEDRICH VON MATTHISSON
## 1760–1831

### ADELAIDE

Einsam wandelt dein Freund im Frühlingsgarten,
Mild vom lieblichen Zauberlicht umflossen,
Das durch wankende Blütenzweige zittert,
    Adelaide !

In der spiegelnden Flut, im Schnee der Alpen,
In des sinkenden Tages Goldgewölken,
Im Gefilde der Sterne strahlt dein Bildnis,
    Adelaide !

Abendlüftchen im zarten Laube flüstern,
Silberglöckchen des Mais im Grase säuseln,
Wellen rauschen und Nachtigallen flöten :
    Adelaide!

Einst, o Wunder ! entblüht, auf meinem Grabe,
Eine Blume der Asche meines Herzens ;
Deutlich schimmert auf jedem Purpurblättchen :
    Adelaide !

### ABENDLANDSCHAFT

    Goldner Schein
    Deckt den Hain.
Mild beleuchtet Zauberschimmer
Der umbüschten Waldburg Trümmer.

Still und hehr
Strahlt das Meer ;
Heimwärts gleiten, sanft wie Schwäne,
Fern am Eiland Fischerkähne.


Silbersand
Blinkt am Strand ;
Röter schweben hier, dort blässer,
Wolkenbilder in Gewässer.


Rauschend kränzt,
Goldbeglänzt,
Wankend Ried des Vorlands Hügel,
Wild umschwärmt vom Seegeflügel.


Malerisch
Im Gebüsch
Winkt, mit Gärtchen, Laub' und Quelle,
Die bemooste Klausnerzelle.


Pappeln wehn
Auf den Höh'n ;
Eichen glühn, zum Schattendome
Dicht verschränkt, am Felsenstrome.


Nebelgrau
Weht im Tau
Elfenreigen, dort wo Rüstern
Am Druidenaltar flüstern.


Auf der Flut
Stirbt die Glut ;
Schon verblasst der Abendschimmer
An der hohen Waldburg Trümmer.

Vollmondschein
Deckt den Hain;
Geisterlispel wehn im Tale
Um versunkne Heldenmale.


### BERUHIGUNG

Wo durch dunkle Buchengänge
Blasser Vollmondsschimmer blickt,
Wo um schroffe Felsenhänge
Sich die Efeuranke strickt;
Wo aus halbverfallnem Turme
Ein verlassnes Bäumchen ragt
Und, emporgescheucht vom Sturme,
Schauervoll die Eule klagt;

Wo um sterbende Gesträuche
Sich der graue Nebel dehnt,
Wo im trüben Erlenteiche
Dürres Rohr im Winde tönt;
Wo in wild verwachsnen Gründen
Dumpf der Bergstrom wiederhallt,
Und, ein Spiel von Abendwinden,
Welkes Laub auf Gräber wallt;

Wo, im bleichen Sternenscheine,
Um den früh verlornen Freund
Einsam im Zypressenhaine
Hoffnungslose Sehnsucht weint;
Da, da wandelt, von den Spielen
Angestaunter Torheit fern,
Unter ahnenden Gefühlen,
Schwermut, dein Vertrauter gern!

Da erfüllt ein stilles Sehnen
Nach des Grabes Ruh sein Herz!
Da ergiesst in milden Tränen
Sich der Seele banger Schmerz!

Und sein Blick durchschaut die trübe
Zukunft ruhig bis ans Grab,
Und es ruft; ,, Gott ist die Liebe!"
Jeder Stern auf ihn herab.

# JOHANN GAUDENZ FREIHERR
## VON SALIS-SEEWIS
### 1762–1834

#### ABENDBILDER

WENN der Abend
    Kühl und labend
Sich auf Tal und Waldung senkt;
Wenn die Wolken röter werden,
Und der Hirt des Dorfes Herden
Am beschilften Teiche tränkt;

Wenn der Hase
    Leis' im Grase
Nascht, und im betauten Kraut;
Wenn der Hirsch aus dem Gehege
Wandelt, und das Reh am Wege
Steht und traulich um sich schaut;

Wenn mit Blüten
    Auf den Hüten
Sens' und Rechen auf dem Arm,
Unter stetem Festgeleier
Heimwärts kehrt der Zug der Heuer
Und der Schnitterinnen Schwarm:

Wonneträumend
    Staun' ich, säumend,
Dann vom Damm die Gegend an;
Freu' so herrlich mich der hehren

Schönen Erd', und süsse Zähren
Sagen, was kein Ausdruck kann.

    Froh und bange
    Lausch' ich lange
Auf der Amsel Abendlied :
Wie, umhüllt von Erlenblättern,
Nachtigallen ziehend schmettern,
Und der Kiebitz lockt im Ried ;

    Bis nur Grillen
    Noch im stillen
Zirpen, und der Käfer streift,
Und der Landmann, wenn's noch
    dämmert,
Seine Sens' im Hofe hämmert,
Und ein Mäherliedchen pfeift ;

    Bis der Liebe
    Stern so trübe
In der Abendröte schwimmt ;
Dann der perlenfarbne Himmel
Dunkelt, und das Glanzgewimmel
Der Gestirne sacht entglimmt.


### HERBSTLIED

Bunt sind schon die Wälder,
Gelb die Stoppelfelder,
Und der Herbst beginnt.
Rote Blätter fallen,
Graue Nebel wallen,
Kühler weht der Wind.

Wie die volle Traube
Aus dem Rebenlaube
Purpurfarbig strahlt !

Am Geländer reifen
Pfirsiche, mit Streifen
Rot und weiss bemalt.

Sieh, wie hier die Dirne
Emsig Pflaum' und Birne
In ihr Körbchen legt !
Dort mit leichten Schritten
Jene goldne Quitten
In den Landhof trägt !

Flinke Träger springen,
Und die Mädchen singen,
Alles jubelt froh !
Bunte Bänder schweben
Zwischen hohen Reben
Auf dem Hut von Stroh.

Geige tönt und Flöte
Bei der Abendröte
Und im Mondenglanz ;
Junge Winzerinnen
Winken und beginnen
Deutschen Ringeltanz.


### LIED

Ins stille Land !
Wer leitet uns hinüber ?
Schon wölkt sich uns der Abendhimmel trüber,
Und immer trümmervoller wird der Strand.
Wer leitet uns mit sanfter Hand
Hinüber, ach ! hinüber
Ins stille Land ?

Ach Land! ach Land!
Für alle Sturmbedrohten;
Der mildeste von unsers Schicksals Boten
Winkt uns, die Fackel umgewandt,
Und leitet uns mit sanfter Hand
Ins Land der grossen Toten,
Ins stille Land!


## JEAN PAUL
### 1763–1825

#### DISTICHON

FRÜHLING ist Leben der Liebe und Liebe Frühling des
    Lebens,
    Lebst du der Liebe, so lebt ewiger Frühling in dir.


#### DER LIEBENDE

O WÄR' ich ein Stern —
Ich wollte ihr leuchten.
Wär' ich eine Rose —
Ich wollte ihr blühen.
Wär' ich ein Ton —
Ich dräng' in ihr Herz.
Wär' ich die Liebe, die glücklichste,
Ich bliebe darin.
Ja wär' ich nur der Traum —
Ich wollt' in ihren Schlummer ziehen
Und der Stern und die Rose
Und die Liebe und alles sein
Und gern verschwinden,
Wenn sie erwachte.

\*

Ich sah dich.
Und liebte dich.

Ich sah dich nicht mehr
Und liebte dich.
So muss ich dich immer lieben,
Ich mag nun frohlocken oder weinen
Tief im Herzen.


## ERNST MORITZ ARNDT
### 1769–1860

#### DIE STERNLEIN

UND die Sonne machte den weiten Ritt
Um die Welt,
Und die Sternlein sprachen : wir reisen mit
Um die Welt ;
Und die Sonne, sie schalt sie : ihr bleibt zu Haus
Denn ich brenn' euch die goldenen Äuglein aus
Bei dem feurigen Ritt um die Welt.


Und die Sternlein gingen zum lieben Mond
In der Nacht,
Und sie sprachen : du, der auf Wolken thront
In der Nacht,
Lass uns wandeln mit dir, denn dein milder Schein
Er verbrennet uns nimmer die Äugelein.
Und er nahm sie, Gesellen der Nacht.


Nun willkommen, Sternlein und lieber Mond,
In der Nacht !
Ihr versteht, was still in dem Herzen wohnt
In der Nacht.
Kommt und zündet die himmlischen Lichter an,
Dass ich lustig mitschwärmen und spielen kann
In den freundlichen Spielen der Nacht.

### VATERLANDSLIED 1813

Der Gott, der Eisen wachsen liess,
Der wollte keine Knechte;
Drum gab er Säbel, Schwert und Spiess
Dem Mann in seine Rechte,
Drum gab er ihm den kühnen Mut,
Den Zorn der freien Rede,
Dass er bestände bis aufs Blut,
Bis in den Tod die Fehde.


So wollen wir, was Gott gewollt,
Mit rechten Treuen halten
Und nimmer im Tyrannensold
Die Menschenschädel spalten.
Doch wer für Tand und Schande ficht,
Den hauen wir zu Scherben,
Der soll im deutschen Lande nicht
Mit deutschen Männern erben.


O Deutschland, heil'ges Vaterland!
O deutsche Lieb' und Treue!
Du hohes Land! du schönes Land!
Dir schwören wir aufs neue:
,, Dem Buben und dem Knecht die Acht!
Der speise Krähn und Raben! "
So ziehn wir aus zur Hermannsschlacht
Und wollen Rache haben.


Lasst brausen, was nur brausen kann,
In hellen, lichten Flammen!
Ihr Deutschen alle, Mann für Mann,
Fürs Vaterland zusammen!
Und hebt die Herzen himmelan
Und himmelan die Hände!
Und rufet alle, Mann für Mann:
,, Die Knechtschaft hat ein Ende! "

Lasst klingen, was nur klingen kann,
Die Trommeln und die Flöten!
Wir wollen heute, Mann für Mann,
Mit Blut das Eisen röten,
Mit Henkersblut, Franzosenblut —
O süsser Tag der Rache!
Das klinget allen Deutschen gut,
Das ist die gute Sache.

Lasst wehen, was nur wehen kann!
Standarten wehn und Fahnen!
Wir wollen heut uns, Mann für Mann,
Zum Heldentode mahnen;
Auf! fliege, stolzes Siegspanier,
Voran dem kühnen Reihen!
Wir siegen oder sterben hier
Den süssen Tod der Freien.


### DES DEUTSCHEN VATERLAND

Was ist des Deutschen Vaterland?
Ist's Preussenland? ist's Schwabenland?
Ist's, wo am Rhein die Rebe blüht?
Ist's, wo am Belt die Möwe zieht?
O nein, nein, nein!
Sein Vaterland muss grösser sein!

Was ist des Deutschen Vaterland?
Ist's Bàyerland? ist's Steierland?
Ist's, wo des Marsen Rind sich streckt?
Ist's, wo der Märker Eisen reckt?
O nein, nein, nein!
Sein Vaterland muss grösser sein!

Was ist des Deutschen Vaterland?
Ist's Pommerland? Westfalenland?
Ist's, wo der Sand der Dünen weht?

Ist's, wo die Donau brausend geht?
O nein, nein, nein!
Sein Vaterland muss grösser sein!

Was ist des Deutschen Vaterland?
So nenne mir das grosse Land!
Ist's Land der Schweizer? ist's Tirol?
Das Land und Volk gefiel mir wohl:
O nein, nein, nein!
Sein Vaterland muss grösser sein!

Was ist des Deutschen Vaterland?
So nenne mir das grosse Land!
Gewiss, es ist das Österreich,
An Ehren und an Siegen reich?
O nein, nein, nein!
Sein Vaterland muss grösser sein!

Was ist des Deutschen Vaterland?
So nenne endlich mir das Land!
So weit die deutsche Zunge klingt
Und Gott im Himmel Lieder singt,
Das soll es sein! das soll es sein!
Das, wackrer Deutscher, nenne dein!

Das ist des Deutschen Vaterland,
Wo Eide schwört ein Druck der Hand,
Wo Treue hell vom Auge blitzt,
Und Liebe warm im Herzen sitzt —
Das soll es sein! das soll es sein!
Das, wackrer Deutscher, nenne dein!

Das ganze Deutschland soll es sein!
O Gott vom Himmel, sieh darein,
Und gib uns rechten deutschen Mut,
Dass wir es lieben treu und gut!
Das soll es sein!
Das ganze Deutschland soll es sein!

## FRIEDRICH HÖLDERLIN
### 1770–1843

#### AN DIE PARZEN

NUR einen Sommer gönnt, ihr Gewaltigen,
Und einen Herbst zu reifem Gesange mir,
    Dass williger mein Herz, vom süssen
        Spiele gesättiget, dann mir sterbe !

Die Seele, der im Leben ihr göttlich Recht
Nicht ward, sie ruht auch drunten im Orkus nicht ;
    Doch ist mir einst das Heil'ge, das am
        Herzen mir liegt, das Gedicht gelungen :

Willkommen dann, o Stille der Schattenwelt !
Zufrieden bin ich, wenn auch mein Saitenspiel
    Mich nicht hinabgeleitet ; einmal
        Lebt' ich wie Götter, und mehr bedarf's nicht.

#### SOKRATES UND ALKIBIADES

,, WARUM huldigest du, heiliger Sokrates,
Diesem Jünglinge stets ? kennest du Grössers nicht ?
    Warum siehet mit Liebe,
        Wie auf Götter, dein Aug' auf ihn ? "

Wer das Tiefste gedacht, liebt das Lebendigste,
Hohe Tugend versteht, wer in die Welt geblickt,
    Und es neigen die Weisen
        Oft am Ende zu Schönem sich.

#### MENSCHENBEIFALL

IST nicht heilig mein Herz, schöneren Lebens voll,
Seit ich liebe ?  Warum achtetet ihr mich mehr,
    Da ich stolzer und wilder,
        Wortreicher und leerer war ?

Ach ! der Menge gefällt, was auf den Marktplatz taugt,
Und es ehret der Knecht nur den Gewaltsamen ;
    An das Göttliche glauben
      Die allein, die es selber sind.


## AN DIE HOFFNUNG

O Hoffnung ! holde ! gütiggeschäftige !
Die du das Haus der Trauernden nicht verschmähst,
    Und gerne dienend, Edle ! zwischen
      Sterblichen waltest und Himmelsmächten,

Wo bist du ? Wenig lebt' ich. Doch atmet kalt
Mein Abend schon. Und stille, den Schatten gleich,
    Bin ich schon hier ; und schon gesanglos
      Schlummert das schauernde Herz im Busen.

Im grünen Tale, dort, wo der frische Quell
Vom Berge täglich rauscht und die liebliche
    Zeitlose mir am Herbsttag aufblüht,
      Dort, in der Stille, du Holde ! will ich

Dich suchen, oder wenn in der Mitternacht
Das unsichtbare Leben im Haine wallt,
    Und über mir die immerfrohen
      Blumen, die sicheren Sterne, glänzen,

O du, des Äthers Tochter, erscheine dann
Aus deines Vaters Gärten, und darfst du nicht
    Mir sterblich Glück verheissen, schreck', o
      Schrecke mit anderem nur das Herz mir !


## DIE HEIMAT

Froh kehrt der Schiffer heim an den stillen Strom,
Von Inseln fernher, wenn er geerntet hat ;
    So käm' auch ich zur Heimat, hätt' ich
      Güter so viele wie Leid geerntet.

Ihr teuern Ufer, die mich erzogen einst,
Stillt ihr der Liebe Leiden, versprecht ihr mir,
   Ihr Wälder meiner Jugend, wenn ich
      Komme, die Ruhe noch einmal wieder?

Am kühlen Bache, wo ich der Wellen Spiel,
Am Strome, wo ich gleiten die Schiffe sah,
   Dort bin ich bald; euch, traute Berge,
      Die mich behüteten einst, der Heimat

Verehrte sichre Grenzen, der Mutter Haus
Und liebender Geschwister Umarmungen
   Begrüss' ich bald; und ihr umschliesst mich,
      Dass, wie in Banden, das Herz mir heile,

Ihr treu geblieb'nen! Aber ich weiss, ich weiss,
Der Liebe Leid, dies heilet so bald mir nicht,
   Dies singt kein Wiegengesang, den tröstend
      Sterbliche singen, mir aus dem Busen.

Denn sie, die uns das himmlische Feuer leihn,
Die Götter, schenken heiliges Leid uns auch.
   Drum bleibe dies. Ein Sohn der Erde
      Schein' ich, zu lieben gemacht, zu leiden.


### DES MORGENS

Vom Taue glänzt der Rasen; beweglicher
Eilt schon die wache Quelle; die Birke neigt
   Ihr schwankes Haupt, und im Geblätter
      Rauscht es und schimmert; und um die grauen

Gewölke streifen rötliche Flammen dort,
Verkündende, sie wallen geräuschlos auf;
   Wie Fluten am Gestade wogen
      Höher und höher die wandelbaren.

Komm nun, o komm, und eile mir nicht zu schnell,
Du goldner Tag, zum Gipfel des Himmels fort!
  Denn offner fliegt, vertrauter dir mein
    Auge, du Freudiger! zu, solang du

In deiner Schöne jugendlich blickst, und noch
Zu herrlich nicht, zu stolz mir geworden bist;
  Du möchtest immer eilen, könnt' ich,
    Göttlicher Wandrer, mit dir! Doch lächelst

Des frohen Übermütigen du, dass er
Dir gleichen möchte; segne mir lieber denn
  Mein sterblich Tun und heitre wieder,
    Gütiger! heute den stillen Pfad mir!

## AM ABEND

GEH unter, schöne Sonne, sie achteten
Nur wenig dein, sie kannten dich, Heilige, nicht,
  Denn mühelos und stille bist du
    Über den Mühsamen aufgegangen.

Mir gehst du freundlich unter und auf, o Licht
Und wohl erkennt mein Auge dich, herrliches!
  Denn göttlich stille ehren lernt' ich,
    Da Diotima den Sinn mir heilte.

O du, des Himmels Botin! wie lauscht' ich dir!
Dir, Diotima! Liebe! wie sah von dir
  Zum goldnen Tage dieses Auge
    Staunend und dankend empor. Da rauschten

Lebendiger die Quellen, es atmeten
Der dunkeln Erde Blüten mich liebend an,
  Und lächelnd über Silberwolken
    Neigte sich segnend herab der Äther.

## ABENDPHANTASIE

Vor seiner Hütte ruhig im Schatten sitzt
Der Pflüger ; dem Genügsamen raucht sein Herd.
   Gastfreundlich tönt dem Wanderer im
      Friedlichen Dorfe die Abendglocke.

Wohl kehren jetzt die Schiffer zum Hafen auch,
In fernen Städten fröhlich verrauscht des Markts
   Geschäft'ger Lärm ; in stiller Laube
      Glänzt das gesellige Mahl den Freunden.

Wohin denn ich ?   Es leben die Sterblichen
Von Lohn und Arbeit ; wechselnd in Müh und Ruh
   Ist alles freudig ; warum schläft denn
      Nimmer nur mir in der Brust der Stachel ?

Am Abendhimmel blühet ein Frühling auf ;
Unzählig blühn die Rosen, und ruhig scheint
   Die goldne Welt ; o dorthin nehmt mich,
      Purpurne Wolken ! und möge droben

In Licht und Luft zerrinnen mir Lieb und Leid ! —
Doch, wie verscheucht von törichter Bitte, flieht
   Der Zauber ; dunkel wird's, und einsam
      Unter dem Himmel, wie immer, bin ich. —

Komm du nun, sanfter Schlummer ! zu viel begehrt
Das Herz ; doch endlich, Jugend, verglühst du ja,
   Du ruhelose, träumerische !
      Friedlich und heiter ist dann das Alter.

## SONNENUNTERGANG

Wo bist du ? trunken hämmert die Seele mir
Von aller deiner Wonne ; denn eben ist's,
   Dass ich gelauscht, wie, goldner Töne
      Voll, der entzückende Sonnenjüngling

Sein Abendlied auf himmlischer Leier spielt';
Es tönten rings die Wälder und Hügel nach,
    Doch fern ist er zu frommen Völkern,
        Die ihn noch ehren, hinweggegangen.


### HEIDELBERG

LANGE lieb' ich dich schon, möchte dich, mir zur Lust,
Mutter nennen und dir schenken ein kunstlos Lied,
    Du, der Vaterlandsstädte
        Ländlichschönste, so viel ich sah.

Wie der Vogel des Walds über die Gipfel fliegt,
Schwingt sich über den Strom, wo er vorbei dir glänzt,
    Leicht und kräftig die Brücke,
        Die von Wagen und Menschen tönt.

Wie von Göttern gesandt, fesselt' ein Zauber einst
Auf der Brücke mich an, da ich vorüberging,
    Und herein in die Berge
        Mir die reizende Ferne schien,

Und der Jüngling, der Strom, fort in die Ebne zog,
Traurig froh, wie das Herz, wenn es, sich selbst zu
        schön,
    Liebend unterzugehen,
        In die Fluten der Zeit sich wirft.

Quellen hattest du ihm, hattest dem Flüchtigen
Kühle Schatten geschenkt, und die Gestade sahn
    All ihm nach, und es bebte
        Aus den Wellen ihr lieblich Bild.

Aber schwer in das Tal hing die gigantische,
Schicksalskundige Burg, nieder bis auf den Grund
    Von den Wettern zerrissen ;
        Doch die ewige Sonne goss

Ihr verjüngendes Licht über das alternde
Riesenbild, und umher grünte lebendiger
   Efeu ; freundliche Wälder
    Rauschten über die Burg herab.


Sträuche blühten herab, bis wo im heitern Tal,
An den Hügel gelehnt, oder dem Ufer hold,
   Deine fröhlichen Gassen
    Unter duftenden Gärten ruhn.


### DIE KÜRZE

„ Warum bist du so kurz ?   Liebst du, wie vormals,
   denn
Nun nicht mehr den Gesang ?   Fandst du als Jüngling
   doch
  In den Tagen der Hoffnung,
    Wenn du sangest, das Ende nie ! "


Wie mein Glück ist mein Lied. — Willst du im
   Abendrot
Froh dich baden ?   Hinweg ist's, und die Erde ist kalt,
  Und der Vogel der Nacht schwirrt
    Unbequem vor das Auge dir.


### RINGSUM RUHET DIE STADT

RINGSUM ruhet die Stadt ; still wird die erleuchtete
   Gasse,
   Und, mit Fackeln geschmückt, rauschen die Wagen
    hinweg.
Satt gehn heim, von Freuden des Tags zu ruhen, die
   Menschen,
   Und Gewinn und Verlust waget ein sinniges Haupt

Wohlzufrieden zu Haus ; leer steht von Trauben und
    Blumen,
    Und von Werken der Hand ruht der geschäftige
    Markt.
Aber das Saitenspiel tönt fern aus Gärten ; vielleicht,
    dass
    Dort ein Liebendes spielt oder ein einsamer Mann
Ferner Freunde gedenkt und der Jugendzeit ; und die
    Brunnen,
    Immerquillend und frisch, rauschen an duftendem
    Beet.
Still in dämmriger Luft ertönen geläutete Glocken,
    Und der Stunden gedenk rufet ein Wächter die
    Zahl.
Jetzt auch kommet ein Wehn und regt die Wipfel des
    Hains auf,
    Sieh ! und das Schattenbild unserer Erde, der
    Mond,
Kommet geheim nun auch ; die Schwärmerische, die
    Nacht kommt
    Voll von Sternen und wohl wenig bekümmert um
    uns
Glänzt die Erstaunende dort, die Fremdlingin unter
    den Menschen,
    Über Gebirgeshöhn traurig und prächtig herauf.


### SCHICKSALSLIED

IHR wandelt droben im Licht
    Auf weichem Boden, selige Genien !
      Glänzende Götterlüfte
      Rühren euch leicht,
        Wie der Finger der Künstlerin
        Heilige Saiten.

Schicksallos, wie der schlafende
Säugling, atmen die Himmlischen;
Keusch bewahrt
In bescheidener Knospe,
Blühet ewig
Ihnen der Geist,
Und die seligen Augen
Blicken in stiller
Ewiger Klarheit.

Doch uns ist es gegeben,
Auf keiner Stätte zu ruhn:
Es schwinden, es fallen
Die leidenden Menschen
Blindings von einer
Stunde zur andern,
Wie Wasser von Klippe
Zu Klippe geworfen,
Jahrlang ins Ungewisse hinab.

# NOVALIS
## (Friedrich von Hardenberg)
### 1772–1801

#### WENN ICH IHN NUR HABE

Wenn ich ihn nur habe,
Wenn er mein nur ist,
Wenn mein Herz bis hin zum Grabe
Seine Treue nie vergisst,
Weiss ich nichts von Leide,
Fühle nichts als Andacht, Lieb' und Freude.

Wenn ich ihn nur habe,
Lass' ich alles gern,
Folg' an meinem Wanderstabe

Treugesinnt nur meinem Herrn,
Lasse still die andern
Breite, lichte, volle Strassen wandern.


Wenn ich ihn nur habe,
Schlaf' ich fröhlich ein ;
Ewig wird zu süsser Labe
Seines Herzens Flut mir sein,
Die mit sanftem Zwingen
Alles wird erweichen und durchdringen.


Wenn ich ihn nur habe,
Hab' ich auch die Welt ;
Selig wie ein Himmelsknabe,
Der der Jungfrau Schleier hält.
Hingesenkt im Schauen
Kann mir vor dem Irdischen nicht grauen.


Wo ich ihn nur habe,
Ist mein Vaterland ;
Und es fällt mir jede Gabe
Wie ein Erbteil in die Hand ;
Längst vermisste Brüder
Find' ich nun in seinen Jüngern wieder.


### WENN ALLE UNTREU WERDEN

WENN alle untreu werden,
So bleib' ich dir doch treu,
Dass Dankbarkeit auf Erden
Nicht ausgestorben sei.
Für mich umfing dich Leiden,
Vergingst für mich in Schmerz ;
Drum geb' ich dir mit Freuden
Auf ewig dieses Herz.

Oft muss ich bitter weinen,
Dass du gestorben bist,
Und mancher von den deinen
Dich lebenslang vergisst.
Von Liebe nur durchdrungen
Hast du so viel getan,
Und doch bist du verklungen,
Und keiner denkt daran.

Du stehst voll treuer Liebe
Noch immer jedem bei ;
Und wenn dir keiner bliebe,
So bleibst du dennoch treu.
Die treuste Liebe sieget,
Am Ende fühlt man sie,
Weint bitterlich und schmieget
Sich kindlich an dein Knie.

Ich habe dich empfunden,
O lasse nicht von mir !
Lass innig mich verbunden
Auf ewig sein mit dir.
Einst schauen meine Brüder
Auch wieder himmelwärts
Und sinken liebend nieder
Und fallen dir ans Herz.

### ES GIBT SO BANGE ZEITEN

Es gibt so bange Zeiten,
Es gibt so trüben Mut,
Wo alles sich von weitem
Gespenstisch zeigen tut.

Es schleichen wilde Schrecken
So ängstlich leise her,
Und tiefe Nächte decken
Die Seele zentnerschwer.

Die sichern Stützen schwanken,
Kein Halt der Zuversicht;
Der Wirbel der Gedanken
Gehorcht dem Willen nicht.

Der Wahnsinn naht und locket
Unwiderstehlich hin.
Der Puls des Lebens stocket,
Und stumpf ist jeder Sinn.

Wer hat das Kreuz erhoben
Zum Schutz für jedes Herz?
Wer wohnt im Himmel droben
Und hilft in Angst und Schmerz?

Geh zu dem Wunderstamme,
Gib stiller Sehnsucht Raum,
Aus ihm geht eine Flamme
Und zehrt den schweren Traum.

Ein Engel zieht dich wieder
Gerettet auf den Strand,
Und schaust voll Freuden nieder
In das Gelobte Land.

### MARIA

Ich sehe dich in tausend Bildern,
Maria, lieblich ausgedrückt,
Doch keins von allen kann dich schildern,
Wie meine Seele dich erblickt.

Ich weiss nur, dass der Welt Getümmel
Seitdem mir wie ein Traum verweht,
Und ein unnennbar süsser Himmel
Mir ewig im Gemüte steht.

### WENN IN BANGEN, TRÜBEN STUNDEN

WENN in bangen, trüben Stunden
Unser Herz beinah verzagt,
Wenn von Krankheit überwunden
Angst in unserm Innern nagt,
Wir der Treugeliebten denken,
Wie sie Gram und Kummer drückt,
Wolken unsern Blick beschränken,
Die kein Hoffnungsstrahl durchblickt:

O, dann neigt sich Gott herüber,
Seine Liebe kommt uns nah,
Sehnen wir uns dann hinüber,
Steht ein Engel vor uns da,
Bringt den Kelch des frischen Lebens,
Lispelt Mut und Trost uns zu,
Und wir beten nicht vergebens
Auch für die Geliebten Ruh.

### WER EINMAL, MUTTER, DICH ERBLICKT

WER einmal, Mutter, dich erblickt,
Wird vom Verderben nie bestrickt.
Trennung von dir muss ihn betrüben,
Ewig wird er dich brünstig lieben,
Und deiner Huld Erinnerung
Bleibt fortan seines Geistes höchster Schwung.

Ich mein' es herzlich gut mit dir.
Was mir gebricht, siehst du in mir.
Lass, süsse Mutter, dich erweichen,
Einmal gib mir ein frohes Zeichen.
Mein ganzes Dasein ruht in dir,
Nur einen Augenblick sei du bei mir.

Oft, wenn ich träumte, sah ich dich,
So schön, so herzensinniglich.
Der kleine Gott auf deinen Armen

Wollt' des Gespielen sich erbarmen ;
Du aber hobst den hehren Blick
Und gingst in tiefe Wolkenpracht zurück.

Was hab' ich Armer dir getan ?
Noch bet' ich dich voll Sehnsucht an.
Sind deine heiligen Kapellen
Nicht meines Lebens Ruhestellen ?
Gebenedeite Königin,
Nimm dieses Herz mit diesem Leben hin.

Du weisst, geliebte Königin,
Wie ich so ganz dein eigen bin.
Hab' ich nicht schon seit langen Jahren
Im stillen deine Huld erfahren ?
Als ich kaum meiner noch bewusst,
Sog ich schon Milch aus deiner sel'gen Brust.

Unzähligmal standst du bei mir,
Mit Kindeslust sah ich nach dir,
Dein Kindlein gab mir seine Hände,
Dass es dereinst mich wiederfände ;
Du lächeltest voll Zärtlichkeit
Und küsstest mich, o himmelsüsse Zeit !

Fern steht nun diese sel'ge Welt,
Gram hat sich längst zu mir gesellt,
Betrübt bin ich umhergegangen,
Hab' ich mich denn so schwer vergangen ?
Kindlich berühr' ich deinen Saum,
Erwecke mich aus diesem schweren Traum !

Darf nur ein Kind dein Antlitz schaun
Und deinem Beistand fest vertraun,
So löse doch des Alters Binde
Und mache mich zu deinem Kinde !
Die Kindeslieb' und Kindestreu'
Wohnt mir von jener goldnen Zeit noch bei.

## LUDWIG TIECK
### 1773–1853

#### LIEBE

LIEBE denkt in süssen Tönen,
Denn Gedanken stehn zu fern,
Nur in Tönen mag sie gern
Alles, was sie will, verschönen.

#### MONDBEGLÄNZTE ZAUBERNACHT

MONDBEGLÄNZTE Zaubernacht,
Die den Sinn gefangen hält,
Wundervolle Märchenwelt,
Steig auf in der alten Pracht!

## CLEMENS BRENTANO
### 1778–1842

#### ABENDLIED

WIE so leis die Blätter wehn,
In dem lieben, stillen Hain!
Sonne will schon schlafen gehn,
Lässt ihr goldnes Hemdelein
Sinken auf den grünen Rasen,
Wo die schlanken Hirsche grasen
In dem roten Abendschein.

In der Quellen klarer Flut
Treibt kein Fischlein mehr sein Spiel;
Jedes suchet, wo es ruht,
Sein gewöhnlich Ort und Ziel,
Und entschlummert überm Lauschen
Auf der Wellen leises Rauschen
Zwischen bunten Kieseln kühl.

Schlank schaut auf der Felsenwand
Sich die Glockenblume um;
Denn verspätet über Land
Will ein Bienchen mit Gesumm
Sich zur Nachtherberge melden,
In den blauen, zarten Zelten,
Schlüpft hinein und wird ganz stumm.

Vöglein, euer schwaches Nest,
Ist das Abendlied vollbracht,
Wird wie eine Burg so fest;
Fromme Vöglein schützt zur Nacht
Gegen Katz- und Marderkrallen,
Die im Schlaf sie überfallen,
Gott, der über alles wacht.

Treuer Gott, du bist nicht weit,
Und so ziehn wir ohne Harm
In die wilde Einsamkeit
Aus des Hofes eitelm Schwarm.
Du wirst uns die Hütte bauen,
Das wir fromm und voll Vertrauen
Sicher ruhn in deinem Arm.

### ABENDSTÄNDCHEN

Hör', es klagt die Flöte wieder,
Und die kühlen Brunnen rauschen;
Golden wehn die Töne nieder;
Stille, stille, lass uns lauschen!

Holdes Bitten, mild Verlangen,
Wie es süss zum Herzen spricht!
Durch die Nacht, die mich umfangen,
Blickt zu mir der Töne Licht.

## O KÜHLER WALD

O KÜHLER Wald
Wo rauschest du,
In dem mein Liebchen geht,
O Widerhall
Wo lauschest du,
Der gern mein Lied versteht?


O Widerhall,
O sängst du ihr
Die süssen Träume vor,
Die Lieder all,
O bring sie ihr,
Die ich so früh verlor. —


Im Herzen tief,
Da rauscht der Wald,
In dem mein Liebchen geht;
In Schmerzen schlief
Der Widerhall,
Die Lieder sind verweht.


Im Walde bin
Ich so allein,
O Liebchen, wandre hier;
Verschallet auch
Manch Lied so rein,
Ich singe andre dir.


### WIEGENLIED

SINGET leise, leise, leise,
Singt ein flüsternd Wiegenlied,
Von dem Monde lernt die Weise,
Der so still am Himmel zieht.

Singt ein Lied so süss gelinde,
Wie die Quellen auf den Kieseln,
Wie die Bienen um die Linde
Summen, murmeln, flüstern, rieseln,

### SÄUSLE, LIEBE MYRTE

Säusle, liebe Myrte!
Wie still ist's in der Welt!
Der Mond, der Sternenhirte
Auf klarem Himmelsfeld,
Treibt schon die Wolkenschafe
Zum Born des Lichtes hin.
Schlaf, mein Freund, o schlafe,
Bis ich wieder bei dir bin!

Säusle, liebe Myrte,
Und träum' im Sternenschein!
Die Turteltaube girrte
Auch ihre Brut schon ein.
Still ziehn die Wolkenschafe
Zum Born des Lichtes hin.
Schlaf, mein Freund, o schlafe,
Bis ich wieder bei dir bin!

Hörst du, wie die Brunnen rauschen?
Hörst du, wie die Grille zirpt?
Stille, stille, lass uns lauschen!
Selig, wer in Träumen stirbt;
Selig, wen die Wolken wiegen,
Wem der Mond ein Schlaflied singt;
O, wie selig kann der fliegen,
Dem der Traum den Flügel schwingt,
Dass an blauer Himmelsdecke
Sterne er wie Blumen pflückt!
Schlafe, träume, flieg, ich wecke
Bald dich auf und bin beglückt!

Komm heraus, komm heraus, o du schöne, schöne Braut,
Deine guten Tage sind nun alle, alle aus;
Dein Schleierlein weht so feucht und tränenschwer,
O, wie weinet die schöne Braut so sehr!
Musst die Mägdlein lassen stehn,
Musst nun zu den Frauen gehn.


Lege an, lege an heut' auf kurze, kurze Zeit
Deine Seidenröslein, dein reiches Brustgeschmeid;
Dein Schleierlein weht so feucht und tränenschwer,
O, wie weinet die schöne Braut so sehr!
Musst die Zöpflein schliessen ein
Unterm goldnen Häubelein.


Lache nicht, lache nicht, deine Gold- und Perlenschuh'
Werden dich schon drücken, sind eng genug dazu;
Dein Schleierlein weht so feucht und tränenschwer,
O, wie weinet die schöne Braut so sehr!
Wenn die andern tanzen gehn,
Musst du bei der Wiege stehn.


Winke nur, winke nur, sind gar leichte, leichte Wink',
Bis den Finger drücket der goldne Treuering;
Dein Schleierlein weht so feucht und tränenschwer,
O, wie weinet die schöne Braut so sehr!
Ringlein sehn heut' lieblich aus,
Morgen werden Fesseln draus.


Springe heut', springe heut' deinen letzten, letzten Tanz,
Welken erst die Rosen, stehen Dornen in dem Kranz;
Dein Schleierlein weht so feucht und tränenschwer,
O, wie weinet die schöne Braut so sehr!
Musst die Blümlein lassen stehn,
Musst nun auf den Acker gehn.

### DER SPINNERIN LIED

Es sang vor langen Jahren
Wohl auch die Nachtigall,
Das war wohl süsser Schall,
Da wir zusammen waren.

Ich sing' und kann nicht weinen
Und spinne so allein
Den Faden, klar und rein,
So lang der Mond wird scheinen.

Da wir zusammen waren,
Da sang die Nachtigall,
Nun mahnet mich ihr Schall,
Dass du von mir gefahren.

So oft der Mond mag scheinen,
Gedenk' ich dein allein,
Mein Herz ist klar und rein,
Gott wolle uns vereinen!

Seit du von mir gefahren,
Singt stets die Nachtigall,
Ich denk' bei ihrem Schall,
Wie wir zusammen waren.

Gott wolle uns vereinen,
Hier spinn' ich so allein,
Der Mond scheint klar und rein,
Ich sing' und möchte weinen!

## ADALBERT VON CHAMISSO
### 1781–1838

#### DAS SCHLOSS BONCOURT

Ich träum' als Kind mich zurücke
Und schüttle mein greises Haupt;
Wie sucht ihr mich heim, ihr Bilder,
Die lang' ich vergessen geglaubt!

Hoch ragt aus schatt'gen Gehegen
Ein schimmerndes Schloss hervor;
Ich kenne die Türme, die Zinnen,
Die steinerne Brücke, das Tor.

Es schauen vom Wappenschilde
Die Löwen so traulich mich an,
Ich grüsse die alten Bekannten
Und eile den Burghof hinan.

Dort liegt die Sphinx am Brunnen,
Dort grünt der Feigenbaum,
Dort, hinter diesen Fenstern,
Verträumt' ich den ersten Traum.

Ich tret' in die Burgkapelle
Und suche des Ahnherrn Grab;
Dort ist's, dort hängt vom Pfeiler
Das alte Gewaffen herab.

Noch lesen umflort die Augen
Die Züge der Inschrift nicht,
Wie hell durch die bunten Scheiben
Das Licht darüber auch bricht.

So stehst du, o Schloss meiner Väter,
Mir treu und fest in dem Sinn,

Und bist von der Erde verschwunden,
Der Pflug geht über dich hin.

Sei fruchtbar, o teurer Boden!
Ich segne dich mild und gerührt
Und segn' ihn zwiefach, wer immer
Den Pflug nun über dich führt.

Ich aber will auf mich raffen,
Mein Saitenspiel in der Hand,
Die Weiten der Erde durchschweifen
Und singen von Land zu Land.

### FRISCH GESUNGEN

Hab' oft im Kreise der Lieben
In duftigem Grase geruht
Und mir ein Liedlein gesungen,
Und alles war hübsch und gut.

Hab' einsam auch mich gehärmet
In bangem, düsterem Mut
Und habe wieder gesungen,
Und alles war wieder gut.

Und manches, was ich erfahren,
Verkocht' ich in stiller Wut,
Und kam ich wieder zu singen,
War alles auch wieder gut.

Sollst nicht uns lange klagen,
Was alles dir wehe tut;
Nur frisch, nur frisch gesungen!
Und alles wird wieder gut.

## FRAUEN-LIEBE UND LEBEN

### 1

Seit ich ihn gesehen,
Glaub' ich blind zu sein ;
Wo ich hin nur blicke,
Seh' ich ihn allein ;
Wie im wachen Traume
Schwebt sein Bild mir vor,
Taucht aus tiefstem Dunkel
Heller mir empor.

Sonst ist licht- und farblos
Alles um mich her,
Nach der Schwestern Spiele
Nicht begehr' ich mehr,
Möchte lieber weinen
Still im Kämmerlein ;
Seit ich ihn gesehen,
Glaub' ich blind zu sein.

### 2

Du Ring an meinem Finger,
Mein goldnes Ringelein,
Ich drücke dich fromm an die Lippen,
Dich fromm an das Herze mein.

Ich hatt' ihn ausgeträumet,
Der Kindheit friedlichen Traum,
Ich fand allein mich, verloren
Im öden unendlichen Raum.

Du Ring an meinem Finger,
Da hast du mich erst belehrt,
Hast meinem Blick erschlossen
Des Lebens unendlichen Wert.

Ich werd' ihm dienen, ihm leben,
Ihm angehören ganz,
Hin selber mich geben und finden
Verklärt mich in seinem Glanz.

Du Ring an meinem Finger,
Mein goldnes Ringelein,
Ich drücke dich fromm an die Lippen,
Dich fromm an das Herze mein.

### 3

Nun hast du mir den ersten Schmerz getan,
    Der aber traf.
Du schläfst, du harter, unbarmherz'ger Mann
    Den Todesschlaf.

Es blicket die Verlassne vor sich hin,
    Die Welt ist leer.
Geliebet hab' ich und gelebt, ich bin
    Nicht lebend mehr.

Ich zieh' mich in mein Innres still zurück,
    Der Schleier fällt,
Da hab' ich dich und mein vergangnes Glück,
    Du meine Welt!

#### DER SOLDAT

Es geht bei gedämpfter Trommel Klang;
Wie weit noch die Stätte! der Weg wie lang!
O wär' er zur Ruh und alles vorbei!
Ich glaub', es bricht mir das Herz entzwei.

Ich hab' in der Welt nur ihn geliebt,
Nur ihn, dem jetzt man den Tod doch gibt.
Bei klingendem Spiele wird paradiert,
Dazu bin auch ich kommandiert.

Nun schaut er auf zum letztenmal
In Gottes Sonne freudigen Strahl,
Nun binden sie ihm die Augen zu —
Dir schenke Gott die ewige Ruh !

Es haben die neun wohl angelegt,
Acht Kugeln haben vorbeigefegt ;
Sie zitterten alle vor Jammer und Schmerz —
Ich aber, ich traf ihn mitten ins Herz.

### DAS RIESENSPIELZEUG

BURG NIDECK ist im Elsass der Sage wohlbekannt,
Die Höhe, wo vor Zeiten die Burg der Riesen stand ;
Sie selbst ist nun verfallen, die Stätte wüst und leer,
Du fragest nach den Riesen, du findest sie nicht mehr.

Einst kam das Riesenfräulein aus jener Burg hervor,
Erging sich sonder Wartung und spielend vor dem Tor
Und stieg hinab den Abhang bis in das Tal hinein,
Neugierig zu erkunden, wie's unten möchte sein.

Mit wen'gen raschen Schritten durchkreuzte sie den
        Wald,
Erreichte gegen Haslach das Land der Menschen bald,
Und Städte dort und Dörfer und das bestellte Feld
Erschienen ihren Augen gar eine fremde Welt.

Wie jetzt zu ihren Füssen sie spähend niederschaut,
Bemerkt sie einen Bauer, der seinen Acker baut ;
Es kriecht das kleine Wesen einher so sonderbar,
Es glitzert in der Sonne der Pflug so blank und klar.

,, Ei ! artig Spielding ! '' ruft sie, ,, das nehm' ich mit
        nach Haus ! ''
Sie knieet nieder, spreitet behend ihr Tüchlein aus
Und feget mit den Händen, was sich da alles regt,
Zu Haufen in das Tüchlein, das sie zusammenschlägt ;

Und eilt mit freud'gen Sprüngen — man weiss, wie
    Kinder sind —
Zur Burg hinan und suchet den Vater auf geschwind :
„ Ei Vater, lieber Vater, ein Spielding wunderschön !
So Allerliebstes sah ich noch nie auf unsern Höhn."

Der Alte sass am Tische und trank den kühlen Wein ;
Er schaut sie an behaglich, er fragt das Töchterlein :
„ Was Zappeliges bringst du in deinem Tuch herbei ?
Du hüpfest ja vor Freuden ; lass sehen, was es sei ! "

Sie spreitet aus das Tüchlein und fängt behutsam an,
Den Bauer aufzustellen, den Pflug und das Gespann ;
Wie alles auf dem Tische sie zierlich aufgebaut,
So klatscht sie in die Hände und springt und jubelt
    laut.

Der Alte wird gar ernsthaft und wiegt sein Haupt und
    spricht :
„ Was hast du angerichtet ?   Das ist kein Spielzeug
    nicht !
Wo du es hergenommen, da trag' es wieder hin !
Der Bauer ist kein Spielzeug ; was kommt dir in den
    Sinn ?

Sollst gleich und ohne Murren erfüllen mein Gebot
Denn, wäre nicht der Bauer, so hättest du kein Brot !
Es spriesst der Stamm der Riesen aus Bauernmark
    hervor,
Der Bauer ist kein Spielzeug, da sei uns Gott davor ! "

### DIE ALTE WASCHFRAU

Du siehst geschäftig bei dem Linnen
Die Alte dort in weissem Haar,
Die rüstigste der Wäscherinnen
Im sechsundsiebenzigsten Jahr.

So hat sie stets mit sauerm Schweiss
Ihr Brot in Ehr' und Zucht gegessen
Und ausgefüllt mit treuem Fleiss
Den Kreis, den Gott ihr zugemessen.

Sie hat in ihren jungen Tagen
Geliebt, gehofft und sich vermählt ;
Sie hat des Weibes Los getragen,
Die Sorgen haben nicht gefehlt ;
Sie hat den kranken Mann gepflegt ;
Sie hat drei Kinder ihm geboren ;
Sie hat ihn in das Grab gelegt
Und Glaub' und Hoffnung nicht verloren.

Da galt's, die Kinder zu ernähren ;
Sie griff es an mit heiterm Mut,
Sie zog sie auf in Zucht und Ehren,
Der Fleiss, die Ordnung sind ihr Gut.
Zu suchen ihren Unterhalt,
Entliess sie segnend ihre Lieben,
So stand sie nun allein und alt,
Ihr war ihr heitrer Mut geblieben.

Sie hat gespart und hat gesonnen
Und Flachs gekauft und nachts gewacht,
Den Flachs zu feinem Garn gesponnen,
Das Garn dem Weber hingebracht ;
Der hat's gewebt zu Leinewand ;
Die Schere brauchte sie, die Nadel,
Und nähte sich mit eigner Hand
Ihr Sterbehemde sonder Tadel.

Ihr Hemd, ihr Sterbehemd, sie schätzt es,
Verwahrt's im Schrein am Ehrenplatz ;
Es ist ihr Erstes und ihr Letztes,
Ihr Kleinod, ihr ersparter Schatz.

Sie legt es an, des Herren Wort
Am Sonntag früh sich einzuprägen;
Dann legt sie's wohlgefällig fort,
Bis sie darin zur Ruh' sie legen.

Und ich, an meinem Abend, wollte,
Ich hätte, diesem Weibe gleich,
Erfüllt, was ich erfüllen sollte
In meinen Grenzen und Bereich;
Ich wollt', ich hätte so gewusst,
Am Kelch des Lebens mich zu laben,
Und könnt' am Ende gleiche Lust
An meinem Sterbehemde haben.

## MAX VON SCHENKENDORFF
### 1783–1817

#### MUTTERSPRACHE

Muttersprache, Mutterlaut!
Wie so wonnesam, so traut!
Erstes Wort, das mir erschallet,
Süsses, erstes Liebeswort,
Erster Ton, den ich gelallet,
Klingest ewig in mir fort.

Ach, wie trüb ist meinem Sinn,
Wenn ich in der Fremde bin,
Wenn ich fremde Zungen üben,
Fremde Worte brauchen muss,
Die ich nimmermehr kann lieben,
Die nicht klingen als ein Gruss!

Sprache, schön und wunderbar,
Ach, wie klingest du so klar!

Will noch tiefer mich vertiefen
In den Reichtum, in die Pracht;
Ist mir's doch, als ob mich riefen
Väter aus des Grabes Nacht.

Klinge, klinge fort und fort,
Heldensprache, Liebeswort!
Steig empor aus tiefen Grüften,
Längst verschollnes altes Lied,
Leb' aufs neu in heil'gen Schriften,
Dass dir jedes Herz erglüht!

Überall weht Gottes Hauch,
Heilig ist wohl mancher Brauch.
Aber soll ich beten, danken,
Geb' ich meine Liebe kund:
Meine seligsten Gedanken
Sprech' ich, wie der Mutter Mund.

## JUSTINUS KERNER
### 1786–1862

#### DIE SCHWÄBISCHE DICHTERSCHULE

„ Wohin soll den Fuss ich lenken, ich, ein fremder
  Wandersmann,
Dass ich eure Dichterschule, gute Schwaben, finden
  kann?"
Fremder Wanderer! o gerne will ich solches sagen dir:
Geh durch diese lichten Matten in das dunkle Wald-
  revier,
Wo die Tanne steht, die hohe, die als Mast einst
  schifft durchs Meer;
Wo von Zweig zu Zweig sich schwinget singend lust'ger
  Vögel Heer;
Wo das Reh mit klaren Augen aus dem dunkeln
  Dickicht sieht,

Und der Hirsch, der schlanke, setzet über Felsen von
    Granit ;
Trete dann aus Waldes Dunkel, wo im goldnen Son-
    nenstrahl
Grüssen Berge dich voll Reben, Neckars Blau im tiefen
    Tal ;
Wo ein goldnes Meer von Ähren durch die Eb'nen wogt
    und wallt,
Drüber in den blauen Lüften Jubelruf der Lerche
    schallt ;
Wo der Winzer, wo der Schnitter singt ein Lied durch
    Berg und Flur :
Da ist schwäb'scher Dichter Schule, und ihr Meister
    heisst — Natur !

### POESIE

POESIE ist tiefes Schmerzen,
Und es kommt das echte Lied
Einzig aus dem Menschenherzen,
Das ein tiefes Leid durchglüht.

Doch die höchsten Poesien
Schweigen wie der höchste Schmerz ;
Nur wie Geisterschatten ziehen
Stumm sie durchs gebrochne Herz.

### WANDERLIED

WOHLAUF, noch getrunken
Den funkelnden Wein !
Ade nun, ihr Lieben !
Geschieden muss sein.
Ade nun, ihr Berge,
Du väterlich Haus !
Es treibt in die Ferne
Mich mächtig hinaus.

Die Sonne, sie bleibet
Am Himmel nicht stehn,
Es treibt sie durch Länder
Und Meere zu gehn.
Die Woge nicht haftet
Am einsamen Strand,
Die Stürme, sie brausen
Mit Macht durch das Land.

Mit eilenden Wolken
Der Vogel dort zieht
Und singt in der Ferne
Ein heimatlich Lied.
So treibt es den Burschen
Durch Wälder und Feld,
Zu gleichen der Mutter,
Der wandernden Welt.

Da grüssen ihn Vögel
Bekannt überm Meer,
Sie flogen von Fluren
Der Heimat hieher;
Da duften die Blumen
Vertraulich um ihn,
Sie trieben vom Lande
Die Lüfte dahin.

Die Vögel, die kennen
Sein väterlich Haus;
Die Blumen einst pflanzt' er
Der Liebe zum Strauss;
Und Liebe, die folgt ihm,
Sie geht ihm zur Hand:
So wird ihm zur Heimat
Das fernste Land.

### DER WANDERER IN DER SÄGEMÜHLE

DORT unten in der Mühle
Sass ich in süsser Ruh
Und sah dem Räderspiele
Und sah den Wassern zu.

Sah zu der blanken Säge,
Es war mir wie ein Traum,
Die bahnte lange Wege
In einen Tannenbaum.

Die Tanne war wie lebend;
In Trauermelodie,
Durch alle Fasern bebend,
Sang diese Worte sie:

,, Du kehrst zur rechten Stunde,
O Wanderer, hier ein;
Du bist's, für den die Wunde
Mir dringt ins Herz hinein;

Du bist's, für den wird werden,
Wenn kurz gewandert du,
Dies Holz im Schoss der Erden
Ein Schrein zur langen Ruh.''

Vier Bretter sah ich fallen,
Mir ward's ums Herze schwer,
Ein Wörtlein wollt' ich lallen,
Da ging das Rad nicht mehr.


### DER REICHSTE FÜRST

PREISEND mit viel schönen Reden
Ihrer Länder Wert und Zahl,
Sassen viele deutsche Fürsten
Einst zu Worms im Kaisersaal.

„ Herrlich," sprach der Fürst von Sachsen,
„ Ist mein Land und seine Macht,
Silber hegen seine Berge
Wohl in manchem tiefen Schacht."

„ Seht mein Land in üpp'ger Fülle,"
Sprach der Kurfürst von dem Rhein,
„ Goldne Saaten in den Tälern,
Auf den Bergen edlen Wein ! "

„ Grosse Städte, reiche Klöster,"
Ludwig, Herr zu Bayern, sprach,
„ Schaffen, dass mein Land den euren
Wohl nicht steht an Schätzen nach."

Eberhard, der mit dem Barte,
Württembergs geliebter Herr,
Sprach : „ Mein Land hat kleine Städte,
Trägt nicht Berge silberschwer ;

Doch ein Kleinod hält's verborgen :
Dass in Wäldern, noch so gross,
Ich mein Haupt kann kühnlich legen
Jedem Untertan in Schoss."

Und es rief der Herr von Sachsen,
Der von Bayern, der vom Rhein :
„ Graf im Bart ! Ihr seid der reichste,
Euer Land trägt Edelstein ! "

### DER SCHWERE TRAUM

Mir träumt', ich flög' gar bange
Weit in die Welt hinaus,
Zu Strassburg durch alle Gassen
Bis vor Feinsliebchens Haus.

Feinsliebchen ist betrübet,
Als ich so flieg', und weint:
„ Wer dich so fliegen lehret,
Das ist der böse Feind." —

„ Feinsliebchen! Was hilft lügen,
Da du doch alles weisst!
Wer mich so fliegen lehrte,
Das ist der böse Geist."

Feinsliebchen weint und schreiet,
Dass ich am Schrei erwacht':
Da lieg' ich, ach! in Augsburg
Gefangen auf der Wacht.

Und morgen muss ich hangen,
Feinslieb mich nicht mehr ruft,
Wohl morgen als ein Vogel
Schwank' ich in freier Luft!


### DER WASSERMANN

Es war in des Maien lindem Glanz,
Da hielten die Jungfern von Tübingen Tanz.

Sie tanzten und tanzten wohl allzumal
Um eine Linde im grünen Tal.

Ein fremder Jüngling in stolzem Kleid
Sich wandte bald zu der schönsten Maid.

Er reicht' ihr dar die Hände zum Tanz,
Er setzt' ihr aufs Haar einen meergrünen Kranz.

„ O Jüngling! warum ist so kalt dein Arm?" —
„ In Neckars Tiefen da ist's nicht warm." —

,, O Jüngling ! warum ist so bleich deine Hand ? " —
,, Ins Wasser dringt nicht der Sonne Brand ! "


Er tanzt mit ihr von der Linde weit.
,, Lass, Jüngling !   Horch, die Mutter mir schreit ! "


Er tanzt mit ihr den Neckar entlang :
,, Lass, Jüngling ! weh ! mir wird so bang ! "


Er fasst sie fest um den schlanken Leib.
,, Schön' Maid ! du bist des Wassermanns Weib ! "


Er tanzt mit ihr in die Wellen hinein :
,, O Vater und o du Mutter mein ! "


Er führt sie in einen kristallenen Saal :
,, Ade, ihr Schwestern im grünen Tal ! "


## LUDWIG UHLAND
### 1787–1862

#### DIE FAHRT ZUR GELIEBTEN

O BRICH nicht, Steg ! du zitterst sehr.
O stürz' nicht, Fels ! du dräuest schwer.
Welt, geh nicht unter, Himmel, fall nicht ein,
Eh' ich mag bei der Liebsten sein !


#### LEBEWOHL

LEBE wohl, lebe wohl, mein Lieb !
Muss noch heute scheiden.
Einen Kuss, einen Kuss mir gib !
Muss dich ewig meiden.

Eine Blüt', eine Blüt' mir brich
Von dem Baum im Garten!
Keine Frucht, keine Frucht für mich!
Darf sie nicht erwarten.

### DIE KAPELLE

DROBEN stehet die Kapelle,
Schauet still ins Tal hinab,
Drunten singt bei Wies' und Quelle
Froh und hell der Hirtenknab'.

Traurig tönt das Glöcklein nieder,
Schauerlich der Leichenchor;
Stille sind die frohen Lieder,
Und der Knabe lauscht empor.

Droben bringt man sie zu Grabe,
Die sich freuten in dem Tal.
Hirtenknabe, Hirtenknabe,
Dir auch singt man dort einmal.

### SCHÄFERS SONNTAGSLIED

DAS ist der Tag des Herrn.
Ich bin allein auf weiter Flur.
Noch eine Morgenglocke nur,
Nun Stille nah und fern.

Anbetend knie' ich hier.
O süsses Graun, geheimes Wehn,
Als knieten viele ungesehn
Und beteten mit mir!

Der Himmel, nah und fern,
Er ist so klar und feierlich,
So ganz, als wollt' er öffnen sich.
Das ist der Tag des Herrn.

### FRÜHLINGSGLAUBE

Die linden Lüfte sind erwacht,
Sie säuseln und weben Tag und Nacht,
Sie schaffen an allen Enden.
O frischer Duft, o neuer Klang!
Nun, armes Herze, sei nicht bang!
Nun muss sich alles, alles wenden.

Die Welt wird schöner mit jedem Tag,
Man weiss nicht, was noch werden mag,
Das Blühen will nicht enden.
Es blüht das fernste, tiefste Tal:
Nun, armes Herz, vergiss der Qual!
Nun muss sich alles, alles wenden.

### DAS SCHLOSS AM MEERE

„Hast du das Schloss gesehen,
Das hohe Schloss am Meer?
Golden und rosig wehen
Die Wolken drüber her.

Es möchte sich niederneigen
In die spiegelklare Flut,
Es möchte streben und steigen
In der Abendwolken Glut ". —

„Wohl hab' ich es gesehen,
Das hohe Schloss am Meer,
Und den Mond darüber stehen
Und Nebel weit umher." —

„Der Wind und des Meeres Wallen,
Gaben sie frischen Klang?
Vernahmst du aus hohen Hallen
Saiten und Festgesang? " —

„ Die Winde, die Wogen alle
Lagen in tiefer Ruh;
Einem Klagelied aus der Halle
Hört' ich mit Tränen zu." —

„ Sahest du oben gehen
Den König und sein Gemahl,
Der roten Mäntel Wehen,
Der goldnen Kronen Strahl?

Führten sie nicht mit Wonne
Eine schöne Jungfrau dar,
Herrlich wie eine Sonne,
Strahlend im goldnen Haar?" —

„ Wohl sah ich die Eltern beide,
Ohne der Kronen Licht,
Im schwarzen Trauerkleide;
Die Jungfrau sah ich nicht."

### DER GUTE KAMERAD

Ich hatt' einen Kameraden,
Einen bessern findst du nit.
Die Trommel schlug zum Streite,
Er ging an meiner Seite
In gleichem Schritt und Tritt.

Eine Kugel kam geflogen;
Gilt's mir oder gilt es dir?
Ihn hat es weggerissen,
Er liegt mir vor den Füssen,
Als wär's ein Stück von mir.

Will mir die Hand noch reichen,
Derweil ich eben lad':
„ Kann dir die Hand nicht geben,
Bleib du im ew'gen Leben
Mein guter Kamerad!"

### DER WIRTIN TÖCHTERLEIN

Es zogen drei Bursche wohl über den Rhein,
Bei einer Frau Wirtin da kehrten sie ein.

,, Frau Wirtin, hat Sie gut Bier und Wein?
Wo hat Sie ihr schönes Töchterlein? "

,, Mein Bier und Wein ist frisch und klar,
Mein Töchterlein liegt auf der Totenbahr'."

Und als sie traten zur Kammer hinein,
Da lag sie in einem schwarzen Schrein.

Der erste, der schlug den Schleier zurück
Und schaute sie an mit traurigem Blick:

,, Ach, lebtest du noch, du schöne Maid!
Ich würde dich lieben von dieser Zeit."

Der zweite deckte den Schleier zu
Und kehrte sich ab und weinte dazu:

,, Ach, dass du liegst auf der Totenbahr'!
Ich hab' dich geliebet so manches Jahr."

Der dritte hub ihn wieder sogleich
Und küsste sie an den Mund so bleich:

,, Dich lieb' ich immer, dich lieb' ich noch heut
Und werde dich lieben in Ewigkeit."

### DER WEISSE HIRSCH

Es gingen drei Jäger wohl auf die Birsch,
Sie wollten erjagen den weissen Hirsch.

Sie legten sich unter den Tannenbaum,
Da hatten die drei einen seltsamen Traum.

*Der erste :*

„ Mir hat geträumt, ich klopf' auf den Busch,
Da rauschte der Hirsch heraus, husch husch ! "

*Der zweite :*

„ Und als er sprang mit der Hunde Geklaff,
Da brannt' ich ihn auf das Fell, piff paff ! "

*Der dritte :*

„ Und als ich den Hirsch an der Erde sah,
Da stiess ich lustig ins Horn, trara ! "

So lagen sie da und sprachen, die drei,
Da rannte der weisse Hirsch vorbei.

Und eh' die drei Jäger ihn recht gesehn,
So war er davon über Tiefen und Höhn.
        Husch husch ! piff paff ! trara !

### SIEGFRIEDS SCHWERT

Jung Siegfried war ein stolzer Knab',
Ging von des Vaters Burg herab,

Wollt' rasten nicht in Vaters Haus,
Wollt' wandern in alle Welt hinaus.

Begegnet' ihm manch Ritter wert
Mit festem Schild und breitem Schwert.

Siegfried nur einen Stecken trug,
Das war ihm bitter und leid genug.

Und als er ging im finstern Wald,
Kam er zu einer Schmiede bald.

Da sah er Eisen und Stahl genug,
Ein lustig Feuer Flammen schlug.

„ O Meister, liebster Meister mein,
Lass du mich deinen Gesellen sein

Und lehr' du mich mit Fleiss und Acht,
Wie man die guten Schwerter macht! "

Siegfried den Hammer wohl schwingen kunnt',
Er schlug den Amboss in den Grund.

Er schlug, dass weit der Wald erklang
Und alles Eisen in Stücke sprang.

Und von der letzten Eisenstang'
Macht' er ein Schwert so breit und lang:

„ Nun hab' ich geschmiedet ein gutes Schwert,
Nun bin ich wie andre Ritter wert;

Nun schlag' ich wie ein andrer Held
Die Riesen und Drachen in Wald und Feld."

### BERTRAN DE BORN

DROBEN auf dem schroffen Steine
Raucht in Trümmern Autafort,
Und der Burgherr steht gefesselt
Vor des Königs Zelte dort:
„ Kamst du, der mit Schwert und Liedern
Aufruhr trug von Ort zu Ort,
Der die Kinder aufgewiegelt
Gegen ihres Vaters Wort?

Steht vor mir, der sich gerühmet
In vermessener Prahlerei,
Dass ihm nie mehr als die Hälfte
Seines Geistes nötig sei?

Nun der halbe dich nicht rettet,
Ruf den ganzen doch herbei,
Dass er neu dein Schloss dir baue,
Deine Ketten brech' entzwei!" —

„Wie du sagst, mein Herr und König,
Steht vor dir Bertran de Born,
Der mit einem Lied entflammte
Perigord und Ventadorn,
Der dem mächtigen Gebieter
Stets im Auge war ein Dorn,
Dem zu Liebe Königskinder
Trugen ihres Vaters Zorn.

„Deine Tochter sass im Saale,
Festlich, eines Herzogs Braut,
Und da sang vor ihr mein Bote,
Dem ein Lied ich anvertraut,
Sang, was einst ihr Stolz gewesen,
Ihres Dichters Sehnsuchtlaut,
Bis ihr leuchtend Brautgeschmeide
Ganz von Tränen war betaut.

Aus des Ölbaums Schlummerschatten
Fuhr dein bester Sohn empor,
Als mit zorn'gen Schlachtgesängen
Ich bestürmen liess sein Ohr.
Schnell war ihm das Ross gegürtet,
Und ich trug das Banner vor,
Jenem Todespfeil entgegen,
Der ihn traf vor Montforts Tor.

Blutend lag er mir im Arme;
Nicht der scharfe, kalte Stahl —
Dass er sterb' in deinem Fluche,
Das war seines Sterbens Qual.

Strecken wollt' er dir die Rechte
Über Meer, Gebirg' und Tal,
Als er deine nicht erreichet,
Drückt' er meine noch einmal.

Da, wie Autafort dort oben,
Ward gebrochen meine Kraft,
Nicht die ganze, nicht die halbe
Blieb mir, Saite nicht, noch Schaft.
Leicht hast du den Arm gebunden,
Seit der Geist mir liegt in Haft ;
Nur zu einem Trauerliede
Hat er sich noch aufgerafft.''

Und der König senkt die Stirne :
,, Meinen Sohn hast du verführt,
Hast der Tochter Herz verzaubert,
Hast auch meines nun gerührt.
Nimm die Hand, du Freund des Toten,
Die, verzeihend, ihm gebührt !
Weg die Fesseln ! Deines Geistes
Hab' ich einen Hauch verspürt.''

# JOSEPH FREIHERR VON EICHENDORFF
## 1788–1857

### WÜNSCHELRUTE

Schläft ein Lied in allen Dingen,
Die da träumen fort und fort ;
Und die Welt hebt an zu singen,
Triffst du nur das Zauberwort.

### DER FROHE WANDERSMANN

Wem Gott will rechte Gunst erweisen,
Den schickt er in die weite Welt ;

Dem will er seine Wunder weisen
In Berg und Wald und Strom und Feld.

Die Trägen, die zu Hause liegen,
Erquicket nicht das Morgenrot,
Sie wissen nur von Kinderwiegen,
Von Sorgen, Last und Not um Brot.

Die Bächlein von den Bergen springen,
Die Lerchen schwirren hoch vor Lust;
Was sollt' ich nicht mit ihnen singen
Aus voller Kehl' und frischer Brust?

Den lieben Gott lass' ich nur walten;
Der Bächlein, Lerchen, Wald und Feld
Und Erd' und Himmel will erhalten,
Hat auch mein' Sach' aufs best' bestellt.

## ABSCHIED

O TÄLER weit, o Höhen,
O schöner, grüner Wald,
Du meiner Lust und Wehen
Andächt'ger Aufenthalt!
Da draussen, stets betrogen,
Saust die geschäft'ge Welt;
Schlag noch einmal die Bogen
Um mich, du grünes Zelt!

Wenn es beginnt zu tagen,
Die Erde dampft und blinkt,
Die Vögel lustig schlagen,
Dass dir dein Herz erklingt:
Da mag vergehn, verwehen
Das trübe Erdenleid,
Da sollst du auferstehen
In junger Herrlichkeit!

Da steht im Wald geschrieben
Ein stilles, ernstes Wort
Von rechtem Tun und Lieben,
Und was des Menschen Hort.
Ich habe treu gelesen
Die Worte schlicht und wahr,
Und durch mein ganzes Wesen
Ward's unaussprechlich klar.

Bald werd' ich dich verlassen,
Fremd in die Fremde gehn,
Auf buntbewegten Gassen
Des Lebens Schauspiel sehn;
Und mitten in dem Leben
Wird deines Ernsts Gewalt
Mich Einsamen erheben,
So wird mein Herz nicht alt.

### DER JÄGER ABSCHIED

WER hat dich, du schöner Wald,
Aufgebaut so hoch da droben?
Wohl den Meister will ich loben,
Solang' noch mein' Stimm' erschallt.
Lebe wohl!
Lebe wohl, du schöner Wald!

Tief die Welt verworren schallt,
Oben einsam Rehe grasen,
Und wir ziehen fort und blasen,
Dass es tausendfach verhallt:
Lebe wohl!
Lebe wohl, du schöner Wald!

Banner, der so kühle wallt!
Unter deinen grünen Wogen
Hast du treu uns auferzogen,

Frommer Sagen Aufenthalt!
Lebe wohl!
Lebe wohl, du schöner Wald!

Was wir still gelobt im Wald,
Wollen's draussen ehrlich halten,
Ewig bleiben treu die Alten:
Deutsch Panier, das rauschend wallt,
Lebe wohl!
Schirm' dich Gott, du schöner Wald!

### MORGENGEBET

O WUNDERBARES, tiefes Schweigen,
Wie einsam ist's noch auf der Welt!
Die Wälder nur sich leise neigen,
Als ging' der Herr durchs stille Feld.

Ich fühl' mich recht wie neu geschaffen,
Wo ist die Sorge nun und Not?
Was mich noch gestern wollt' erschlaffen,
Ich schäm' mich des im Morgenrot.

Die Welt mit ihrem Gram und Glücke
Will ich, ein Pilger, frohbereit
Betreten nur wie eine Brücke
Zu dir, Herr, übern Strom der Zeit.

Und buhlt mein Lied, auf Weltgunst lauernd,
Um schnöden Sold der Eitelkeit:
Zerschlag mein Saitenspiel, und schauernd
Schweig' ich vor dir in Ewigkeit.

### MONDNACHT

Es war, als hätt' der Himmel
Die Erde still geküsst,
Dass sie im Blütenschimmer
Von ihm nun träumen müsst'.

Die Luft ging durch die Felder,
Die Ähren wogten sacht,
Es rauschten leis die Wälder,
So sternklar war die Nacht.

Und meine Seele spannte
Weit ihre Flügel aus,
Flog durch die stillen Lande,
Als flöge sie nach Haus.

### SEHNSUCHT

Es schienen so golden die Sterne,
Am Fenster ich einsam stand
Und hörte aus weiter Ferne
Ein Posthorn im stillen Land.
Das Herz mir im Leibe entbrennte,
Da hab' ich mir heimlich gedacht:
Ach! wer da mitreisen könnte
In der prächtigen Sommernacht!

Zwei junge Gesellen gingen
Vorüber am Bergeshang;
Ich hörte im Wandern sie singen
Die stille Gegend entlang:
Von schwindelnden Felsenschlüften,
Wo die Wälder rauschen so sacht,
Von Quellen, die von den Klüften
Sich stürzen in die Waldesnacht.

Sie sangen von Marmorbildern,
Von Gärten, die überm Gestein
In dämmernden Lauben verwildern,
Palästen im Mondenschein,
Wo die Mädchen am Fenster lauschen,
Wenn der Lauten Klang erwacht,
Und die Brunnen verschlafen rauschen
In der prächtigen Sommernacht.

### DAS ZERBROCHENE RINGLEIN

IN einem kühlen Grunde
Da geht ein Mühlenrad,
Mein' Liebste ist verschwunden,
Die dort gewohnet hat.

Sie hat mir Treu versprochen,
Gab mir ein'n Ring dabei,
Sie hat die Treu gebrochen,
Mein Ringlein sprang entzwei.

Ich möchte als Spielmann reisen
Weit in die Welt hinaus
Und singen meine Weisen
Und gehn von Haus zu Haus.

Ich möcht' als Reiter fliegen
Wohl in die blut?ge Schlacht,
Um stille Feuer liegen
Im Feld bei dunkler Nacht.

Hör' ich das Mühlrad gehen:
Ich weiss nicht, was ich will —
Ich möcht' am liebsten sterben,
Da wär's auf einmal still!

### IM WALDE

Es zog eine Hochzeit den Berg entlang,
Ich hörte die Vögel schlagen,
Da blitzten viel' Reiter, das Waldhorn klang,
Das war ein lustiges Jagen!

Und eh ich's gedacht, war alles verhallt,
Die Nacht bedecket die Runde,
Nur von den Bergen noch rauschet der Wald,
Und mich schauert im Herzensgrunde.
20

### WALDGESPRÄCH

Es ist schon spät, es wird schon kalt,
Was reit'st du einsam durch den Wald ?
Der Wald ist lang, du bist allein,
Du schöne Braut ! Ich führ' dich heim !

,, Gross ist der Männer Trug und List,
Vor Schmerz mein Herz gebrochen ist.
Wohl irrt das Waldhorn her und hin,
O flieh ! Du weisst nicht, wer ich bin.''

So reich geschmückt ist Ross und Weib,
So wunderschön der junge Leib,
Jetzt kenn' ich dich — Gott steh mir bei !
Du bist die Hexe Lorelei.

,, Du kennst mich wohl — von hohem Stein
Schaut still mein Schloss tief in den Rhein.
Es ist schon spät, es wird schon kalt,
Kommst nimmermehr aus diesem Wald ! ''

### WANDERLIED DER PRAGER STUDENTEN

Nach Süden nun sich lenken
Die Vöglein allzumal,
Viel' Wandrer lustig schwenken
Die Hüt' im Morgenstrahl.
Das sind die Herrn Studenten,
Zum Tor hinaus es geht,
Auf ihren Instrumenten
Sie blasen zum Valet :
Ade in die Läng' und Breite,
O Prag, wir ziehn in die Weite :
*Et habeat bonam pacem,*
*Qui sedet post fornacem !*

Nachts wir durchs Städtlein schweifen,
Die Fenster schimmern weit,
Am Fenster drehn und schleifen
Viel' schön geputzte Leut'.
Wir blasen vor den Türen
Und haben Durst genung,
Das kommt vom Musizieren,
,, Herr Wirt, ein'n frischen Trunk ! "
Und siehe, über ein kleines
Mit einer Kanne Weines
*Venit ex sua domo*
*Beatus ille homo !*

Nun weht schon durch die Wälder
Der kalte Boreas,
Wir streichen durch die Felder,
Von Schnee und Regen nass,
Der Mantel fliegt im Winde,
Zerrissen sind die Schuh',
Da blasen wir geschwinde
Und singen noch dazu :
*Beatus ille homo,*
*Qui sedet in sua domo,*
*Et sedet post fornacem*
*Et habet bonam pacem !*

### AUF MEINES KINDES TOD

Von fern die Uhren schlagen,
Es ist schon tiefe Nacht,
Die Lampe brennt so düster,
Dein Bettlein ist gemacht.

Die Winde nur noch gehen
Wehklagend um das Haus,
Wir sitzen einsam drinne
Und lauschen oft hinaus.

Es ist, als müsstest leise
Du klopfen an die Tür,
Du hätt'st dich nur verirret
Und kämst nun müd' zurück.

Wir armen, armen Toren!
Wir irren ja im Graus
Des Dunkels noch verloren —
Du fandest längst nach Haus.

### MARIÄ SEHNSUCHT

Es ging Maria in den Morgen hinein,
Tat die Erd' einen lichten Liebesschein,
Und über die fröhlichen, grünen Höhn
Sah sie den bläulichen Himmel stehn.
„ Ach, hätt' ich ein Brautkleid von Himmelsschein,
Zwei goldene Flüglein — wie flög' ich hinein! "

Es ging Maria in stiller Nacht,
Die Erde schlief, der Himmel wacht',
Und durchs Herze, wie sie ging und sann und dacht',
Zogen die Sterne mit goldener Pracht.
„ Ach, hätt' ich das Brautkleid von Himmelsschein,
Und goldene Sterne gewoben drein! "

Es ging Maria im Garten allein,
Da sangen so lockend bunt' Vögelein,
Und Rosen sah sie im Grünen stehn,
Viel rote und weisse so wunderschön.
„ Ach, hätt' ich ein Knäblein, so weiss und rot,
Wie wollt' ich's lieb haben bis in den Tod! "

Nun ist wohl das Brautkleid gewoben gar,
Und goldene Sterne im dunkelen Haar,
Und im Arme die Jungfrau das Knäblein hält,

Hoch über der dunkelerbrausenden Welt,
Und vom Kindlein gehet ein Glänzen aus,
Das ruft uns nur ewig : nach Haus, nach Haus !

# FRIEDRICH RÜCKERT

## 1788–1866

### LIEBESFRÜHLING

Ich liebe dich, weil ich dich lieben muss ;
Ich liebe dich, weil ich nicht anders kann ;
Ich liebe dich nach einem Himmelsschluss ;
Ich liebe dich durch einen Zauberbann.

Dich lieb' ich, wie die Rose ihren Strauch ;
Dich lieb' ich, wie die Sonne ihren Schein ;
Dich lieb' ich, weil du bist mein Lebenshauch ;
Dich lieb' ich, weil dich lieben ist mein Sein.

### BARBAROSSA

Der alte Barbarossa,
Der Kaiser Friederich,
Im unterird'schen Schlosse
Hält er verzaubert sich.

Er ist niemals gestorben,
Er lebt darin noch jetzt ;
Er hat im Schloss verborgen
Zum Schlaf sich hingesetzt.

Er hat hinabgenommen
Des Reiches Herrlichkeit
Und wird einst wiederkommen
Mit ihr zu seiner Zeit.

Der Stuhl ist elfenbeinern,
Darauf der König sitzt ;
Der Tisch ist marmelsteinern,
Worauf sein Haupt er stützt.


Sein Bart ist nicht von Flachse,
Er ist von Feuersglut,
Ist durch den Tisch gewachsen,
Worauf sein Kinn ausruht.


Er nickt als wie im Traume,
Sein Aug' halb offen zwinkt,
Und je nach langem Raume
Er einem Knaben winkt.


Er spricht im Schlaf zum Knaben :
„ Geh hin vors Schloss, o Zwerg,
Und sieh, ob noch die Raben
Herfliegen um den Berg.


Und wenn die alten Raben
Noch fliegen immerdar,
So muss ich auch noch schlafen
Verzaubert hundert Jahr."


### ABENDLIED

Ich stand auf Berges Halde,
Als heim die Sonne ging,
Und sah wie überm Walde
Des Abends Goldnetz hing.


Des Himmels Wolken tauten
Der Erde Frieden zu,
Bei Abendglockenlauten
Ging die Natur zur Ruh.

Ich sprach : O Herz, empfinde
Der Schöpfung Stille nun
Und schick' mit jedem Kinde
Der Flur dich auch zu ruhn.

Die Blumen alle schliessen
Die Augen allgemach,
Und alle Wellen fliessen
Besänftiget im Bach.

Nun hat der müde Sylphe
Sich unters Blatt gesetzt,
Und die Libell' am Schilfe
Entschlummert taubenetzt.

Es ward dem goldnen Käfer
Zur Wieg' ein Rosenblatt ;
Die Herde mit dem Schäfer
Sucht ihre Lagerstatt.

Die Lerche sucht aus Lüften
Ihr feuchtes Nest im Klee,
Und in des Waldes Schlüften
Ihr Lager Hirsch und Reh.

Wer sein ein Hüttchen nennet,
Ruht nun darin sich aus ;
Und wen die Fremde trennet,
Den trägt ein Traum nach Haus.

Mich fasset ein Verlangen,
Da ich zu dieser Frist
Hinauf nicht kann gelangen,
Wo meine Heimat ist.

### HERBSTHAUCH

Herz, nun so alt und noch immer nicht klug,
Hoffst du von Tagen zu Tagen,
Was dir der blühende Frühling nicht trug,
Werde der Herbst dir noch tragen !

Lässt doch der spielende Wind nicht vom Strauch,
Immer zu schmeicheln, zu kosen ;
Rosen entfaltet am Morgen sein Hauch,
Abends verstreut er die Rosen.

Lässt doch der spielende Wind nicht vom Strauch,
Bis er ihn völlig gelichtet.
Alles, o Herz, ist ein Wind und ein Hauch,
Was wir geliebt und gedichtet.

### AUS DER JUGENDZEIT

Aus der Jugendzeit, aus der Jugendzeit
Klingt ein Lied mir immerdar ;
O wie liegt so weit, o wie liegt so weit,
Was mein einst war !

Was die Schwalbe sang, was die Schwalbe sang,
Die den Herbst und Frühling bringt,
Ob das Dorf entlang, ob das Dorf entlang
Das jetzt noch klingt ?

,, Als ich Abschied nahm, als ich Abschied nahm,
Waren Kisten und Kasten schwer ;
Als ich wieder kam, als ich wieder kam,
War alles leer.``

O du Kindermund, o du Kindermund,
Unbewusster Weisheit froh,
Vogelsprachekund, vogelsprachekund,
Wie Salomo !

O du Heimatflur, o du Heimatflur,
Lass zu deinem heil'gen Raum
Mich noch einmal nur, mich noch einmal nur
Entfliehn im Traum !

Als ich Abschied nahm, als ich Abschied nahm,
War die Welt mir voll so sehr ;
Als ich wieder kam, als ich wieder kam,
War alles leer.

Wohl die Schwalbe kehrt', wohl die Schwalbe kehrt',
Und der leere Kasten schwoll ;
Ist das Herz geleert, ist das Herz geleert,
Wird's nie mehr voll.

Keine Schwalbe bringt, keine Schwalbe bringt,
Dir zurück, wonach du weinst ;
Doch die Schwalbe singt, doch die Schwalbe singt
Im Dorf wie einst :

,, Als ich Abschied nahm, als ich Abschied nahm,
Waren Kisten und Kasten schwer ;
Als ich wieder kam, als ich wieder kam,
War alles leer.''

#### SPRÜCHE

#### 1

PRAHL' nicht heute : ,, Morgen will
Dieses oder das ich tun.''
Schweige doch bis morgen still,
Sage dann : ,, Das tat ich nun.''

#### 2

Willst du, dass wir mit hinein
In das Haus dich bauen,
Lass es dir gefallen, Stein,
Dass wir dich behauen.

### 3

O blicke, wenn den Sinn dir will die Welt verwirren,
Zum ew'gen Himmel auf, wo nie die Sterne irren.

### 4

Nie stille steht die Zeit, der Augenblick entschwebt,
Und den du nicht benutzt, den hast du nicht gelebt.

Und du auch stehst nicht still, der Gleiche bist du
    nimmer,
Und wer nicht besser wird, ist schon geworden
    schlimmer,

### 5

Dass sie die Perle trägt, das macht die Muschel krank ;
Dem Himmel sag' für Schmerz, der dich veredelt,
    Dank.

## THEODOR KÖRNER
### 1791–1813

##### GEBET WÄHREND DER SCHLACHT

VATER, ich rufe dich !
Brüllend umwölkt mich der Dampf der Geschütze,
Sprühend umzucken mich rasselnde Blitze,
    Lenker der Schlachten, ich rufe dich !
    Vater du, führe mich !

    Vater du, führe mich !
Führ' mich zum Siege, führ' mich zum Tode
Herr, ich erkenne deine Gebote ;
    Herr, wie du willst, so führe mich.
    Gott, ich erkenne dich !

Gott, ich erkenne dich!
So im herbstlichen Rauschen der Blätter
Als im Schlachtendonnerwetter,
Urquell der Gnade, erkenn' ich dich.
Vater du, segne mich!

Vater du, segne mich!
In deine Hand befehl' ich mein Leben,
Du kannst es nehmen, du hast es gegeben;
Zum Leben, zum Sterben segne mich!
Vater, ich preise dich!

Vater, ich preise dich!
Es ist ja kein Kampf für die Güter der Erde;
Das Heiligste schützen wir mit dem Schwerte:
Drum, fallend und siegend preis' ich dich.
Gott, dir ergeb' ich mich!

Gott, dir ergeb' ich mich!
Wenn mich die Donner des Todes begrüssen,
Wenn meine Adern geöffnet fliessen:
Dir, mein Gott, dir ergeb' ich mich!
Vater, ich rufe dich!

## ZUR NACHT

Gute Nacht!
Allen Müden sei's gebracht.
Neigt der Tag sich still zum Ende,
Ruhen alle fleiss'gen Hände,
Bis der Morgen neu erwacht.
Gute Nacht!

Geht zur Ruh!
Schliesst die müden Augen zu.
Stiller wird es auf den Strassen,

Und den Wächter hört man blasen,
Und die Nacht ruft allen zu :
Geht zur Ruh !

Schlummert süss !
Träumt euch euer Paradies.
Wem die Liebe raubt den Frieden,
Sei ein schöner Traum beschieden,
Als ob Liebchen ihn begrüss'.
Schlummert süss !

Gute Nacht !
Schlummert, bis der Tag erwacht,
Schlummert, bis der neue Morgen
Kommt mit seinen neuen Sorgen,
Ohne Furcht ; der Vater wacht.
Gute Nacht !

## GUSTAV SCHWAB
### 1792–1850

LIED EINES ABZIEHENDEN BURSCHEN

BEMOOSTER Bursche zieh' ich aus,
Behüt' dich Gott, Philisters Haus !
Zur alten Heimat geh' ich ein,
Muss selber nun Philister sein.

Fahrt wohl, ihr Strassen grad' und krumm,
Ich zieh' nicht mehr in euch herum,
Durchtön' euch nicht mehr mit Gesang,
Mit Lärm nicht mehr und Sporenklang !

Was wollt ihr Kneipen all von mir ?
Mein Bleiben ist nicht mehr allhier ;

Winkt nicht mit eurem langen Arm,
Macht mir mein durstig Herz nicht warm!

Ei, grüss' euch Gott, Kollegia!
Wie steht ihr in Parade da!
Ihr dumpfen Säle gross und klein,
Jetzt kriegt ihr mich nicht mehr herein!

Auch du von deinem Giebeldach,
Siehst mir umsonst, o Karzer, nach!
Für schlechte Herberg', Tag und Nacht,
Sei dir ein Pereat gebracht!

Du aber blüh' und schalle noch,
Leb', alter Waffenboden, hoch!
Es stärkt den Geist die Wissenschaft,
So stärke du des Armes Kraft.

Da komm' ich, ach, an Liebchens Haus;
O Kind, schau' noch einmal heraus,
Heraus mit deinen Äuglein klar,
Mit deinem dunkeln Lockenhaar!

Und hast du mich vergessen schon,
So wünsch' ich dir nicht bösen Lohn;
Such' dir nur einen Buhlen neu,
Doch sei er flott, gleich mir, und treu!

Und weiter, weiter, geht mein Lauf:
Tut euch, ihr alten Tore, auf!
Leicht ist mein Sinn und frei mein Pfad;
Gehab' dich wohl, du Musenstadt!

Ihr Freunde, drängt euch um mich her,
Macht mir mein leichtes Herz nicht schwer!
Auf frischem Ross, mit frohem Sang
Geleitet mich den Weg entlang!

Im nächsten Dorfe kehret ein,
Trinkt noch mit mir von einem Wein! —
Und nun denn, Brüder, sei's, weil's muss,
Das letzte Glas, den letzten Kuss!


# WILHELM MÜLLER

## 1794–1827

### WOHIN?

Ich hört' ein Bächlein rauschen
Wohl aus dem Felsenquell,
Hinab zum Tale rauschen
So frisch und wunderhell.

Ich weiss nicht, wie mir wurde,
Nicht, wer den Rat mir gab,
Ich musste gleich hinunter
Mit meinem Wanderstab.

Hinunter und immer weiter,
Und immer dem Bache nach,
Und immer frischer rauschte
Und immer heller der Bach.

Ist das denn meine Strasse?
O Bächlein, sprich wohin?
Du hast mit deinem Rauschen
Mir ganz berauscht den Sinn.

Was sag' ich denn von Rauschen?
Das kann kein Rauschen sein:
Es singen wohl die Nixen
Dort unten ihren Reihn.

Lass singen, Gesell, lass rauschen,
Und wandre fröhlich nach!
Es gehn ja Mühlenräder
In jedem klaren Bach.


### UNGEDULD

Ich schnitt' es gern in alle Rinden ein,
Ich grüb' es gern in jeden Kieselstein,
Ich möcht' es sä'n auf jedes frische Beet
Mit Kressensamen, der es schnell verrät,
Auf jeden weissen Zettel möcht' ich's schreiben:
Dein ist mein Herz und soll es ewig bleiben.


Ich möcht' mir ziehen einen jungen Star,
Bis dass er spräch' die Worte rein und klar,
Bis er sie spräch' mit meines Mundes Klang,
Mit meines Herzens vollem, heissem Drang;
Dann säng' er hell durch ihre Fensterscheiben:
Dein ist mein Herz und soll es ewig bleiben.


Den Morgenwinden möcht' ich's hauchen ein,
Ich möcht' es säuseln durch den regen Hain;
O, leuchtet' es aus jedem Blumenstern!
Trüg' es der Duft zu ihr von nah' und fern!
Ihr Wogen, könnt ihr nichts als Räder treiben?
Dein ist mein Herz und soll es ewig bleiben.


Ich meint', es müsst' in meinen Augen stehn,
Auf meinen Wangen müsst' man's brennen sehn,
Zu lesen wär's auf meinem stummen Mund,
Ein jeder Atemzug gäb's laut ihr kund;
Und sie merkt nichts von all dem bangen Treiben:
Dein ist mein Herz und soll es ewig bleiben!

### WANDERSCHAFT

Das Wandern ist des Müllers Lust,
  Das Wandern!
Das muss ein schlechter Müller sein,
Dem niemals fiel das Wandern ein,
  Das Wandern.

Vom Wasser haben wir's gelernt,
  Vom Wasser!
Das hat nicht Rast bei Tag und Nacht,
Ist stets auf Wanderschaft bedacht,
  Das Wasser.

Das sehn wir auch den Rädern ab,
  Den Rädern!
Die gar nicht gerne stille stehn,
Die sich mein Tag nicht müde drehn,
  Die Räder.

Die Steine selbst, so schwer sie sind,
  Die Steine!
Sie tanzen mit den muntern Reihn
Und wollen gar noch schneller sein,
  Die Steine.

O Wandern, Wandern, meine Lust,
  O Wandern!
Herr Meister und Frau Meisterin,
Lasst mich in Frieden weiter ziehn
  Und wandern!

### HEIMKEHR

Vor der Türe meiner Lieben
  Häng' ich auf den Wanderstab;
Was mich durch die Welt getrieben,
  Leg' ich ihr zu Füssen ab.

Wanderlustige Gedanken,
Die ihr flattert nah und fern,
Fügt euch in die engen Schranken
Ihrer treuen Arme gern!

Was uns in der weiten Ferne
Suchen hiess ein eitler Traum,
Zeigen uns der Liebe Sterne
In dem traulich kleinen Raum.

Schwalben kommen hergezogen —
Setzt euch, Vöglein, auf mein Dach!
Habt euch müde schon geflogen,
Und noch ist die Welt nicht wach.

Baut in meinen Fensterräumen
Eure Häuschen weich und warm!
Singt mir zu in Morgenträumen
Wanderlust und Wanderharm!

### VINETA

Aus des Meeres tiefem, tiefem Grunde
Klingen Abendglocken dumpf und matt,
Uns zu geben wunderbare Kunde
Von der schönen alten Wunderstadt.

In der Fluten Schoss hinabgesunken
Blieben unten ihre Trümmer stehn.
Ihre Zinnen lassen goldne Funken
Widerscheinend auf dem Spiegel sehn.

Und der Schiffer, der den Zauberschimmer
Einmal sah im hellen Abendrot,
Nach derselben Stelle schifft er immer,
Ob auch rings umher die Klippe droht.

Aus des Herzens tiefem, tiefem Grunde
Klingt es mir wie Glocken dumpf und matt.
Ach, sie geben wunderbare Kunde
Von der Liebe, die geliebt es hat.

Eine schöne Welt ist da versunken,
Ihre Trümmer blieben unten stehn,
Lassen sich als goldne Himmelsfunken
Oft im Spiegel meiner Träume sehn.

Und dann möcht' ich tauchen in die Tiefen,
Mich versenken in den Widerschein,
Und mir ist, als ob mich Engel riefen
In die alte Wunderstadt herein.

## AUGUST, GRAF VON PLATEN
### 1796–1835

#### DAS GRAB IM BUSENTO

NÄCHTLICH am Busento lispeln bei Cosenza dumpfe
    Lieder,
Aus den Wassern schallt es Antwort, und in Wirbeln
    klingt es wieder.

Und den Fluss hinauf, hinunter ziehn die Schatten
    tapfrer Goten,
Die den Alarich beweinen, ihres Volkes besten Toten.

Allzufrüh und fern der Heimat mussten hier sie ihn
    begraben,
Während noch die Jugendlocken seine Schulter blond
    umgaben.

Und am Ufer des Busento reihten sie sich um die
    Wette ;
Um die Strömung abzuleiten, gruben sie ein frisches
    Bette.

In der wogenleeren Höhlung wühlten sie empor die
    Erde,
Senkten tief hinein den Leichnam mit der Rüstung
    auf dem Pferde ;

Deckten dann mit Erde wieder ihn und seine stolze
    Habe,
Dass die hohen Stromgewächse wüchsen aus dem
    Heldengrabe.

Abgelenkt zum zweiten Mahle, ward der Fluss her-
    beigezogen ;
Mächtig in ihr altes Bette schäumten die Busentowogen.

Und es sang ein Chor von Männern : ,, Schlaf in
    deinen Heldenehren !
Keines Römers schnöde Habsucht soll dir je das
    Grab versehren ! "

Sangen's, und die Lobgesänge tönten fort im Goten-
    heere ;
Wälze sie, Busentowelle, wälze sie von Meer zu Meere !

### DER PILGRIM VOR ST. JUST

NACHT ist's, und Stürme sausen für und für,
Hispanische Mönche, schliesst mir auf die Tür !

Lasst hier mich ruhn, bis Glockenton mich weckt,
Der zum Gebet euch in die Kirche schreckt !

Bereitet mir, was euer Haus vermag,
Ein Ordenskleid und einen Sarkophag!

Gönnt mir die kleine Zelle, weiht mich ein!
Mehr als die Hälfte dieser Welt war mein.

Das Haupt, das nun der Schere sich bequemt,
Mit mancher Krone war's bediademt.

Die Schulter, die der Kutte nun sich bückt,
Hat kaiserlicher Hermelin geschmückt.

Nun bin ich vor dem Tod den Toten gleich,
Und fall' in Trümmer wie das alte Reich.


## VENEDIG

### 1

MEIN Auge liess das hohe Meer zurücke,
Als aus der Flut Palladios Tempel stiegen,
An deren Staffeln sich die Wellen schmiegen,
Die uns getragen ohne Falsch und Tücke.

Wir landen an, wir danken es dem Glücke,
Und die Lagune scheint zurück zu fliegen,
Der Dogen alte Säulengänge liegen
Vor uns gigantisch mit der Seufzerbrücke.

Venedigs Löwen, sonst Venedigs Wonne,
Mit eh'rnen Flügeln sehen wir ihn ragen
Auf seiner kolossalischen Kolonne.

Ich steig' ans Land, nicht ohne Furcht und Zagen,
Da glänzt der Markusplatz im Licht der Sonne:
Soll ich ihn wirklich zu betreten wagen?

### 2

Dies Labyrinth von Brücken und von Gassen,
Die tausendfach sich ineinanderschlingen,
Wie wird hindurchzugehn mir je gelingen?
Wie werd' ich je dies grosse Rätsel fassen?

Ersteigend erst des Markusturms Terrassen,
Vermag ich vorwärts mit dem Blick zu dringen,
Und aus den Wundern, welche mich umringen,
Entsteht ein Bild, es teilen sich die Massen.

Ich grüsse dort den Ozean, den blauen,
Und hier die Alpen, die im weiten Bogen
Auf die Laguneninseln niederschauen.

Und sieh! da kam ein mut'ges Volk gezogen,
Paläste sich und Tempel sich zu bauen
Auf Eichenpfähle mitten in die Wogen.

### 3

Wie lieblich ist's, wenn sich der Tag verkühlet,
Hinauszusehn, wo Schiff und Gondel schweben,
Wenn die Lagune ruhig, spiegeleben,
In sich verfliesst, Venedig sanft umspület!

Ins Innre wieder dann gezogen fühlet
Das Auge sich, wo nach den Wolken streben
Palast und Kirche, wo ein lautes Leben
Auf allen Stufen des Rialto wühlet.

Ein frohes Völkchen lieber Müssiggänger,
Es schwärmt umher, es lässt durch nichts sich stören
Und stört auch niemals einen Grillenfänger.

Des Abends sammelt sich's zu ganzen Chören,
Denn auf dem Markusplatze will's den Sänger
Und den Erzähler auf der Riva hören.

4

Venedig liegt nur noch im Land der Träume
Und wirft nur Schatten her aus alten Tagen,
Es liegt der Leu der Republik erschlagen,
Und öde feiern seines Kerkers Räume.

Die eh'rnen Hengste, die, durch salz'ge Schäume
Dahergeschleppt, auf jener Kirche ragen,
Nicht mehr dieselben sind sie, ach! sie tragen
Des korsikan'schen Überwinders Zäume.

Wo ist das Volk von Königen geblieben,
Das diese Marmorhäuser durfte bauen,
Die nun verfallen und gemach zerstieben?

Nur selten finden auf der Enkel Brauen
Der Ahnen grosse Züge sich geschrieben,
An Dogengräbern in den Stein gehauen.

### TRISTAN

WER die Schönheit angeschaut mit Augen,
Ist dem Tode schon anheimgegeben,
Wird für keinen Dienst auf Erden taugen,
Und doch wird er vor dem Tode beben,
Wer die Schönheit angeschaut mit Augen!

Ewig währt für ihn der Schmerz der Liebe,
Denn ein Tor nur kann auf Erden hoffen
Zu genügen einem solchen Triebe:
Wen der Pfeil des Schönen je getroffen,
Ewig währt für ihn der Schmerz der Liebe!

Ach, er möchte wie ein Quell versiechen,
Jedem Hauch der Luft ein Gift entsaugen
Und den Tod aus jeder Blume riechen:
Wer die Schönheit angeschaut mit Augen,
Ach, er möchte wie ein Quell versiechen!

### WIE RAFFT' ICH MICH AUF

WIE rafft' ich mich auf in der Nacht, in der Nacht,
Und fühlte mich fürder gezogen!
Die Gassen verliess ich, vom Wächter bewacht,
Durchwandelte sacht,
In der Nacht, in der Nacht,
Das Tor mit dem gotischen Bogen.

Der Mühlbach rauschte durch felsigen Schacht,
Ich lehnte mich über die Brücke,
Tief unter mir nahm ich der Wogen in acht,
Die wallten so sacht
In der Nacht, in der Nacht,
Doch wallte nicht eine zurücke.

Es drehte sich oben, unzählig entfacht,
Melodischer Wandel der Sterne,
Mit ihnen der Mond in beruhigter Pracht,
Sie funkelten sacht
In der Nacht, in der Nacht,
Durch täuschend entlegene Ferne.

Ich blickte hinauf in der Nacht, in der Nacht,
Ich blickte hinunter aufs neue:
O wehe, wie hast du die Tage verbracht!
Nun stille du sacht
In der Nacht, in der Nacht,
Im pochenden Herzen die Reue!


### SPRACHE

WER sich zu dichten erkühnt und die Sprache ver-
    schmäht und den Rhythmus,
    Gliche dem Plastiker, der Bilder gehaun in die
    Luft!

Nicht der Gedanke genügt; die Gedanken gehören
    der Menschheit,
    Die sie verstreut und benutzt, aber die Sprache
      dem Volk.
Der wird währen am längsten von allen germanischen
    Dichtern,
    Der des germanischen Worts Weisen am besten
      verstand.

### GRABSCHRIFT

Ich war ein Dichter und empfand die Schläge
Der bösen Zeit, in welcher ich entsprossen;
Doch schon als Jüngling hab' ich Ruhm genossen,
Und auf die Sprache drückt' ich mein Gepräge.

Die Kunst zu lernen, war ich nicht zu träge,
Drum hab' ich neue Bahnen aufgeschlossen,
In Reim und Rhythmus meinen Geist ergossen,
Die dauernd sind, wofern ich recht erwäge.

Gesänge formt' ich aus verschiednen Stoffen,
Lustspiele sind und Märchen mir gelungen
In einem Stil, den keiner übertroffen:

Der ich der Ode zweiten Preis errungen
Und im Sonett des Lebens Schmerz und Hoffen
Und diesen Vers für meine Gruft gesungen.

### ICH MÖCHTE, WENN ICH STERBE

Ich möchte, wenn ich sterbe, wie die lichten
Gestirne schnell und unbewusst erbleichen,
Erliegen möcht' ich einst des Todes Streichen
Wie Sagen uns von Pindaros berichten.

Ich will ja nicht im Leben oder Dichten
Den grossen Unerreichlichen erreichen,
Ich möcht', ö Freund, ihm nur im Tode gleichen ;
Doch höre nun die schönste der Geschichten.

Er sass im Schauspiel, vom Gesang beweget,
Und hatte, der ermüdet war, die Wangen
Auf seines Lieblings schönes Knie geleget :

Als nun der Chöre Melodien verklangen,
Will wecken ihn, der ihn so sanft geheget,
Doch zu den Göttern war er heimgegangen.

## GHASELEN

### 1

Im Wasser wogt die Lilie, die blanke, hin und her,
Doch irrst du, Freund, sobald du sagst, sie schwanke
    hin und her !
Es wurzelt ja so fest ihr Fuss im tiefen Meeresgrund,
Ihr Haupt nur wiegt ein lieblicher Gedanke hin und
    her !

### 2

O weh dir, der die Welt verachtet, allein zu sein,
Und dessen ganze Seele trachtet, allein zu sein !
Es schuf der unerschöpfte Schöpfer Geschöpfe rings,
Und nicht ein einzig Wesen trachtet, allein zu sein :
Allein zu sein, verschmäht die Tulpe des Tulpenbeets,
Es scheut der Stern sich, wenn es nächtet, allein zu
    sein.
Verlass den Stolz, der deine Seele so tief betört,
Der sich und seine Freuden schlachtet, allein zu sein !
Sogar vom Throne reicht der Herrscher die Hand
    herab.

Ihm schwindelt, wenn er sich betrachtet, allein zu
    sein ;
Dem Klausner selbst im Wald gesellt sich ein Got-
    tesbild,
Weil betend er's für sündlich achtet, allein zu sein.

### 3

Der Strom, der neben mir verrauschte, wo ist er nun ?
Der Vogel, dessen Lied ich lauschte, wo ist er nun ?
Wo ist die Rose, die die Freundin am Herzen trug,
Und jener Kuss, der mich berauschte, wo ist er nun ?
Und jener Mensch, der ich gewesen, und den ich
    längst
Mit einem andern Ich vertauschte, wo ist er nun ?


## HEINRICH HEINE
### 1797–1856

#### DU BIST WIE EINE BLUME

Du bist wie eine Blume,
So hold und schön und rein ;
Ich schau' dich an, und Wehmut
Schleicht mir ins Herz hinein.

Mir ist, als ob ich die Hände
Aufs Haupt dir legen sollt',
Betend, dass Gott dich erhalte
So rein und schön und hold.

#### AUS MEINEN TRÄNEN SPRIESSEN

Aus meinen Tränen spriessen
Viel blühende Blumen hervor,
Und meine Seufzer werden
Ein Nachtigallenchor.

Und wenn du mich lieb hast, Kindchen,
Schenk' ich dir die Blumen all',
Und vor deinem Fenster soll klingen
Das Lied der Nachtigall.


### IM WUNDERSCHÖNEN MONAT MAI

Im wunderschönen Monat Mai,
Als alle Knospen sprangen,
Da ist in meinem Herzen
Die Liebe aufgegangen.

Im wunderschönen Monat Mai,
Als alle Vögel sangen,
Da hab' ich dir gestanden
Mein Sehnen und Verlangen.


### EIN FICHTENBAUM STEHT EINSAM

Ein Fichtenbaum steht einsam
Im Norden auf kahler Höh'.
Ihn schläfert; mit weisser Decke
Umhüllen ihn Eis und Schnee.

Er träumt von einer Palme,
Die fern im Morgenland
Einsam und schweigend trauert
Auf brennender Felsenwand.


### EIN JÜNGLING LIEBT EIN MÄDCHEN

Ein Jüngling liebt ein Mädchen,
Die hat einen Andern erwählt;
Der Andre liebt eine Andre,
Und hat sich mit dieser vermählt.

Das Mädchen heiratet aus Ärger
Den ersten, besten Mann,
Der ihr in den Weg gelaufen ;
Der Jüngling ist übel dran.

Es ist eine alte Geschichte,
Doch bleibt sie immer neu ;
Und wem sie just passieret,
Dem bricht das Herz entzwei.

### DER WIND ZIEHT SEINE HOSEN AN

DER Wind zieht seine Hosen an,
Die weissen Wasserhosen !
Er peitscht die Wellen so stark er kann,
Die heulen und brausen und tosen.

Aus dunkler Höh', mit wilder Macht,
Die Regengüsse träufen ;
Es ist, als wollt' die alte Nacht
Das alte Meer ersäufen.

An den Mastbaum klammert die Möwe sich
Mit heiserem Schrillen und Schreien ;
Sie flattert und will gar ängstiglich
Ein Unglück prophezeien.

### DU SCHÖNES FISCHERMÄDCHEN

DU schönes Fischermädchen,
Treibe den Kahn ans Land ;
Komm zu mir und setze dich nieder,
Wir kosen Hand in Hand.

Leg' an mein Herz dein Köpfchen,
Und fürchte dich nicht zu sehr;
Vertraust du dich doch sorglos
Täglich dem wilden Meer.

Mein Herz gleicht ganz dem Meere,
Hat Sturm und Ebb' und Flut,
Und manche schöne Perle
In seiner Tiefe ruht.


### WIR SASSEN AM FISCHERHAUSE

WIR sassen am Fischerhause
Und schauten nach der See;
Die Abendnebel kamen
Und stiegen in die Höh'.

Im Leuchtturm wurden die Lichter
Allmählich angesteckt,
Und in der weiten Ferne
Ward noch ein Schiff entdeckt.

Wir sprachen von Sturm und Schiffbruch,
Vom Seemann, und wie er lebt,
Und zwischen Himmel und Wasser
Und Angst und Freude schwebt.

Wir sprachen von fernen Küsten,
Vom Süden und vom Nord,
Und von den seltsamen Völkern
Und seltsamen Sitten dort.

Am Ganges duftet's und leuchtet's,
Und Riesenbäume blühn,
Und schöne, stille Menschen
Vor Lotosblumen knien.

In Lappland sind schmutzige Leute,
Plattköpfig, breitmäulig und klein ;
Sie kauern ums Feuer und backen
Sich Fische, und quäken und schrein.

Die Mädchen horchten ernsthaft,
Und endlich sprach niemand mehr ;
Das Schiff war nicht mehr sichtbar,
Es dunkelte gar zu sehr.

### DIE LOTOSBLUME

DIE Lotosblume ängstigt
Sich vor der Sonne Pracht,
Und mit gesenktem Haupte
Erwartet sie träumend die Nacht.

Der Mond, der ist ihr Buhle,
Er weckt sie mit seinem Licht,
Und ihm entschleiert sie freundlich
Ihr frommes Blumengesicht.

Sie blüht und glüht und leuchtet
Und starret stumm in die Höh' ;
Sie duftet und weinet und zittert
Vor Liebe und Liebesweh.

### AUF FLÜGELN DES GESANGES

AUF Flügeln des Gesanges,
Herzliebchen, trag' ich dich fort,
Fort nach den Fluren des Ganges,
Dort weiss ich den schönsten Ort.

Dort liegt ein rotblühender Garten
Im stillen Mondenschein ;
Die Lotosblumen erwarten
Ihr trautes Schwesterlein.

Die Veilchen kichern und kosen,
Und schaun nach den Sternen empor;
Heimlich erzählen die Rosen
Sich duftende Märchen ins Ohr.

Es hüpfen herbei und lauschen
Die frommen, klugen Gazell'n;
Und in der Ferne rauschen
Des heiligen Stromes Well'n.

Dort wollen wir niedersinken
Unter dem Palmenbaum,
Und Liebe und Ruhe trinken
Und träumen seligen Traum.

### VERGIFTET SIND MEINE LIEDER

VERGIFTET sind meine Lieder —
Wie könnt' es anders sein?
Du hast mir ja Gift gegossen
Ins blühende Leben hinein.

Vergiftet sind meine Lieder —
Wie könnt' es anders sein?
Ich trage im Herzen viel Schlangen
Und dich, Geliebte mein.

### SIE HABEN MICH GEQUÄLET

SIE haben mich gequälet,
Geärgert blau und blass,
Die Einen mit ihrer Liebe,
Die Andern mit ihrem Hass.

Sie haben das Brot mir vergiftet,
Sie gossen mir Gift ins Glas,
Die Einen mit ihrer Liebe,
Die Andern mit ihrem Hass.

Doch sie, die mich am meisten
Gequält, geärgert, betrübt,
Die hat mich nie gehasset,
Und hat mich nie geliebt.

### DU HAST DIAMANTEN UND PERLEN

Du hast Diamanten und Perlen,
Hast alles, was Menschenbegehr,
Und hast die schönsten Augen —
Mein Liebchen, was willst du mehr?

Auf deine schöne Augen
Hab' ich ein ganzes Heer
Von ewigen Liedern gedichtet —
Mein Liebchen, was willst du mehr?

Mit deinen schönen Augen
Hast du mich gequält so sehr,
Und hast mich zugrunde gerichtet —
Mein Liebchen, was willst du mehr?

### MEIN KIND, WIR WAREN KINDER

Mein Kind, wir waren Kinder,
Zwei Kinder, klein und froh;
Wir krochen ins Hühnerhäuschen,
Versteckten uns unter das Stroh.

Wir krähten wie die Hähne,
Und kamen Leute vorbei —
,, Kikeriki! " sie glaubten,
Es wäre Hahnengeschrei.

Die Kisten auf unserem Hofe,
Die tapezierten wir aus
Und wohnten drin beisammen
Und machten ein vornehmes Haus.

Des Nachbars alte Katze
Kam öfters zum Besuch;
Wir machten ihr Bückling' und Knickse
Und Komplimente genug.

Wir haben nach ihrem Befinden
Besorglich und freundlich gefragt;
Wir haben seitdem dasselbe
Mancher alten Katze gesagt.

Wir sassen auch oft und sprachen
Vernünftig wie alte Leut',
Und klagten, wie alles besser
Gewesen zu unserer Zeit,

Wie Lieb' und Treu' und Glauben
Verschwunden aus der Welt,
Und wie so teuer der Kaffee,
Und wie so rar das Geld! —

Vorbei sind die Kinderspiele,
Und alles rollt vorbei —
Das Geld und die Welt und die Zeiten,
Und Glauben und Lieb' und Treu'.


### DIE LORELEI

Ich weiss nicht, was soll es bedeuten,
Dass ich so traurig bin;
Ein Märchen aus alten Zeiten,
Das kommt mir nicht aus dem Sinn.

Die Luft ist kühl, und es dunkelt,
Und ruhig fliesst der Rhein;
Der Gipfel des Berges funkelt
Im Abendsonnenschein.

Die schönste Jungfrau sitzet
Dort oben wunderbar,
Ihr goldnes Geschmeide blitzet,
Sie kämmt ihr goldenes Haar.

Sie kämmt es mit goldenem Kamme
Und singt ein Lied dabei ;
Das hat eine wundersame,
Gewaltige Melodei.

Den Schiffer im kleinen Schiffe
Ergreift es mit wildem Weh ;
Er schaut nicht die Felsenriffe,
Er schaut nur hinauf in die Höh'.

Ich glaube, die Wellen verschlingen
Am Ende Schiffer und Kahn ;
Und das hat mit ihrem Singen
Die Lorelei getan.

### DER TOD, DAS IST DIE KÜHLE NACHT

DER Tod, das ist die kühle Nacht,
Das Leben ist der schwüle Tag.
Es dunkelt schon, mich schläfert,
Der Tag hat mich müd' gemacht.

Über mein Bett erhebt sich ein Baum,
Drin singt die junge Nachtigall ;
Sie singt von lauter Liebe,
Ich hör' es sogar im Traum.

### AN MEINE MUTTER

#### 1

Ich bin's gewohnt, den Kopf recht hoch zu tragen,
Mein Sinn ist auch ein bisschen starr und zähe ;
Wenn selbst der König mir ins Antlitz sähe,
Ich würde nicht die Augen niederschlagen.

Doch, liebe Mutter, offen will ich's sagen :
Wie mächtig auch mein stolzer Mut sich blähe,
In deiner selig süssen, trauten Nähe
Ergreift mich oft ein demutvolles Zagen.

Ist es dein Geist, der heimlich mich bezwinget,
Dein hoher Geist, der alles kühn durchdringet
Und blitzend sich zum Himmelslichte schwinget ?

Quält mich Erinnerung, dass ich verübet
So manche Tat, die dir das Herz betrübet,
Das schöne Herz, das mich so sehr geliebet ?

#### 2

Im tollen Wahn hatt' ich dich einst verlassen ;
Ich wollte gehn die ganze Welt zu Ende
Und wollte sehn, ob ich die Liebe fände,
Um liebevoll die Liebe zu umfassen.

Die Liebe suchte ich auf allen Gassen,
Vor jeder Türe streckt' ich aus die Hände
Und bettelte um geringe Liebesspende —
Doch lachend gab man mir nur kaltes Hassen.

Und immer irrte ich nach Liebe, immer
Nach Liebe, doch die Liebe fand ich nimmer
Und kehrte um nach Hause, krank und trübe.

Doch da bist du entgegen mir gekommen,
Und ach! was da in deinem Aug' geschwommen,
Das war die süsse, langgesuchte Liebe.

### DIE GRENADIERE

NACH Frankreich zogen zwei Grenadier',
Die waren in Russland gefangen;
Und als sie kamen ins deutsche Quartier,
Sie liessen die Köpfe hangen.

Da hörten sie beide die traurige Mär':
Dass Frankreich verloren gegangen,
Besiegt und zerschlagen das grosse Heer —
Und der Kaiser, der Kaiser gefangen.

Da weinten zusammen die Grenadier'
Wohl ob der kläglichen Kunde.
Der eine sprach: ,, Wie weh wird mir,
Wie brennt meine alte Wunde! "

Der andre sprach: ,, Das Lied ist aus,
Auch ich möcht' mit dir sterben;
Doch hab' ich Weib und Kind zu Haus,
Die ohne mich verderben."

,, Was schert mich Weib, was schert mich Kind?
Ich trage weit bessres Verlangen;
Lass sie betteln gehn, wenn sie hungrig sind —
Mein Kaiser, mein Kaiser gefangen!

Gewähr' mir, Bruder, eine Bitt':
Wenn ich jetzt sterben werde,
So nimm meine Leiche nach Frankreich mit,
Begrab mich in Frankreichs Erde.

Das Ehrenkreuz am roten Band
Sollst du aufs Herz mir legen !
Die Flinte gib mir in die Hand,
Und gürt' mir um den Degen.

So will ich liegen und horchen still,
Wie eine Schildwach', im Grabe,
Bis einst ich höre Kanonengebrüll
Und wiehernder Rosse Getrabe.

Dann reitet mein Kaiser wohl über mein Grab,
Viel Schwerter klirren und blitzen ;
Dann steig' ich gewaffnet hervor aus dem Grab —
Den Kaiser, den Kaiser zu schützen ! "


### BELSAZER

DIE Mitternacht zog näher schon ;
In stiller Ruh' lag Babylon.

Nur oben in des Königs Schloss,
Da flackert's, da lärmt des Königs Tross.

Dort oben in dem Königssaal
Belsazer hielt sein Königsmahl.

Die Knechte sassen in schimmernden Reihn
Und leerten die Becher mit funkelndem Wein.

Es klirrten die Becher, es jauchzten die Knecht' ;
So klang es dem störrischen Könige recht.

Des Königs Wangen leuchten Glut ;
Im Wein erwuchs ihm kecker Mut.

Und blindlings reisst der Mut ihn fort ;
Und er lästert die Gottheit mit sündigem Wort.

Und er brüstet sich frech und lästert wild;
Die Knechtenschar ihm Beifall brüllt.


Der König rief mit stolzem Blick;
Der Diener eilt und kehrt zurück.


Er trug viel gülden Gerät auf dem Haupt;
Das war aus dem Tempel Jehovahs geraubt.


Und der König ergriff mit frevler Hand
Einen heiligen Becher, gefüllt bis am Rand.


Und er leert ihn hastig bis auf den Grund
Und rufet laut mit schäumendem Mund:


„ Jehovah! dir künd' ich auf ewig Hohn, —
Ich bin der König von Babylon!"


Doch kaum das grause Wort verklang,
Dem König ward's heimlich im Busen bang.


Das gellende Lachen verstummte zumal;
Es wurde leichenstill im Saal.


Und sieh! und sieh! an weisser Wand
Da kam's hervor wie Menschenhand;


Und schrieb und schrieb an weisser Wand
Buchstaben von Feuer, und schrieb und schwand.


Der König stieren Blicks da sass,
Mit schlotternden Knien und totenblass.


Die Knechtenschar sass kalt durchgraut,
Und sass gar still, gab keinen Laut.

Die Magier kamen, doch keiner verstand
Zu deuten die Flammenschrift an der Wand.

Belsazer ward aber in selbiger Nacht
Von seinen Knechten umgebracht.


### DIE HEIL'GEN DREI KÖNIGE

Die heil'gen drei Könige aus Morgenland,
Sie frugen in jedem Städtchen :
Wo geht der Weg nach Bethlehem,
Ihr lieben Buben und Mädchen ?

Die Jungen und Alten, sie wussten es nicht,
Die Könige zogen weiter ;
Sie folgten einem goldenen Stern,
Der leuchtete lieblich und heiter.

Der Stern blieb stehn über Josephs Haus,
Da sind sie hineingegangen ;
Das Öchslein brüllte, das Kindlein schrie,
Die heil'gen drei Könige sangen.


### DIE NORDSEE

#### ABENDDÄMMERUNG

Am blassen Meeresstrande
Sass ich gedankenbekümmert und einsam.
Die Sonne neigte sich tiefer und warf
Glührote Streifen auf das Wasser,
Und die weissen, weiten Wellen,
Von der Flut gedrängt,
Schäumten und rauschten näher und näher —
Ein seltsam Geräusch, ein Flüstern und Pfeifen,
Ein Lachen und Murmeln, Seufzen und Sausen,
Dazwischen ein wiegenliedheimliches Singen —

Mir war, als hört' ich verschollne Sagen,
Uralte, liebliche Märchen,
Die ich einst, als Knabe,
Von Nachbarskindern vernahm,
Wenn wir am Sommerabend,
Auf den Treppensteinen der Haustür,
Zum stillen Erzählen niederkauerten,
Mit kleinen, horchenden Herzen
Und neugierklugen Augen;
Während die grossen Mädchen,
Neben duftenden Blumentöpfen,
Gegenüber am Fenster sassen,
Rosengesichter,
Lächelnd und mondbeglänzt.

### FRAGEN

AM Meer, am wüsten, nächtlichen Meer,
Steht ein Jüngling-Mann,
Die Brust voll Wehmut, das Haupt voll Zweifel,
Und mit düstern Lippen fragt er die Wogen:

,, O, löst mir das Rätsel des Lebens,
Das qualvoll uralte Rätsel,
Worüber schon manche Häupter gegrübelt,
Häupter in Hieroglyphenmützen,
Häupter in Turban und schwarzem Barett,
Perückenhäupter und tausend andre
Arme, schwitzende Menschenhäupter —
Sagt mir, was bedeutet der Mensch?
Woher ist er kommen? Wo geht er hin?
Wer wohnt dort oben auf goldenen Sternen? "

Es murmeln die Wogen ihr ew'ges Gemurmel,
Es wehet der Wind, es fliehen die Wolken,
Es blinken die Sterne, gleichgültig und kalt,
Und ein Narr wartet auf Antwort.

### SEEGESPENST

Ich aber lag am Rande des Schiffes
Und schaute, träumenden Auges,
Hinab in das spiegelklare Wasser,
Und schaute tiefer und tiefer —
Bis tief, im Meeresgrunde,
Anfangs wie dämmernde Nebel,
Jedoch allmählich farbenbestimmter,
Kirchenkuppel und Türme sich zeigten,
Und endlich, sonnenklar, eine ganze Stadt,
Altertümlich niederländisch,
Und menschenbelebt.
Bedächtige Männer, schwarzbemäntelt,
Mit weissen Halskrausen und Ehrenketten
Und langen Degen und langen Gesichtern,
Schreiten über den wimmelnden Marktplatz
Nach dem treppenhohen Rathaus,
Wo steinerne Kaiserbilder
Wacht halten mit Zepter und Schwert.
Unferne, vor langen Häuserreihn,
Wo spiegelblanke Fenster
Und pyramidisch beschnittene Linden,
Wandeln seidenrauschende Jungfern,
Schlanke Leibchen, die Blumengesichter
Sittsam umschlossen von schwarzen Mützchen
Und hervorquellendem Goldhaar.
Bunte Gesellen in spanischer Tracht
Stolzieren vorüber und nicken.
Bejahrte Frauen,
In braunen, verschollnen Gewändern,
Gesangbuch und Rosenkranz in der Hand,
Eilen, trippelnden Schritts,
Nach dem grossen Dome,
Getrieben von Glockengeläute
Und rauschendem Orgelton.

Mich selbst ergreift des fernen Klangs
Geheimnisvoller Schauer !
Unendliches Sehnen, tiefe Wehmut
Beschleicht mein Herz,
Mein kaum geheiltes Herz ;
Mir ist, als würden seine Wunden
Von lieben Lippen aufgeküsst
Und täten wieder bluten —
Heisse, rote Tropfen,
Die lang und langsam niederfall'n
Auf ein altes Haus, dort unten
In der tiefen Meerstadt,
Auf ein altes hochgegiebeltes Haus,
Das melancholisch menschenleer ist,
Nur dass am untern Fenster
Ein Mädchen sitzt,
Den Kopf auf den Arm gestützt,
Wie ein armes, vergessenes Kind —
Und ich kenne dich, armes, vergessenes Kind !

So tief, meertief also
Verstecktest du dich vor mir
Aus kindischer Laune,
Und konntest nicht mehr herauf
Und sassest fremd unter fremden Leuten,
Jahrhundertelang,
Derweilen ich, die Seele voll Gram,
Auf der ganzen Erde dich suchte,
Und immer dich suchte,
Du Immergeliebte,
Du Längstverlorene,
Du Endlichgefundene —
Ich hab' dich gefunden und schaue wieder
Dein süsses Gesicht,
Die klugen, treuen Augen,
Das liebe Lächeln —
Und nimmer will ich dich wieder verlassen,

Und ich komme hinab zu dir,
Und mit ausgebreiteten Armen
Stürz' ich hinab an dein Herz —

Aber zur rechten Zeit noch
Ergriff mich beim Fuss der Kapitän,
Und zog mich vom Schiffsrand
Und rief, ärgerlich lachend :
Doktor, sind Sie des Teufels ?


## WILHELM  HAUFF

### 1802–1827

#### REITERS MORGENGESANG

MORGENROT,
Leuchtest mir zum frühen Tod ?
Bald wird die Trompete blasen,
Dann muss ich mein Leben lassen,
Ich und mancher Kamerad !

Kaum gedacht,
Ward der Lust ein End' gemacht.
Gestern noch auf stolzen Rossen,
Heute durch die Brust geschossen,
Morgen in das kühle Grab !

Ach, wie bald
Schwindet Schönheit und Gestalt !
Tust du stolz mit deinen Wangen,
Die wie Milch und Purpur prangen ?
Ach ! die Rosen welken all' !

Darum still
Füg' ich mich, wie Gott es will.
Nun so will ich wacker streiten,
Und sollt' ich den Tod erleiden,
Stirbt ein braver Reitersmann.

# NOTES

The Roman figures denote the stanza, the Arabic figures the lines.

## BARTHOLD HEINRICH BROCKES

p. 1 : KIRSCHBLÜTE BEI DER NACHT. I, 1 : *Ich, er sahe*: archaic and Biblical for the historically correct form *sah* (M.H.G. *sach*). The *e* by analogy with the 1st and 3rd pers. of weak verbs.

## JOHANN CHRISTIAN GÜNTHER

p. 2 : STUDENTENLIED. An imitation of *Gaudeamus igitur, juvenes dum sumus*. I, 2 : *Weil* (temporal) = *solange als, während, dieweil*, while ; this original meaning changes to ' because ' (causal). *Derweil* is still used with temporal meaning. 6 : *jetzo* : the historically correct form (M.H.G. *iezuo*.)

## FRIEDRICH VON HAGEDORN

p. 5 : DER ERSTE MAI. Imitation of a triolet (' *le roi des triolets* ', Ménage called it) by Ranchin : *Le premier jour du mois de Mai* | *Fut le plus beau jour de ma vie*. In a triolet the rhymes are : cat dog bat fat hog cat dog.

## CHRISTIAN FÜRCHTEGOTT GELLERT

p. 7 : DER TANZBÄR. 1 : read *hatte ertanzen müssen*. 2 = went back to where he came from.
p. 8 : DIE BEIDEN MÄDCHEN. 1 : *Zwo* : the original forms masc. *zwēne*, fem. *zwō, zwuo*, neut. *zwei* were generalized to *zwei*.

## EWALD CHRISTIAN VON KLEIST

p. 9 : DITHYRAMBE, f., or *Dithyrambus*, m. = *Bacchuslied*, then *begeisterter Gesang, Loblied* generally ; dithyramb(us).
p. 10 : LIED EINES LAPPLÄNDERS. See note to Herder's *Die Fahrt zur Geliebten*.

## JOHANN WILHELM LUDWIG GLEIM

p. 11 : PFLICHT ZU VERLIEBTEN GESPRÄCHEN. 5 : *Enter*, now *Enterich*. Cf. *Gänserich* and *Taube*, f., *Tauber*, m. (*Tauberich* is archaic).

## JOHANN NIKOLAUS GÖTZ

p. 13 : DAS LEBEN. 1 : *schnelle ;* archaic and poetical
adverbial form ; M.H.G. adj. *snel,* adv. *snelle,* O.H.G.
*snello.*  Adverbs are normally formed from the adjective
by the addition of *e* (from O.H.G. *o* : *ferne, lange, stille ;*
(*Dichtersprache*) *balde, gerne.*  6 : *fleucht* : the 2nd and
3rd pers. pres. indic. of *fliehen* occur poetically as *fleuchst,
fleucht,* with imper. *fleuch* < M.H.G. *vliuhest, vliuhet,
vliuch.*  This is common in other strong verbs with *ie* in
infin. ; cf. *was da kreucht und fleugt* (Schiller).  But 1st
pers. and pl. forms always keep *ie* of the infin.  *ch* for *h*
occurs frequently in poetry : *geschicht* for *geschieht.*
This interchange of *h* and *ch* is normal in nouns : *cf*
*geschehen, Geschichte* ;   *sehen, Sicht, Gesicht* ;   *ziehen,
Zucht.*

## FRIEDRICH GOTTLIEB KLOPSTOCK

p. 13 : DER EISLAUF.  A pseudo-classical strophe invented
by Klopstock for this ode.  The scheme is :

$$\times \left| \frac{\prime}{-} \times \right| \frac{\prime}{-} \times \left| \frac{\prime}{-} \times \times \ \frac{\prime}{-} \right.$$

$$\times \times \left| \frac{\prime}{-} \times \right| \frac{\prime}{-} \times \left| \frac{\prime}{-} \times \times \ \frac{\prime}{-} \right.$$

$$\frac{\prime}{-} \times \left| \frac{\prime}{-} \right| \frac{\prime}{-} \times \times - \left| \frac{\prime}{-} \times \ \frac{\prime}{-} \right.$$

$$\frac{\prime}{-} \times \times - \left| \frac{\prime}{-} \times \times \ \frac{\prime}{-} \right.$$

The rhythm is intended to reproduce the rhythmic
movement of the skate-dance.  When Klopstock visited
Goethe at Frankfurt in 1774, instead of discoursing on
literature they discussed Frisian *Schrittschuhe* and other
athletic subjects : ' *Neben der Reit- und Fechtkunst
wurde auf Klopstocks Anregung das Schlittschuhlaufen mit
Begeisterung getrieben.  Seine "Eisoden" waren in aller
Munde* ' (Haarhaus, *Goethe,* p. 73).  The older term for
' skate ' is *Schrittschuh* (M.H.G. *schritschuoch*) ; *Schlitt-
schuh* is a new formation based on *Schlitten* ; other
terms were Rhenish *Glittschuh* and *Schleifschuh.*  III,
4 : *Reihen = Reigen,* dance.  X, 4 : *fleug* : see Götz,
note 6.  XI, 4 : Johann Martin Preisler, copper-plate
engraver at the court in Copenhagen, was a friend of
Klopstock.
p. 16 : DER ERLÖSER.  In Klopstock's favourite strophe, the
Alcaic.  The scheme is :

$$× \stackrel{/}{-} \mid × \stackrel{/}{-} × \parallel \stackrel{/}{-} × × \stackrel{/}{-} \mid × \stackrel{/}{-}$$

$$× \stackrel{/}{-} \mid × \stackrel{/}{-} × \parallel \stackrel{/}{-} × × \stackrel{/}{-} \mid × \stackrel{/}{-}$$

$$× \stackrel{/}{-} \mid × \stackrel{/}{-} \mid × \stackrel{/}{-} \mid × \stackrel{/}{-} ×$$

$$\stackrel{/}{-} × × \mid \stackrel{/}{-} × × \mid \stackrel{/}{-} × \mid \stackrel{/}{-} ×$$

In classical feet the first two lines are : iambus, amphi-brach, choriambus, iambus ; the third, three iambuses followed by an amphibrach ; the fourth, dactyl, dactyl, trochee, trochee. The German poets allow themselves variations in all these classical strophes. A salient feature of the Alcaic strophe is that the first two lines have masculine ending, the last two a feminine ending. X, 1–4 : the poem was written in 1765 ; the last cantos of *Der Messias* were published in 1773. Cf. Hölderlin's *An die Parzen*.

p. 18 : DIE FRÜHEN GRÄBER. III, 4 : *sahe* : see Brockes, note 1.

## MATTHIAS CLAUDIUS

p. 22 : RHEINWEINLIED. I, 3 : *Europia* : the inserted *i* fills the line and fits the jocular mood of the poem. IV, 3 ; *die weiland Krater* = craters of olden time. Some editions have *Kreter. weiland*, adv., here used adjectivally. IV, 4 : *nicht der Stelle wert* : not worth the space they occupy. VI, 4 : *Lausegold* : lousy gold ; *lausig* = arm-selig ; cf. *Lausbube*, young scamp, ragamuffin. VII, 1 : *der Blocksberg* is another name for der Brocken, the highest summit of the Harz Mountains, where witches forgather on the witches' sabbath (*Walpurgisnacht*), 30th April to 1st May. The second name comes from the granite blocks which cover the treeless summit. See Goethe's *Faust*, Part 1, *Walpurgisnacht*, and his poem *Harzreise im Winter*. VII, 3 : *der Kuckuck* : euphe-mistical and popular (like *der Gottseibeiuns*) for *der Teufel*. In north Germany *des Kuckucks Küster* = *der Wiedehopf*, hoopoe, a bird that comes in spring with the cuckoo. Cf. *das weiss der Kuckuck und sein Küster* = God knows, that beats me.

p. 24 : ABENDLIED. II, 4 : *als* = *wie, als wie*. IV, 2 : *eitel* = *nichts als*.

p. 28 : DER TOD. ' *Vielleicht die schönsten Verse der deutschen Sprache* '. Heinz Steinberg, *Welt und Wort*, 1949, p. 49.

## JOHANN GOTTFRIED HERDER

p. 28 : ERLKÖNIGS TOCHTER is a version of a Danish folk-
song. *Erlkönig* is a mistranslation of the Danish *ellerkonge* for *elverkonge*, king of the elves. III, 2 : *Reihen* :
see Klopstock, note III, 4, to *Der Eislauf*. V, 2 :
*Sporne* for *Sporen* still occurs in Bavaria ; O.H.G. *sporo*,
M.H.G. *spor*[*e*] > N.H.G. *Sporn*, pl. *Sporen*. The French
borrowed the word as *éperon*. XI, 1 : *tät* < M.H.G.
*tet*[*e*] > *tat*, infin. *tuon* > *tun*. XIII, 2 *dafür = davor* ;
see note 1, p. xxi. XV, 2 : *traf = kam*.

p. 30 : *Die Fahrt zur Geliebten*. Another version of this
Lapland song is by Ewald Christian von Kleist (p. 10).
The original of the two adaptations is in *Historia
Lapponiae* (1673), a Latin book on Lapland by Johannes
Scheffer (1621–79), a professor at Upsala. Kleist's
direct source was probably Elizabeth Rowe's *A Lap-
lander's Song to his Mistress* ; she herself, no doubt, used
Scheffer. Herder in a letter to Karoline Flachsland
says : ' *Wundern Sie sich nicht, dass ein Lappländischer
Jüngling, der keinen Buchstaben kennet . . ., besser singt
als der Major Kleist ! Denn jener sang das Lied eben
aus dem Fluge, da er mit seinen Renntieren über den
Schnee hinschlüpfte, und ihm die Zeit lang ward, den
Orrasee zu sehen, wo sein Mädchen wohnte. Kleist aber
ahmte es aus dem Buche nach.*' This admirably fits the
folk-song theory (p. xl), which from now on is to be
such a vital factor in German poetry. The Lapp song
referred to was discussed by Herder in his *Ossian und
die Lieder alter Völker* and included by him in his *Alte
Volkslieder* (1774), Part II, and in his *Volkslieder*, Part II
(1779). A critical comparison favours Kleist's version
in a few details. Kleist has the vague word *Bäume*, while
Herder has the icy Northern word *Fichten* ; here Herder
scores. But Kleist has *Grönlands weisse Küsten*, with
its blinding vision of snow-bound distances, and the
vital idea : *die lange Nacht kommt schon* (the long Polar
night !). Part of this Lapland poem haunts the memory
of all of us ; in Scheffer's version we find : *Puerorum
voluntas, voluntas venti ; juvenum cogitationes, longae
cogitationes*, and this we remember from Longfellow's
poem *My Lost Youth* : ' And a verse of a Lapland
song | Is haunting my memory still : " A boy's will is
the wind's will, | And the thoughts of youth are long,
long thoughts." '

p. 31 : DER AUGENBLICK. I, 2 : Einen ; either a capital
initial or spacing may be used to emphasize a numeral.

## GOTTFRIED AUGUST BÜRGER

p. 33 : DER BAUER. II, 2 ; *ungebleut* ; *bleuen* = *(heftig)
schlagen*, to beat black and blue. IV, 1 : *so* = *die*. *So*
as relative pronoun occurs mostly in South German.
Cf. *die Erlösung, so durch Christum Jesum geschehen ist.*

p. 34 : MUTTERTÄNDELEI. IV, 2 : *eine böse Sieben* = *ein
bitterböses Weib*, vixen, demon. The term derives from
the ' seven ' of playing cards.

p. 35 : DAS MÄDEL, DAS ICH MEINE. *meinen* = (1) *woraufhin
denken* ; (2) *zugeneigt denken an, lieben*. The correspond-
ing noun is *Minne* ; in the Middle Ages the word had
mostly a sexual significance, but after the publication
of Bodmer's and Breitinger's *Sammlung von Minnesingern*
(p. xxviii) it was restored, together with *minnen, minniglich,
Minnelied*, &c.), to respectability and was used by the
poets of the *Göttinger Almanach* (p. xlii) as a noble
archaic term.

p. 40 : FÜR SIE MEIN EINS UND ALLES. II, 1 : *Wesir* (with
first syllable stressed) is now *Wesi[e]r* [ve·′zi:r]. IV, 1 :
*so ich weiss* : *so* = *wie*.

## LUDWIG HÖLTY

p. 43. Of Hölty's classical strophes here selected *Der Tod* and
*Auftrag* are Alcaic, the scheme of which is given in notes
to Klopstock's *Der Erlöser* ; *Die Mainacht* and *Die Liebe*
are in the 4th Asclepiad strophe, which scans as follows :

$$
\begin{array}{l}
\dfrac{/}{-} \times \left| \dfrac{/}{-} \times \times \dfrac{/}{-} \right\| \dfrac{/}{-} \times \times \dfrac{/}{-} \left| \times \dfrac{/}{-} \right. \\[2mm]
\dfrac{/}{-} \times \left| \dfrac{/}{-} \times \times \dfrac{/}{-} \right\| \dfrac{/}{-} \times \times \dfrac{/}{-} \left| \times \dfrac{/}{-} \right. \\[2mm]
\qquad \dfrac{/}{-} \times \left| \dfrac{/}{-} \times \times \right. \dfrac{/}{-} \times \\[2mm]
\qquad \dfrac{/}{-} \times \left| \dfrac{/}{-} \times \times \dfrac{/}{-} \right| \times \dfrac{/}{-}
\end{array}
$$

DIE MAINACHT. ' *Die sanftklagende Melancholie der Hölty-
schen* " *Mainacht* ", *von Brahms so zauberhaft ins
Tragische gesteigert, sie ist Klopstocks Ton aus den
*" Frühen Gräbern ", genau wie die Mond- und Tod-
gedichte von Matthias Claudius Klopstocks Ton sind.*'
Ernst Bertram, *Deutsche Gestalten*, p. 50.

p. 43 : DIE LIEBE. II, 4 : *geusst* : see Götz, *Das Leben*,
note l. 6. VII, 4 : *wann* = *wenn* ; *wenn* and *wann* were
not definitely separated till the middle of the eighteenth
century. *Wann* = [at the time] when, occurs in the
poetical language : *In schönen Sommertagen, wann lau die*

*Lüfte wehn* (Uhland); *Im Herbste, wann die Trauben glühn* (Geibel). *Wenn* is the weakened form of original *wann*, as *denn* is of *dann*. *Wenn* implies a condition, *wann* is temporal only.

## JOHANN WOLFGANG VON GOETHE

p. 48: MIT EINEM GEMALTEN BAND. See p. lix. Goethe in *Dichtung und Wahrheit* says he wished to send Friederike a present, and: ' *Gemalte Bänder waren damals erst Mode geworden ; ich malte ihr gleich ein paar Stücke und sendete sie mit einem kleinen Gedicht voraus* '. III, 4 : *genung* was used in Middle German dialects ; hence it came natural to Goethe.

p. 48: MAILIED. The poem was probably written for the Sesenheim May festival of 1771, in which Goethe took part at the invitation of Friederike. IV, 4: *auf jenen Höhn*. Probably the Black Forest mountains.

p. 50: WILLKOMMEN UND ABSCHIED. Another Friederike poem.

p. 51: HEIDENRÖSLEIN. The *Röslein* is Friederike. The poem was published with the title *Fabelliedchen* by Herder as a *Volkslied* in his *Briefwechsel über Ossian* (1773) ; here Herder says it was written down ' *aus dem Gedächtnis* ' and classifies it as a song for children. He included it again in his *Stimmen der Völker* (1779) and here he says he had it ' *aus der mündlichen Sage* '. It is assumed that Goethe did indeed recast an old folk song. I, 7 : *Heiden* : strong feminine nouns in -e are often declined weak in the *Dichtersprache* and in set phrases : *Heide[n]* (but *Heidekraut*), *erdennah*, *Erdenrund*, *Frauenarzt*, *Sonnenstrahl*, *zu Erden*, *auf Erden*.

p. 52: PROMETHEUS. For style and meaning, see Introduction, p. lxii. ' *Die Stimmung des genialen Individualismus hat niemals grossartigeren Ausdruck gefunden. Aber Prometheus ist nicht schlechtweg Goethe*'. R. M. Meyer.

p. 54: NEUE LIEBE NEUES LEBEN. The first of the poems inspired by Lili Schönemann.

p. 55: AN BELINDEN. The second of the Lili-Lieder. II, 2 : *Mondenschein*. The *d* in *Mond* is excrescent ; the M.H.G. form *mān[e]*, *mōn[e]* survives in *Montag*, ' the moon's day '. The strong noun *Mond* was often declined weak in the eighteenth century : *des Mondes, dem Monden* ; *Mondenschein*, poetic for *Mondschein*.

p. 55: RASTLOSE LIEBE. On May 5th, 1776, Goethe wrote from Ilmenau his first letter to Frau von Stein ; on that day it snowed the whole morning. This is the first of

the Lida-Lieder, the poems inspired by Frau von Stein.
Note the change of metre, indicative of a quieter mood,
in the second stanza.

p. 58 : GRENZEN DER MENSCHHEIT contrasts with the mood
of revolt in the dithyramb *Prometheus* ; here gods and
men are content with their separate spheres of action
and there is harmony between the infinite and the finite.
II, 5–6 derives presumably from Horace's Ode I, i :
*sublimi feriam sidera vertice*. III, 8 : he does not reach
up even to oak or vine, the first the emblem of strength,
the second of fruitfulness.

p. 60 : DAS GÖTTLICHE. This dithyramb was first printed
in 1785 together with *Prometheus* in J. H. Jacobi's *Briefe
über die Lehre des Spinoza* (p. lxii). II, 3 : *ahnen* = are
(vaguely) conscious of, contrasts with *kennen*, I, 6.
V, 1 : *Glück* = fate, fortune. VIII, 2 : *lohnen* = be-
*lohnen*. Some editions have *Dem Guten lohnen*. But
acc. occurs in N.H.G. : *einen Arbeiter lohnen*.

p. 62 : DER SCHÄFER PUTZTE SICH ZUM TANZ. From *Faust*,
Part 1, *Vor dem Tor*. II, 4 : *frische Dirne* = lively
lassie. *Dirne* may still be used without disrespect
of a girl, but the usual meaning today is *Lustdirne*.
*frisch* : cf. the English vulgarism : ' Don't be so fresh '
(= cheeky). III, 1–2 : *ging's . . . links* ; the M.H.G.
pronunciation of *ng* as *nk* survives in north Germany,
Saxony, and Silesia, and in surnames (Jungk = *junk*,
Gökingk ; here the latter *k* makes a double symbol).

p. 63 : DER KÖNIG IN THULE : from *Faust*, Part 1, *Abend*.
*Thule* = the *ultima Thule* of the Romans, usually thought
of as the mainland nearest to the Shetland Islands.
Today Thule is known as a town on the west coast of
Greenland. I, 3 : like *Dirne* (see above), *der* or *die
Buhle* has now acquired a pejorative meaning, but here
it still keeps the good sense it has in the Bible ; ' his
leman so true ' would render the meaning Goethe intends
to convey. *Buhle* was originally a weak masculine.
The sense is always pejorative in *die Buhlin*, in com-
pounds such as *Buhlschwester*, *Buhldirne*, and in the adj.
*verbuhlt*. II, 1 : *Es ging ihm nichts darüber*, there was
nothing he prized more highly. II, 2 : *jeden Schmaus*
= *bei jedem Schmaus*. VI, 4 : *sinken* : his eyes half
closed.

p. 64 : MEINE RUH IST HIN. From *Faust*, Part 1, *Gretchens
Stube*. X, 3–4 : *scil., auch wenn ich*.

p. 66 : DER FISCHER. Herder includes this poem in his
*Stimmen der Völker* and comments : ' *Die deutsche Poesie*

*muss, wenn sie wirklich Volksdichtung werden will, den Weg gehen, den dieses Gedicht zeigt.*' 1, 5 : *lauschen* has also (archaically and poetically) the sense of *lauern*, to lie in wait, *heimlich aufhorchen*. I, 8 : *Ein feuchtes Weib* ; she is a species of water-witch or Lorelei. The poem is one of those which poetize the demonic fascination of flowing water. II, 4 : *Todesglut* ; the death-giving heat of the sun.

p. 67 : DER SÄNGER. Probably written 1783. The first song of the harper when he appears in *Wilhelm Meister*, Book II, Chap. II. The ballad is set in the Middle Ages, the time when the Minnesingers roamed from castle to castle and sang their lays of love to gathered knights and ladies ; this and the general tone of the ballad points forward to romanticism. See p. xcviii. Cf. Uhland, *Des Sängers Fluch*. I, 2 : *Brücke = Zugbrücke*, drawbridge. I, 6 : *Knabe = Edelknabe*, page. *kam = came back*. III, 1 : (half) closed his eyes. III, 2 : *schlug* : *scil. die Harfe*, the strings of his harp.

p. 68 : ERLKÖNIG. The ballad, written 1781, has the mood of Herder's *Erlkönigs Tochter* and was no doubt suggested by it. The theme was repeatedly treated : Matthisson's *Die Elfenkönigin*, Uhland's *Die Elfen* and *Harald*, &c. Herder's and Goethe's ballads, with their Danish proto-type, are based on the Germanic belief in elves and their stealing of children and young men. II, 1 : *birgst = verbirgst*. II, 3 : *Schweif* = his cloak flowing out behind him. *die Erle* = alder tree, but *Erlenkönig*, as we have seen (p. 210), transposes the Danish *ellerkonge* for *elverkonge*, king of the elves. In legendary lore the king of the elves (*der Elf, die Elfe*, pl. of both *Elfen*) is Oberon. *Die Lichtelfen* are lovely to look at and helpful to mortals ; they shun daylight but dance in moonshine ; the *Schwarzelfen* are long-nosed and pot-bellied, and steal human babies to replace their own ugly offspring. II, 4 : *Nebelstreif* : *Streif* for *Streifen* : a long strip of misty cloud. III, 4 : *gülden* : archaic form of *golden*. IV, 4 : *säuseln*, to sough, is diminutive form of *sausen*. V, 2 : *warten = pflegen, hüten* ; cf. *Krankenwärter*. Borrowed into French as *garder*. See p. 202, *Der Alpen-jäger*, note III, 1. V, 3 : *Reihn = Rundtanz* ; see p. 208, *Der Eislauf*, note III, 4. V, 4 : the three verbs are a cumulative polysynthesis. *singen dich ein* = sing you to sleep, *einlullen*. VII, 4 : partitive genitive, dependent on a numeral ; cf. *kein Aufhebens machen, kein Feder-lesens mit etwas machen*. Occasionally this gen. is found with *ein* : *ein Aufhebens machen*, to make a fuss, *nur der Stadt kein Leids tun* (Goethe, *Götz von Berlichingen*, IV, 2, 170). The partitive genitive is mostly archaic, dependent on certain verbs (particularly *geniessen*), and used instead of the acc. : *Er genoss des nötigen Unterrichts ; Sorgsam brachte die Mutter des klaren herrlichen Weines* (Goethe) ; *Es schenkte der Böhme des perlenden Weins* (Schiller). VIII, 3 : *Hof* indicates an isolated castle or manor house.

p. 69 : DER SCHATZGRÄBER. Written 1797. Goethe had come upon a picture in a translation of Petrarch's *De remediis utriusque fortunae* which showed a boy bringing a gleaming bowl to a person digging for treasure. In his ballad the child is a good genius and the bowl a symbol of the true enjoyment of life. I, 3–4 : cf. *Nach Golde drängt, | Am Golde hängt | Doch alles ! Ach wir Armen !* (*Faust* I, l. 2808). I, 7 : invocation to the Evil Spirit. I, 8 : cf. *Du unterzeichnest dich mit einem Tröpfchen Blut* (*Faust*, I, l. 1737). II, 1 : *Kreis' um Kreise = Zauberkreise*. II, 3 : Certain herbs and human bones for the magic fire are part of the ritual ; cf. *Macbeth* IV, l. III, 1 : *von weiten = von weitem*. III, 4 : *zwölfe* was often used if the name of no object followed. ' *Die dumpfe Geisterstunde* ' begins with the stroke of twelve and lasts till one o'clock. III, 5 : there could be no question of preparing—the boy appeared suddenly in the circle of light cast by the bright bowl. IV, 4 : *Kreis =* the magic circle ; see note II, 1 above. V : *Trinke Mut* ; the stanza gives the import of the parable.

p. 70 : MIGNONS LIEDER. I. *Kennst du das Land . . .* is spoken by Mignon, an Italian girl abducted by travelling acrobats and rescued in Germany by Wilhelm Meister, to whom the poem is addressed. The first stanza describes her homeland, the second the villa she remembers from her childhood, the third the Alps she had crossed at the frontier. Goethe's own longing for Italy, which ' *in den achtziger Jahren sich zu einer Art Krankheit gesteigert hatte* ' finds expression in the song. See p. lxxi. II, l. 10 : *mein Eingeweide*, my heart, my innermost being. Both these Mignon poems were set to music by Beethoven, Schubert, and Schumann.

p. 72 : KOPHTISCHES LIED. 5 : *steht . . . ein*, is seldom at rest.

p. 72 : LEGENDE VOM HUFEISEN. Written 1797. In this poem Goethe for the first time since his return from Italy in 1788 gives up the classical metres which had pre-occupied him and returns to the popular diction of his early verse. The more or less doggerel rhythm is fitting, for the legend reflects Goethe's reading of Hans Sachs, whose *Sankt Peter mit der Geis* was possibly his model. See Goethe's *Hans Sachsens poetische Sendung*, written, like the first scene of *Faust*, in the *Knüttelverse* which are Hans Sachs's metre (p. xi). I, 5 : *lieb' er sich*, he was fond of ; *sich lieben* with reflexive pronoun for *lieben*. I, 6 : *Strassen* ; see note I, 7 to *Heidenröslein*. p. 212. II, 4 : *was* is in M.H.G. the correct sg. of *wären* ; it is still used by Luther and occurs sporadically till well into the N.H.G. period. II, 9 : *was = etwas*. III, 3 : = and makes no further ado about it. IV, 11 : The form *Gaum = Gaumen < M.H.G. goum[e]* occurs only in the *Dichtersprache*. IV, 12 : *Raum = Zeitraum*.

p. 74 :  WANDRERS NACHTLIED. 2 :  *Schmerzen = alles Schmerzen*. Or possibly the line means *Alles Leid und alle Schmerzen*, especially since in line 6 we have *all der Schmerz und all die Lust*.

p. 74 :  ÜBER ALLEN GIPFELN. Written in Goethe's own handwriting in September, 1783, on the window-frame of the Duke's wooden shooting-box on the Gickelhahn, one of the hills near Ilmenau.

p. 74 :  GOTT UND WELT.  The three poems which are here combined define Goethe's most mature conception of God and nature. The concept of divine immanence is in accord with Schelling's philosophy (see p. xcviii). God and nature, the ' *All-Eins* ', are one. The title of the series might in any case echo Spinoza's thinking : ' *deus sive natura* '. *Proömion = Vorrede, Einleitung* ; that is, introduction to the new section *Gott, Gemüt, und Welt* in the 1815 edition of Goethe's works ; the second poem of the series is *Weltseele*, the third is *Eins und Alles*, and the fourth *Vermächtnis*. Last line : *wo möglich = wenn es möglich ist* ; *womöglich = vielleicht*.

p. 75 :  GESANG DER GEISTER ÜBER DEN WASSERN was inspired by Goethe's visit to the Staubbach, near Lauterbrunnen in the Bernese Oberland, in 1779. V, 2 : *Buhler = wooer* (*Hofmacher*), noun to *buhlen*, to woo, to pay court to. Quite different in meaning from *Buhle* (see note I, 3 to *Der König in Thule*, p. 213), which means established lover. For the meaning of the poem, cf. Hölderlin's *Schicksalslied*.

p. 77 :  SPRÜCHE : from *West-Östlicher Divan* (p. lxxxiii).

p. 77 :  *Lynceus der Türmer*. From *Faust* 11, Act V (*Tiefe Nacht*.) This, the last of Goethe's great poems, written probably in the late twenties, shows that he had not lost that keen zest in living which rings out from so many of his earlier poems. In Eckermann's conversation with Goethe on March 11, 1828, the two discussed great men who keep their youth, and Goethe said: *Solche Männer . . . erleben eine wiederholte Pubertät, während andere Leute nur einmal jung sind.* By *Pubertät* he means, in his own case, the urge to literary activity.

» 78 : GEDICHTE. One of the *Sechzehn Parabeln* written by Goethe in his last years. I, 1. *gemalte Fensterscheiben,* stained glass windows. 11, 4 : *Geschicht' und Zierat* ; verb sg. because the two nouns are taken to be one idea ; history and legend vividly rendered as (in each case) a picture. 11, 5 : *Bedeutend* = full of meaning ; *bedeuten = zum Verständnis bringen* ; bringing home to the mind a noble image in glowing colours. 11, 6 : *den Kindern Gottes,* the chosen ones of the Lord (who, unlike the Philistines, can appreciate poetry).

## FRIEDRICH VON SCHILLER

» 81 : DAS MÄDCHEN AUS DER FREMDE. I, 1 : *Tal = die Erde. die armen Hirten = die Menschen.* I, 4 : *Ein Mädchen = die Poesie.*

» 82 : DIE DEUTSCHE MUSE. I, 1 : *Augustisch Alter (Alter = Zeitalter),* Augustan Age, the age of Augustus Octavianus Caesar (63 B.C.–14 A.D.), the second emperor of Rome. He was the patron of Virgil, Horace, Ovid, and Livy. The Augustan Age in France, the age of ' classical ' literature, defined strictly as such by form and treatment, is the reign of Louis XIV, in England that of Queen Anne. I, 2 : *Medicäers Güte* ; the good will and protection of no Medicean prince. The Medici attained to sovereign power in Florence in the fifteenth century. They are famous for their patronage of art, literature, and scholarship, especially Lorenzo the Magnificent (1448–92). To him is due in large measure the Renaissance with its awakening of an interest in classical scholarship (*Humanismus*). Dante and Boccaccio were Florentines but lived earlier. II, 1 : Frederick the Great (like Leibniz) wrote in French (see p. xiii).

» 83 : DIE GÖTTER GRIECHENLANDS. For this poem, see Walther Rehm, *Götterstille und Göttertrauer,* Munich, 1951, pp. 127 ff. I, 8 : so named from Amathus ('Ἀμαθοῦς) or Amathusia, a town in Cyprus, where

Aphrodite (or Venus) is said to have risen from the sea. Venus was particularly worshipped in Cyprus; there was a famous temple dedicated to her worship at Amathus. III, 4: Helios = *der Sonnengott*. III, 5: *Oreade*, f. = *Bergnymphe*. III, 6: *Dryas* or *Dryade* = *weibliche Baumgottheit*, dryad, wood-nymph. III, 7: *Najade*, f. = *Quellnymphe*. The naiades or naides were inferior deities who presided over rivers, springs, and wells. IV, 1: Daphne, pursued by Apollo, implored the help of the gods and was changed into a laurel tree. Apollo crowned his head with the leaves of the laurel; hence the reverence we show to laurel wreaths (*Lorbeerkränze*), &c., for Apollo was god of the arts. IV, 2: the daughter of Tantalus, king of Lydia, was Niobe, whose arrogant pride, because she had more children than the two of the goddess Latona, was punished by Apollo, who slew all her sons; Niobe's wailing ceased only when she was changed into stone. IV, 3: Pan fell in love with Syrinx, a nymph of Arcadia, and offered her violence; she fled, and was changed by the gods into a reed called syrinx, from which Pan fashioned a pipe ('the pipes of Pan,' &c.). IV, 4: Philomela, inconsolable at the death of her son, was changed into a nightingale. IV, 5: Demeter in Greek = Ceres in Latin, goddess of corn and harvests. Her daughter Proserpine was carried off by Pluto. IV, 8: Cythere here = Cytheræa, another name of Aphrodite, the Greek name of Venus, whose favourite was Adonis (= *der schöne Freund*), who was killed by the bite of a wild boar. Cythere or Cythera is the island (now Cerigo) where she was worshipped. V, 1–2: after the great deluge Deucalion and Pyrrha re-created mankind by throwing stones behind them, which changed into men. V, 4: *der Leto Sohn*: Apollo was the son of Leto (Greek form; Latona in Latin) and Zeus. V, 8: Amathunt, for Amathus; see note I, 8. VI, 7: *Kamöne* = Muse. In Latin the muses are Camoenae or Camenae. VIII, 8: *Grazie* = the three Graces, Aglaia, Thalia, and Euphrosyne. The Greek name of the Latin *Gratiae* is *Charites*, *die Charitinnen*. They were in constant attendance on Venus and were in charge of all good offices. VIII, 1: *das Evoe* = Greek ευοι, the cry of the Bacchantes, who are represented as running before the chariot, drawn by panthers, of Bacchus, almost naked and with dishevelled hair crowned with ivy, each swinging a thyrsus, a staff wreathed with ivy and vine leaves. The German form for the staff is *Thyrsos* or *Thyrsus[stab]*. VIII, 5 : *Mänade*, f., maenad. Latin *Maenades* is another name (derived from μαινομαι, to be furious) for the Bacchantes. IX, 4 : *ein Genius* = death. IX, 5 : *der Orkus* = *die Unterwelt*, Hades, the infernal regions, or the god of Hell, Pluto. The three judges Minos, Äakos, and Rhadamanthus had been mortals. IX, 7 : *der Thraker* = Orpheus, who descended, lyre in hand, to the infernal regions to plead for the return of his wife Euridice. IX, 8 : die Erinnye or Erinnys, or Euminide, goddess of vengeance ; pl. = the Furies. X, 5 : Linus, a Greek singer who was killed in youth. X, 6 : Alceste or Alcestis was, at her request, sacrificed to redeem her husband Admetus from death. X, 7 : the friend of Orestes is Pylades. X, 8 : Philoctetes was given the arrows of Hercules when the latter was burnt to death ; with them he killed Paris, son of Priam, at the siege of Troy. XI, 5 : *Wiederfoderer der Toten* = Herakles = Hercules. According to some he brought Alcestis back from Hell. *fodern*, archaic for *fordern*. XI, 8 : *Zwillingspaar* = Castor and Pollux, sons of Jupiter by Leda. They cleared the Hellespont of pirates and for this reason have always been considered the friends of navigation. XIII, 6 : Selene = *Mondgöttin*. XVI, 6 : Pindus, a mountain range in Greece sacred to the Muses and Apollo.

87 : HEKTORS ABSCHIED. I, 1 : Hector, son of King Priam and Hecuba, was captain of the Trojans when Troy was besieged by the Greeks. I, 2 : Achilles, the most valiant of the Greek warriors, was killed by Hector. I, 4 : *deinen Kleinen* = Astyanax. II, 3 : Pergamus = Troy. II, 6 : *der styg'sche Fluss* = the Styx, which flows round Hell. III, 5–6 : Cocytus, Lethe two rivers which flow through Hell. Lethe in Greek means oblivion, forgetfulness ; the dead drank of its waters and forgot their past. See Keats, *Ode to a Nightingale*, lines 1–4.

88 : DIE TEILUNG DER ERDE. 2, 4 ; *birschen = jagen*. III, 2 : *Firnewein* = old wine, really of last year (*vorjähriger Wein*). IV, 2 : *aus weiter Ferne*, from his world of dreams (see VI). V, 4 : Jovis is gen. of Jupiter.

89 : HOFFNUNG. II, 1 : the hope of parents.

89 : SEHNSUCHT. III, 5 : *des Stromes Toben*, the raging river of life.

91 : AN DIE FREUDE. The poem, written in 1785, gives expression to the poet's newly found joy and satisfaction

24

in his circle of friends after he had met Körner and was free to devote himself to creative work. IV, 8 : *des Sehers Rohr*, the astronomer's telescope. IV, 10 : *Plan* = fields.

p. 94 : NÄNIE. Latin *nenia* = *Trauerlied, Klagegesang (bei der Leiche)*. 1 : *Das* = *Was*. 2 : *der stygische Zeus* = Pluto. See *Die Götter Griechenlands*, note IX, 5, and *Hektors Abschied*, note II, 6 : the appeal of Orpheus for the release of Eurydice ; see *Die Götter Griechenlands*, note IX, 7. He was given permission to take her to the upper world on condition that he did not look round, but at the very threshold of Hades yearning overcame him, he glanced over his shoulder, and she vanished. 5–6 : Adonis, the favourite of Aphrodite, the goddess of love, paid no heed to an injunction not to hunt wild beasts, and was killed by a wild boar. Venus then changed him into an anemone. 7 : *Held* = Achilles. *Mutter* = Thetis, one of the sea-deities. *Held* for *Helden* ; the noun was originally strong. 8 : *skäisch* Skaea was one of the gates of Troy. 9 : Nereus, a sea-god, had fifty daughters called the Nerides (in Engl Nereids).

p. 95 : AUS ' WILHELM TELL '. 2. *Lied des Hirten*. I, 3 *Senne* = *Senn*, a shepherd who lives in a *Sennhütte* *Alpenhirt*. 3. *Lied des Alpenjägers*. I, 2 : *schwindlicht* poetical for *schwind[e]lig*. II, 1 : *neblicht*, for *neb[e]lig* 4. *Jägerliedchen*. II, 1 : *der Weih* = kite. III, 4 *fleugt und kreucht* : see Götz, note 6, p. 208.

p. 97 : DER ALPENJÄGER. I, 4 : *Ranft*, f., originally = *Brotrinde* ; here = *Rand*, edge, brink. III, 1 : *de Blümlein warten*. See *Erlkönig*, note V, 2, p. 214. Th gen. with *warten* is archaic and poetical. IV, 6 *Gazelle* for *Gemse*, chamois. VI, 1 : *Jetzo* ; see Günther note 6, p. 207.

p. 99 : DER HANDSCHUH. Leigh Hunt's *The Glove and th Lions* and Browning's *The Glove* both treat the sam subject. I, 2 : *Kampfspiel* = *Tierkampf*. I, 3 : Franci I (1515–47). II, 2 : *Zwinger* = *Platz zwischen innere und äusserer Burgmauer ;* here *auf allen Seiten einge schlossener Raum, wo man wilde Tiere bezwingt*, bear-pit arena. Then it comes to mean ' dungeon,' ' keep V, 1 : *Altan* = *der Balkon, der Söller*. VII, 5 : *kec* = audacious, recklessly daring. VIII, 8 : *wirft in Gesicht*. Here Schiller follows his source, *Essais his toriques sur Paris* by Germain Saint-Fois, whose text is *le jette au nez de la dame*. Frau von Stein objected t the brutality of this line and Schiller changed the reading to *Und der Ritter sich verbeugend spricht*, but later restored the first reading. Browning's *The Glove* has : ' And full into the face of the owner flung the glove.'

p. 101 : NADOWESSISCHES TOTENLIED. The Nadowessier are an Indian tribe between the Mississippi and the Rocky Mountains.

p. 102 : SPRÜCHE und DISTICHEN. *Weisheit und Klugheit.* 3. *Die Kurzsichtige = die Klugheit. Tonkunst :* 1, *fodr' ich* ; see *Die Götter Griechenlands*, note XI, 5, p. 219. 2. Polyhymnia = *Muse des Gesanges.*

## FRIEDRICH VON MATTHISSON

p. 105 : ADELAIDE [aˑdeˑlaˑˈiːdə]

p. 105 : ABENDLANDSCHAFT. IV, 3 : *wankend Ried*, waving reeds. IV, 5 : *Vorland* : in English ' foreland ' means ' cape ', ' promontory '; cf. North and South Foreland on Kentish coast. IX, 3 : *Geisterlispel . . . lispel* for *Gelispel*, whispering.

## JOHANN GAUDENZ FREIHERR VON SALIS-SEEWIS

p. 108 : ABENDBILDER. III, 4 : *-geleier*, continuous playing, strumming. IV, 5 : *Zähre*, f., poetical for *Träne*. *Zähre* is etymologically identical with ' tear '.

p. 109 : HERBSTLIED. III, 1 : see *Der Schäfer putzte sich zum Tanz*, note II, 4, p. 213.

p. 110. Translated by Longfellow as *Song of the Silent Land*.

## ERNST MORITZ ARNDT

p. 113 : *Vaterlandslied* 1813. The date indicates the theme ; see p. cxv. Written in 1812 before the rising of Prussia against the French. Still a popular students' song. I, 4 : *Rechte = rechte Hand.* II, 2 : *Mit . . . halten*, hold to and fight for with the fidelity that is rightly due. The pl. of *die Treue* is poetical. III, 5 : Put to the ban rascal and slave ! III, 7 : *Hermannsschlacht*, battle A.D. 9 in which Hermann der Cherusker (Arminius to the Romans) routed the armies of Varus in the Teutoburg Forest and freed the Germans from the Roman yoke. The theme of Klopstock's *Hermanns Schlacht* (1769) and Heinrich von Kleist's tragedy *Die Hermannsschlacht* (1808), in which Varus stands for Napoleon, while the Romans are the French.

p. 114 : DES DEUTSCHEN VATERLAND was more or less the national song until it was replaced by Max Schnecken-burger's *Die Wacht am Rhein* (1840) and Hoffman von Fallersleben's (1798–1874) *Deutschlandlied* or *Das Lied der Deutschen* (' *Deutschland, Deutschland über alles* '. . .), the latter written 1841 and sung to the tune (composed by Haydn) of the Austrian *Kaiserhymne* : ' *Gott erhalte Franz den Kaiser* '). II, 2 : *Steierland* = Steiermark, Styria. II, 3 : *des Marsen Rind* ; *die Marser* live in history for their resistance to the Romans in the first century A.D. and then disappear. ' *An der oberen Ruhr bis zur oberen Lippe sassen die Marsi* ' (Meyer's *Konversationslexikon*). *sich streckt* : where the farmer's cattle stretch themselves out, lie full length. II, 4 : . . . *der Märker* refers to the inhabitants of a district in Westphalia, where mining and metal work are the chief occupations. *Märker* usually means ' inhabitant of the March of Brandenburg '. *recken* = to stretch, draw out. IV, 4 : = the land and folks I like full well. An allusion to the rising of the Tyrolese under Andreas Hofer in 1809. The two nouns coalesce in meaning, therefore sg. verb. V, 3–6 : that is, the restored empire must include Austria. This belief was termed *grossdeutsch*.

## FRIEDRICH HÖLDERLIN

p. 116. Of Hölderlin's classical strophes here selected *An die Parzen, An die Hoffnung, Die Heimat, Des Morgens, Am Abend, Abendphantasie, Sonnenuntergang* are Alcaic, while *Sokrates und Alkibiades, Menschenbeifall, Heidelberg, Die Kürze* are the 4th Asclepiad ; for scansion, see pp. 209 and 211. Students should note the skilful use of enjambment as compared with the monotonous *Endstil* of other poets who stop or cut the sentence at the end of the line.

p. 117 : AN DIE HOFFNUNG. III, 2–3 : *die . . . Zeitlose* = *Herbstzeitlose*, meadow-saffron.

p. 117 : DIE HEIMAT. Printed 1799, the year after Hölderlin had given up his post in Diotima's home in Frankfurt. See p. c. III, 2 : *am Strome*. Hölderlin was born on the right bank of the Neckar, at Lauffen. Nürtingen, where his mother lived, and to where he returned in 1802 after her death, is also on the Neckar.

p. 118 : DES MORGENS. V, 3 : *heitre* = *erheitre*.

p. 120 : ABENDPHANTASIE. III, 3 : the Alcaic scansion requires ['va·rum].

## NOVALIS

p. 125 : WENN ALLE UNTREU WERDEN. I, 2 : *dir = Christus.*
p. 127 : MARIA and the two following poems. After the death of his betrothed (p. cvii) and in the distress caused by his own illness Novalis dreamed himself into a mysticism in which Maria and his beloved are one and the same, and he wove into his verse his vision of what he dreamed the world beyond the grave to be.

## CLEMENS BRENTANO

p. 131 : ABENDSTÄNDCHEN. II, 4 : *der Töne Licht.* A good example of the synaesthesia of which the romanticists were fond ; see p. cv. *Die Synästhesie = Zuordnung von Tönen zu Farben und umgekehrt ;* here = sight + hearing. Cf. Heine's *Ein Meer von blauen Gedanken.*

## ADALBERT VON CHAMISSO

p. 136 : DAS SCHLOS BONCOURT ; see p. cxviii.
p. 139 : DER SOLDAT. A rendering of a Danish poem by Hans Christian Andersen.
p. 140 : DAS RIESENSPIELZEUG. Rückert handles the same story in *Die Riesen und die Zwerge.*
p. 141 : DIE ALTE WASCHFRAU. For *Armeleutepoesie,* see p. cxix.

## JUSTINUS KERNER

p. 145 : WANDERLIED. III, 5 : *Burschen* = student. IV, 7 : *Sie* is acc. pl. referring to *Vögel* in line 1.
p. 147 : DER REICHSTE FÜRST is in Swabia more or less a national hymn. II, 3 : *Silber* is mined in the Erzgebirge. VI, 4 : *in* = in'n = in den.
p. 148 : DER SCHWERE TRAUM. 1, 4 : *Feinsliebchen = feines Liebchen,* sweetheart.

## LUDWIG UHLAND

p. 150 : DIE FAHRT ZUR GELIEBTEN. 2 : *dräuen,* poetical for *drohen.*
p. 151 : DIE KAPELLE is the Wurmlinger Kapelle on a hill near Tübingen which affords an extensive view.
p. 152 : FRÜHLINGSGLAUBE. I, 3 : *an allen Enden* = everywhere ; *Ende* here = *Ort.* II, 5 : *vergessen* with the gen. is archaic and poetical. It survives in the old noun *Vergissmeinnicht* : *mein* is the old gen. of *ich.*
p. 152 : DAS SCHLOSS AM MEERE. Translated by Longfellow. I, 3–4 : *wehen . . . drüber her,* come floating over it.

IV, 4 : *Saiten* = *Saitenspiel*. VI, 2 : *das Gemahl* = wife in archaic German ; now *der Gemahl, die Gemahlin*. VII, 2 : *dar* = *daher*, along.

p. 153 : DER GUTE KAMERAD. I, 2 : *nit*, dialectal (South and Middle German) for *nicht*.

p. 154 : DER WIRTIN TÖCHTERLEIN. I, 1 : *drei Bursche* three students ; there are two sg. forms of *Bursch*, which is weak or strong, and *Bursche*, which is always weak. *Burschenschaft*, students association. See p. 226, note to title. II, 2 : *hat Sie* ; *Sie* (you) with the verb in the sg. was formerly used in addressing social inferiors (*in der Anrede an Untergebene*). *Er* was similarly used in addressing males ; e.g. *Geh' er, und lasse er sich nicht wieder erblicken*.

p. 155 : SIEGFRIEDS SCHWERT. The source of the poem is the sixteenth-century song *Das Lied vom hürnen* (horny) *Seyfrid* together with the *Volksbuch* '*Wunderschöne Historie vom gehörnten Siegfried*'. Seyfrid is the Early New High German form of M.H.G. Sivrit < Sigefrit. Siegfried is the hero of the M.H.G. epic *Das Nibelungenlied*. I, 1 : *ein stolzer Knab'*! *Knabe*, besides its usual meaning of ' boy ', meant in the older language, but mostly in poetry, ' youth '. *Knappe*, its *Nebenform*, has usually the meaning of ' page '. *Knabe* and *Knappe* are the same word as Engl. ' knave ', which in Shakespeare keeps its original meaning of page. *stolz* has here a good sense : ' proud of himself ', ' gallant '. III, 1 : *manch Ritter wert* ; in the early stages of the language and still in poetry the adjective (uninflected) may follow the noun (*nachgestelltes Adjektiv*) ; cf. *Röslein rot, mein Mann selig* (my late husband), *ein armes Mädel jung, liebster Meister mein*. IV, I : *Stecken*, a staff ; he has no sword because he has not yet been dubbed a knight. VII, 2 : *Gesell[e]*, apprentice. Usually in this sense *ausgelernter Handwerksgehilfe*. Mostly = fellow. See Eichendorff, *Sehnsucht*, note II, 1, p. 225. VIII, 1 : *Acht* = *Achtsamkeit, Fürsorge*. IX, 1 : *kunnt'*. The preterite of M.H.G. *kunnen* or *künnen* is *kunte* or *kunde* or *konde*. XIII, 1 : *schlag'*; *schlagen* may originally mean *tödlich treffen, erschlagen*. Etymologically *schlagen* is the same word as ' to slay'.

p. 156 : BERTRAN DE BORN was a famous troubadour who incited the sons of Henry II of England to rebel against their father and in 1183 was besieged and taken prisoner by the king. Uhland's source was Diez's *Leben und Werke der Troubadours*, which, together with the translations of the Minnesingers (see p. cv), was a starting-point of comparative literature and philology. III, 4 : Périgord and Ventadorn were French provinces in the south of France then ruled by Henry II. IV, 1 : *Deine Tochter* — Maud, wife of Duke Henry the Lion of Brunswick, for whom Bertran wrote love songs. V, 1 : from his sleepy rest in the shadow of the olive tree.

## JOSEPH FREIHERR VON EICHENDORFF

p. 162 : SEHNSUCHT. I, 4 : see note I, 3, *Im Walde*, below. II, 1 : *Gesellen* = fellows ; see Uhland, *Siegfrieds Schwert*, note VII, 2, p. 224.

p. 163 : DAS ZERBROCHENE RINGLEIN. I, 1 : *Grund = Tal.* II, 4 : *sprang . . . entzwei*, snapped in two. III, 1 : *Spielmann*, wandering minstrel in the sense of troubadour or minnesinger.

p. 163 : IM WALDE. I, 3 : *Waldhorn* and *Posthorn* (see *Sehnsucht* I, 4) are typically romantic terms ; they are heard in enchanted forests in the dead of night (see *Waldgespräch*), or they call from a mystic distance to lone, lorn lovers.

p. 164 : WALDGESPRÄCH. III, 4 : for *Lorelei*, see pp. cxii, cxxxviii.

p. 164 : WANDERLIED DER PRAGER STUDENTEN. I, 8 : *Valet*, n. = *Abschied, Lebewohl.* I, 9 : *ade = lebe wohl.*

## FRIEDRICH RÜCKERT

p. 167 : BARBAROSSA. The Hohenstaufen emperors had their great epoch of splendour during the reign of Frederick I, known as Friedrich Rotbart, who was drowned in 1190 on a crusade ; according to legend he is not dead but sleeping in the Kyffhäuser mountain in Thuringia, biding his time to come again to restore the glory that was. When the legend first took shape it was not Frederick I but his grandson Frederick II of whom it was told ; with his death in 1250 the glory departed. Similarly the Welsh believe that King Arthur is sleeping in the fastnesses of Snowdon and that he too in his own good time (*zu seiner Zeit*) will come forth to restore the kingdom of the Cymry by driving the Saxons into the sea. I, 2 : Friederich is the original full form ; < M.H.G. Friderih. IV, 2 : *Darauf = worauf*, as in l. 4. IV, 3 : *marmelsteinern = aus Marmor, marmorn.* Rückert's poem was written between 1814 and 1817, when the longing of the Germans for national unity and a mighty empire once again was growing. Cf. Geibel's poem,

*Friedrich Rotbart.* V, 4 : *'ausruht* ; poetical shifting of the main stress and pause after *Kinn.* Or in slow reading *'aus'ruht* = spondee for iambus. VI, 2 : *zwinken* or *zwinkern*, to blink ; now mostly *blinzeln.*

p. 168 : ABENDLIED. V, 1 : *Sylphe = Luftgeist*, sylph. V, 3 : *Libelle = Wasserjungfer*, dragonfly.

p. 170 : HERBSTHAUCH. III, 2 : *lichten*, to lighten ; here = *entblättern.*

p. 170 : AUS DER JUGENDZEIT. In this poem the poet is thinking of a swallow's song heard in his youth and never forgotten. I, 2 : *immerdar = immerfort.* III, 2–4 : in autumn chests and boxes are full of the produce of harvest : in the spring they are emptied. IV : the songs of children, instinctively wise and merry, put into words the swallow's twittering. IV, 4 : *wie Salomo* ; Arabian stories relate that Solomon understood the language of birds.

## GUSTAV SCHWAB

p. 174 : LIED EINES ABZIEHENDEN BURSCHEN. Written 1814 ; sung to the tune of Albert Methfessel. This students' song is rich in racy terms *aus der Studentensprache.* For *Bursche* see *Der Wirtin Töchterlein*, note I, 1, p. 224. I, 1 : *bemoost*, moss-grown ; a students' word, as in *bemoostes Haupt*, senior student, (jolly) old buck. I, 2 : *Philister = Spiessbürger, Nichtstudent, alter Herr.* Historically = non-Israelite ; *die Philister = Nachbarvolk der Israeliten.* III, 1 : *Kneipe = Schenke*, pub. III, 4 : *mein durstig Herz* ; the uninflected adjective occurs often : (*a*) in poetry, and (*b*) in set phrases ; (*a*) *Es ist der Krieg ein roh gewaltsam Handwerk* (Schiller) ; *ein liebend Herz ist all mein Gut, jung Roland* (Uhland) ; *einen Buhlen neu* (stanza VIII below) ; (*b*) *ein gut Stück* ; *ein gut Teil, gut* or *schlecht Wetter, gut Ding will Weile haben, ein andermal, manchmal.* IV, 1–2 : *Kolleg*, n., pl. *Kollegien = akademische Vorlesung* ; *Kollegia* for *Kollegien* has a tang of Latin ; it is the pl. of *Kollegium*, a *Nebenform* of *Kolleg. Kollegium* also means *Lehrkörper*, corporate body of professors and lecturers. *Kollegia* here means ' lecture rooms ', now empty, and out of use, there just to look at like soldiers on parade (see next line) ; cf. *Paradezimmer = Prunkzimmer.* V, 2 : *Karzer*, m. or n. (Lat. *carcer*) = *Kerker* ; here = *Hochschulgefängnis.* The jolly old bucks as a matter of course incurred periodic incarceration. V, 4 : *Pereat*, n. ; the verb *pereat, pereat* substantivized. Here = my parting pledge is : to Hell with you ! *bringen* : *eine Gesundheit auf einen ausbringen*, to pledge a person. VI, 2 : *Waffenboden*, fencing ground. A face seamed by fencing scars was considered by ladies a great attraction even in this century. The poet Dehmel had such a scarred face. VIII, 3 : *Buhle*, see *Der König in Thule*, note I, 3, p. 213, and *Gesang der Geister über den Wassern*, note V, 2, p. 216. VIII, 4 : *flott* = jolly, *burschikos* ; *flotter Bursche*, a dashing young buck. IX, 4 : *Gehab' dich wohl* = fare thee well ! good-bye ! *Sich gehaben* is only used in the pres. indic. and imper. *Musenstadt* or *Musensitz* = university, seat of learning. *Musensohn* = poet or student.

## WILHELM MÜLLER

p. 176 : WOHIN ? Translated by Longfellow with the title *Whither*. I, 2 : *wohl* is redundant. See *Die Grenadiere*, note III, 2, p. 229. IV, 3–4 : a pun ! V, 3 : *Nix*, m., *Nixe*, f. = *Wassergeist*, watersprite. V, 4 : *Reihn* : see Klopstock, *Der Eislauf*, note III, 4, p. 208.

p. 178 : WANDERSCHAFT. III, 4 : *mein Tag* = not in my time, never ; *mein* for *mein'n*, *meinen* ; or uninflected in set phrases ; see Gustav Schwab, note III, 4, p. 226.

p. 179 : VINETA. An *Ostseebild* from *Muscheln von der Insel Rügen* (p. cxxi). The poet adds a note saying that there is a *Volkssage* telling of this wealthy city Vineta, which sank into the sea between Pomerania and Rügen. Sailors sometimes hear its bells tolling, and they call the reflection of the city's pinnacles on the smooth sea surface *das Wafeln*, ' *eine nordische Fata Morgana* '. Heine's *Seegespenst* tells of a town submerged in the North Sea (p. 203) and Klaus Groth's *Ol Büsum* handles the same theme.

## AUGUST GRAF VON PLATEN

p. 180 : DAS GRAB IM BUSENTO. After sacking Rome, Alaric, king of the Visigoths (*Westgoten*), died in Cosenza in the year 410 and, so legend relates, was buried in the bed of the river Busento, which had been diverted from its course by the labour of prisoners of war. The natural channel was then restored and all those who had toiled on the task were killed, lest the secret burial-place should be divulged. Cf. Mrs. Hemans's *Alaric in Italy*. I, 2 : *in Wirbeln*, in a roll of mournful sound. III, 2 :

*Jugendlocken* : Alaric was 34 years old when he died.
*blond* : the Germanic races are traditionally fair-haired.

p. 181 : DER PILGRIM VOR ST. JUST.  *Pilgrim* (pronunciation
as in English) : poetical for *Pilger, Wallfahrer*.  Charles V
(Charles-Quint), born at Ghent in 1500 as son of Philip
the Fair of Burgundy and Joanna the Mad (the daughter
of Ferdinand and Isabella of Spain), became King of
Spain in 1516 and in 1529 was crowned by the Pope
King of Lombardy and Emperor of the Romans (' Holy
Roman Emperor ').  Like Germany and Russia in recent
years, he aimed at being ruler of the whole world, and
he was indeed able to boast that the sun never set on
his dominions, seeing that he ruled from the Low
Countries and Italy to the Spanish colonies in America.
But in Germany he had to battle with Luther, the other
dominating personality of the period, and he had to wage
war with Francis I of France and the Ottoman Empire.
Foiled in his ambitions he abdicated in 1555 and retired
to the monastery of San Yuste in Estremadura, where he
died in 1558. I, 1 : *für und für* : without stop or stay. I, 2 :
*hispanisch* and *Hispanien* are archaic for *spanisch, Spanien*.
V, 1 : *sich bequemt*, submits to.  V, 2 : *bediademt* ; this
newly coined word fits the solemn and majestic tone of
the poem.

p. 182 : VENEDIG.  I, 2 : *Tempel*, the churches of San
Giorgio Maggiore and Il Redentore, built by Andrei
Palladio.  II, 4 : *Seufzerbrücke* ;  Ponte dei Sospiri,
Bridge of Sighs, between the palace of the Doge and the
Carceri or public prisons.  III, 2–3 : the winged lion of
St. Mark, near the landing-place for St. Mark's Square,
serves as the coat of arms of Venice.

p. 185 : WIE RAFFT' ICH MICH AUF.  I, 2 : *fürder = weiter* ;
etymologically comparative of *fort*.  II, 3 : *nahm der
Wogen in acht*, observed the waves ;  poetical genitive
for acc.  III, 1 : *entfacht*, lit, kindled.

p. 185 : SPRACHE.  6 : *Weisen* = ways and means, char-
acteristics, inner nature.

p. 186 : GRABSCHRIFT.  III, 2 : see p. cxxxiv.  *Märchen*
refers to his Oriental epic *Die Abassiden* (1833).  IV, 1 :
the first prize he no doubt concedes to Klopstock.  IV, 3 :
Platen's grave is in the garden of a villa at Syracuse,
and on the tombstone is the inscription : *Germaniae
Horatius*.

p. 186 : ICH MÖCHTE, WENN ICH STERBE.  I, 4 : The Greek
poet Pindar is said to have died in the theatre during
the performance of one of his tragedies.

## HEINRICH HEINE

p. 189 : EIN FICHTENBAUM STEHT EINSAM. I, 3 : *Ihn schläfert = es schläfert ihn = er ist schläfrig.*

p. 195 : DIE LORELEI. See pp. cxii, cxxxviii. IV, 4 : *Melodei*, archaic and poetical for *Melodie* ; here = *Wohlklang*.

p. 198 : DIE GRENADIERE. I, 4 : *hangen* is originally the intransitive verb and *hängen* the transitive verb, but the whole of the present of *hangen* and the infin. are now replaced by *hängen*. II, 1 : *Mär'*, f. = *Kunde, Nachricht*. *Mär[e]* may also have the meaning of its diminutive *Märchen*, old tale, fairy tale. II, 3 : *das grosse Heer = la grande armée*. III, 2 : *wohl* is redundant. *ob der = über die, wegen der*. IV, 1 : *Das Lied ist aus = Alles ist vorüber*. V, 1 : *was schiert mich = was kümmert mich ; sich um etwas scheren*, to trouble about a thing. *Das sch[i]ert mich nicht = das geht mich nicht an*. The stanza seems to imitate Herder's translation of the Scotch ballad *Edward* : ' *Und was soll werden dem Weib und Kind,* | *Wann du gehst über Meer ? O ? '* | — ' *Die Welt ist gross, lass sie betteln* | *drin, . . . Ich seh' sie nimmermehr—O* '. VII, 1 : *Das Ehrenkreuz*, the cross of *La Légion d'Honneur*, founded by Napoleon.

p. 199 : BELSAZER. For this Biblical theme, see Dan. V. 1–30. II, 1 : *Tross*, m., usually means ' baggage ', ' baggage train ' ; here it means the king's retainers and personal attendants (*Gefolge*). IV, 1 : *Knechte = Kriegsknechte*, vassals. VI, 1 : *leuchten Glut*, are aflame with enjoyment. X, 1 : *gülden* (M.H.G. *guldîn*) see *Erlkönig*, note III, 4, p. 214. XI, 1 : *frevler . . . frevel* (= wicked) is archaic for *frevelhaft*. The noun is *Frevel*, outrage. XV, 1 : *zumal = sogleich*. XVI, 2 : *kam's = kam etwas*. XVII, 2 : *schwand = verschwand*. XVIII, 1 : *stieren Blicks*, with a hard stare ; here = staring as if hypnotized. XIX, 1 : *kalt durchgraut*, with a cold shiver running through them. *durch* here = thoroughly. *Grauen* has more force than *graulen*, to be afraid of (ghosts, etc.). XX, 1 : *die Magier*, the mages, wise men or priests.

p. 202 : FRAGEN. II, 4 : *Hieroglyphe*, f. = *bildliches Schriftzeichen*, hieroglyph. *Hieroglyphen*, pl. = *ägyptische Bilderschrift*. The caps of Egyptian priests were inscribed with hieroglyphs. II, 5 : *Das Barett* (biretta) is still used by the clergy, judges, and university professors and students. II, 9 : *kommen* ; in older N.H.G. *kommen* for *gekommen* is usual.

p. 203 : SEEGESPENST. For the theme cf. Wilhelm Müller's *Vineta* p. 179. I, 3 : The North Sea is known as Blanker Hans. I, 13 : *Halskrause*, f., ruff. I, 16 : *treppenhohen* = reached by a flight of steps. I, 21 : *Linden, sind* is understood. IV : one of the classical examples of ' romantic irony ' or anticlimax. See p. cv. IV, 4 : . . . *des Teufels?* Are you mad ? The genitive used idiomatically with intransitive verbs is common ; used with *sein* and *werden*, as well as *des Teufels*, are : *des Todes sein*, to be dying ; *guten Mutes, guter Dinge, der Meinung, willens sein.*

## WILHELM HAUFF

p. 205 : REITERS MORGENGESANG. I, 3–4 : *blasen* . . . *lassen* : in South German pronunciation the rhyme is perfect, as *ss* is sounded soft. Similarly Schiller, another Swabian, rhymes *spasse* with *Nase.*

# BIBLIOGRAPHY

*LYRIC POETRY :*

CLOSS, AUGUST. *Die neuere deutsche Lyrik vom Barock bis zur Gegenwart.* Series *Deutsche Philologie im Aufriss.* Berlin/Bielefeld/Munich. 1952 and 1955

ERMATINGER, E. *Die deutsche Lyrik in ihrer geschichtlichen Entwicklung von Herder bis zur Gegenwart.* 3 vols. Leipzig/Berlin. 2nd edition, 1925

FINDEIS, RICHARD. *Geschichte der deutschen Lyrik.* 2 vols. *Sammlung Göschen.* Berlin/Leipzig, 1914

HOFFMEISTER, J. *Nachgoethesche Lyrik.* Bonn, 1948

KAYSER, W. *Geschichte der deutschen Ballade.* Berlin, 1936

LEES, JOHN. *The German Lyric.* London/Toronto, 1914

PRAWER, S. S. *German Lyric Poetry. A Critical Analysis of selected poems from Klopstock to Rilke.* London, 1952

SOMMERFELD, MARTIN. *Romantische Lyrik nach Motiven ausgewählt und geordnet.* Berlin, 1932

SPIERO, HEINRICH. *Geschichte der deutschen Lyrik nach Claudius.* Series *Aus Natur und Geisteswelt.* 2nd edition, Leipzig/Berlin, 1915

VIËTOR, KARL. *Geschichte der deutschen Ode.* Munich, 1923

WITKOP, PHILIPP. *Die deutschen Lyriker von Luther bis Nietzsche.* 2 vols. Leipzig/Berlin, 1921

*CLASSICISM AND ROMANTICISM :*

DILTHEY, W. *Das Erlebnis und die Dichtung. Lessing, Goethe, Novalis, Hölderlin.* Leipzig/Berlin, 1905, 1921

KORFF, H. A. *Geist der Goethezeit.* 4 vols., Leipzig, 3rd ed., 1949–56

SCHULTZ, FRANZ. *Klassik und Romantik der Deutschen.* 2nd edition, 3 vols., Stuttgart

STRICH, FRITZ. *Deutsche Klassik und Romantik oder Vollendung und Unendlichkeit. Ein Vergleich.* 4th edition, Bern, 1949

WILLOUGHBY, L. A. *The Classical Age of German Literature,* 1748–1805. Oxford, 1926

BENZ, RICHARD. *Die deutsche Romantik. Geschichte einer geistigen Bewegung.* 4th edition, Leipzig, 1944

BREUL, KARL. *The Romantic Movement in German Literature. Illustrative Texts—Prose and Verse.* Cambridge, 1927

231

GUNDOLF, FRIEDRICH.  *Romantiker.*  2 vols.  Berlin, 1930–1931

HAYM, RUDOLF.  *Die romantische Schule.*  1870 ;  5th edition, ed. Oskar Walzel, Berlin, 1928

HUCH, RICARDA.  *Blütezeit der Romantik.*  Leipzig, 1899. 3rd edition, 1908.  *Ausbreitung und Verfall der Romantik.*  Leipzig, 1902.  3rd edition, 1908

LEVIN, H.  *Die Heidelberger Romantik.*  Munich, 1922

NADLER, JOSEF.  *Die Berliner Romantik, 1800–14.*  Berlin, 1921

PETERSEN, JULIUS.  *Die Wesensbestimmung der deutschen Romantik.*  Leipzig, 1926

REYNAUD, L.  *Le romantisme.  Les origines anglo-germaniques.*  Paris, 1926

RUPRECHT, E.  *Der Ausbruch der romantischen Bewegung.*  Munich, 1948

TYMMS, RALPH.  *German Romantic Literature.*  London, 1955

WALZEL, OSKAR.  *Deutsche Romantik.*  Series *Aus Natur und Geisteswelt.*  2 vols., 5th ed., Leipzig/Berlin, 1923 and 1926

WILLOUGHBY, L. A.  *The Romantic Movement in Germany.*  Oxford, 1930

WITKOP, PHILIPP.  *Heidelberg und die deutsche Dichtung.*  Leipzig, 1925


*POETS :*

SEIDEL, INA.  *Achim von Arnim.*  Stuttgart, 1944

GUIGNARD, R.  *Achim von Arnim.*  Paris, 1936

GUIGNARD, R.  *Un poète romantique allemand : Clemens Brentano.*  Paris, 1933

SEIDEL, INA.  *Clemens Brentano.*  Stuttgart, 1944

STAMMLER, WOLFGANG.  *Matthias Claudius.*  Halle, 1915

BRANDENBURG, H.  *Joseph von Eichendorff.  Sein Leben und Werk.*  Munich, 1922

KUNZ, J.  *Eichendorff.  Höhepunkte und Krise der Spätromantik.*  Oberwesel, 1951

NADLER, JOSEF.  *Eichendorffs Lyrik.*  Cologne, 1911

BAUMGART, HERMANN.  *Goethes lyrische Dichtung in ihrer Entwicklung und Bedeutung.*  3 vols.  Heidelberg, 1931–1939

BIELSCHOWSKY, ALBERT.  *Goethe.  Sein Leben und seine Werke.*  2 vols.  Revised by W. Linden.  Munich 1928

BOYD, JAMES.  *Notes to Goethe's Poems.*  Vol. I (1749–86). Oxford, 1944.  Vol. II (1786–1832), Oxford, 1949.

FAIRLEY, BARKER.  *A Study of Goethe.*  Oxford, 1947

GUNDOLF, FRIEDRICH.  *Goethe.*  Berlin, 1916 ; 12th edition, 1925

PETERSEN, JULIUS.  *Aus der Goethezeit.*  Leipzig, 1932

ROBERTSON, J. G.  *The Life and Work of Goethe.*  London, 1932

ROSE, WILLIAM.  *From Goethe to Byron.*  London, 1924

VIËTOR, KARL.  *Goethe. Dichtung, Wissenschaft, Weltbild.*  Berne, 1949

BROD, MAX.  *Heinrich Heine.*  Berlin, 1956

BUTLER, E. M.  *Heinrich Heine.*  London, 1956

MAUCLAIR, CAMILLE.  *La vie humiliée de Henri Heine.*  Paris, 1930

ROSE, WILLIAM.  *Heinrich Heine. Two Studies of his Thought and Feeling.*  Clarendon Press, Oxford, 1956

CLARK, R. T.  *Herder, his Life and Thought.*  Berkeley, California, 1955

GILLIES, A.  *Herder und Ossian.*  Berlin, 1933

GILLIES, A.  *Herder.*  Oxford, 1945

BRANDENBURG, H.  *Friedrich Hölderlin. Sein Leben und sein Werk.*  Leipzig, 1924

HEIDEGGER, M.  *Erläuterungen zu Hölderlins Dichtung.*  Frankfurt, 2nd edition, 1951

HELLINGRATH, NORBERT VON.  *Hölderlin und die Deutschen.*  Munich, 1921

LEHMANN, E.  *Hölderlins Lyrik.*  Stuttgart, 1922

MONTGOMERY, M.  *Friedrich Hölderlin and the German Neo-Hellenic Movement.*  London, 1923

MÜLLER, E.  *Hölderlin.*  Stuttgart, 1944

PEACOCK, R.  *Hölderlin.*  London, 1938

STAHL, E. L.  *Hölderlin's Symbolism.*  Oxford, 1945

VIËTOR, KARL.  *Die Lyrik Hölderlins. Eine analytische Untersuchung.*  Deutsche Forschungen, Heft 3, Frankfurt, 1921

FREIVOGEL, MAX.  *Klopstock, der heilige Dichter.*  Berne, 1954

KAUSSMANN, E.  *Der Stil der Oden Klopstocks.*  Leipzig, 1931

KINDT, KARL.  *Klopstock.*  Berlin, 1941

BEHAIM-SCHWARZBACH, M.  *Novalis, Friedrich von Hardenberg.*  2nd edition, Stuttgart, 1948

HEDERER, EDGAR.  *Novalis.*  Vienna, 1949

GARLAND, H. B.  *Schiller.*  London, 1949

WITTE, W.  *Schiller.*  Blackwell's Modern Language Studies, Oxford, 1949

MEISSNER, W.  *Ludwig Tiecks Lyrik.*  Berlin, 1902

SCHNEIDER, HERMANN.  *Uhland. Leben, Dichtung, Forschung.*  Berlin, 1920